# NEW
# CREATIVE
# CUISINE

LYNN BEDFORD HALL

# NEW
# CREATIVE
# CUISINE

PHOTOGRAPHY BY ALAIN PROUST

**Book Express**
*Quality and Value in Every Book....*

*Author's acknowledgements*

Many of my recipes have appeared in *The Star, The Sunday Express* and *The Sunday Times* and I wish to thank, in particular, the editor of *The Sunday Times* for permission to use these recipes in this book.

My grateful thanks as well to Linda de Villiers and Marje Hemp for their invaluable guidance, unflagging enthusiasm and professional editing, which helped to make the compilation of this book such a pleasure. Thank you, too, to Sydney-Anne Wallace and Jennie Hoare for their creative input.

This edition specially produced and published in 1993
for Book Express, Inc.
Airport Business center,
29 Kripes Road
East Granby, Connecticut, USA.

by New Holland (Publishers) Ltd
37 Connaught Street,
London W2 2AZ

North American Direct Sales rights in this edition are
exclusive to Book Express Inc.

ISBN 1 85368 274 8

Editor: Linda de Villiers
Design: Sydney-Anne Wallace
Cover design: Jennie Hoare
Illustrations: Felicity Harris
Phototypeset by: Hewer Text Composition Services, Edinburgh
Reproduction by Unifoto (pry) Ltd
Printed and bound by Tien Wah Press (Pte.) Ltd., Singapore

# CONTENTS

# PREFACE

The majority of the recipes in the *New Creative Cuisine* are from my published works. Paring the selection down to a couple of hundred has been no easy task and many old favorites have had to be side-lined for the simple reason that no cookery book should ever be too fat and heavy to be read in bed or comfortably propped up against a cookie jar. And so, needs must, I have had to choose those that best fit the title.

My basis has been to try and incorporate as many different culinary styles as possible, while still retaining the personal touch which automatically colors the creations of every cook. I certainly have my preferences as regards ingredients and preparation techniques, but at the same time I have tried to take into consideration the frequently changing fashions on the gustatory scene. And so we end up with touches of nouvelle, shades of ethnic cuisine, and a generous portion of vegetarian fare which has become so popular in this health-conscious age. Because natural, unprocessed foods appeal to me very strongly, I have tried to avoid highly processed ingredients and artificial additives, believing that fresh foods, carefully prepared, should not have to be helped along too vigorously.

My selection of recipes ranges from simple, family fare to splendid dishes for elegant entertaining. Because a well-steamed and floured hostess is about as appealing as a stuffed peacock, few of the dishes require much last-minute attention. I have also tried to avoid the temptation of creating dreamy dinner party dishes simply by adding large amounts of butter and cream, and find that lower-calorie sour cream or buttermilk can often be successfully substituted and are more in line with the preference, these days, for somewhat lighter fare. The desserts, however, are unashamedly sweet and indulgent.

Where a recipe requires the addition of flour, all-purpose white flour should be used unless otherwise specified. I have also used extra large eggs in every recipe requiring eggs. Because I prefer natural ingredients, I use butter, but margarine may be substituted according to personal conviction.

Happily, eating, drinking and making merry are part of life, and if I can lay claim to have guided, pleased, or even inspired anyone — whether a nervous new cook or an old hand seeking new ideas — then I shall consider this collection truly complete.

*Lynn Bedford Hall*

## Lemon Crumbed Sole

This type of recipe makes it possible to serve crisp, crumbed fish without any last-minute frying. Allow about 3 small fillets per person, and serve with Tartare sauce (page 55) and lemon wedges.

1–1¼ lb sole fillets
1½ cups fine cereal crumbs
½ tsp salt
oil for baking

LEMON MAYONNAISE
1 egg
5 tsp lemon juice
½ tsp salt
1 tsp sugar
1 cup oil
1 garlic clove, crushed
finely grated zest of ½ lemon

Begin with the mayonnaise. Put egg, lemon juice, salt, sugar and 5 tsp oil into a blender and blend well. With the motor running, pour in the remaining oil in a slow steady stream. Spoon into a bowl and stir in garlic and lemon zest. Cover and chill for several hours for best flavor.

Dip sole fillets into mayonnaise, coating both sides thoroughly, then coat with crumbs mixed with salt. Chill for at least 1 hour to set crumbs.

Preheat oven to 350°F. Heat a thin layer of oil for a few minutes in a large baking dish, then place fillets in dish, turning once in the hot oil. Bake for 10–12 minutes, depending on size.
Serves 4.

## Smoked Salmon and Tuna Ramekins

An elegant appetizer for a special dinner which amazingly stretches less than ¼ lb smoked salmon to 4–5 servings, depending on the size of the ramekins. Ideally choose smoked salmon with no preservatives or coloring. Quantities are easily doubled.

1 x 7 oz can tuna in brine
½ tsp powdered gelatin
⅓ cup mayonnaise
1 tsp lemon juice
1 tbsp sherry
1 egg white
1 tbsp finely chopped chives
⅓ cup cream, whipped
3 oz smoked salmon
black peppercorns

Drain tuna and make up liquid to a scant half cup with water. Sprinkle in gelatin and dissolve over low heat. Add to finely shredded tuna together with mayonnaise, lemon juice and sherry. Purée in blender until smooth, stopping to scrape down the sides. Spoon into a bowl. Beat egg white with a pinch of salt until stiff, then fold into mixture, together with chives and cream. Rinse ramekins and line with smoked salmon slices. Pour in tuna mixture, and chill for a few hours until set. To serve, run a knife round the edges and unmold onto serving plates. Grind a little black pepper over the tops and serve with Melba toast and lemon wedges.
Serves 4.

# Fish Cocktail with Tarragon Mayonnaise

A change from prawns in seafood sauce; use fresh salmon, cod or haddock.

1 lb 14 oz–2 lb firm white fish
4¼ cups water
1 bay leaf
1 carrot, sliced
small bunch of parsley
a few peppercorns
½ onion, sliced
1 tsp salt
2 fresh thyme sprigs
5 tsp lemon juice

TARRAGON MAYONNAISE
2 egg yolks
5 tsp tarragon vinegar
1 tsp dried tarragon
½ tsp salt
1 cup oil
⅓ cup sour cream
3 tbsp chopped chives
1 tbsp capers, drained and
   chopped

Bring all ingredients, from water to lemon juice, to a boil and then simmer, covered, for 10 minutes. Put fish into large saucepan, pour over boiling bouillon (which should just cover fish), bring back to a boil, then cover and simmer very, very gently until just cooked through. Leave to cool in liquid.

Make mayonnaise in advance and chill to develop flavors. Put egg yolks, tarragon vinegar, tarragon, salt and 3 tbsp oil into a blender and blend well. With motor running, slowly pour in the remaining oil. Scoop mayonnaise into a bowl and add cream, chives and capers.

Drain fish thoroughly. Remove any skin and bones, flake, then moisten with mayonnaise. Serve in cocktail glasses or in halved avocados.
Serves 8.

## Note
If the mayonnaise curdles because the oil has been added too quickly, tip it out, wash and dry the blender container very well. Break in another egg and, with motor running, slowly pour the curdled mixture through the hole in the lid.

## Squid Mushroom Salad

Squid marinated in a sharp vinaigrette is squid ruined, so the following dressing is subtle enough not to mask any delicate flavors. The accent in this dish is on the unusual combination of ingredients rather than on the seafood – nevertheless, it is important to use small squid as it has to be cooked in 1 minute. If serving as an hors d'oeuvre rather than at a buffet, pile into scallop shells or halved avocados and serve with fingers of buttered brown bread.

2 slim leeks
2 tsp lemon juice
14 oz squid tubes, sliced into rings
3 cups sliced button mushrooms
salt
2 tsp mayonnaise

BLENDER DRESSING
good ⅓ cup oil
5 tsp lemon juice
1 tbsp anchovy paste
1 small garlic clove, halved
parsley sprigs
1 tsp sugar
1 small green onion, chopped
good ⅓ cup buttermilk (optional)

Slice leeks, white parts only, very thinly. Bring a large saucepan of water to a boil and add lemon juice. Drop in squid, leeks and mushrooms and stir to mix, while the water returns to a boil. Boil for about 1 minute, or just until squid stiffens and turns white. Drain well, tip into bowl and pour dressing over while still hot. To make dressing, put all ingredients into a blender and blend well.

Cool salad and then cover and chill overnight. Just before serving, add salt to taste and bind with mayonnaise.
Serves 6 in scallop shells.

## Avocados with Lumpfish Roe Mousse

By piping the notoriously rich lumpfish roe mousse into the hollows of small avocados, the temptation to over-indulge is neatly avoided.

2 tsp powdered gelatin
5 tsp cold water
½ cup light cream
4 tbsp black lumpfish roe
1 tsp lemon juice
few drops of Tabasco
a little crushed onion
2 tsp mayonnaise
2 egg whites, stiffly beaten
3–4 avocados

Soak gelatin in cold water, then dissolve over low heat. Whip cream, and slowly trickle in melted gelatin. When fairly stiffly whipped, stir in lumpfish roe, lemon juice, Tabasco, onion and mayonnaise. Fold in egg whites, spoon into a bowl and set in the refrigerator.

To serve, pipe the mousse into each avocado half. Serve with lemon wedges, black pepper and Melba toast.
Serves 6–8.

### Hint
To make Melba toast, place loaf in freezer for 2–3 hours, then slice bread very thinly. Remove crusts and, if desired, slice into triangles. Arrange in a single layer on a cookie sheet and dry out in a low oven until crisp. Store in an airtight container.

Monkfish with Mushrooms in Cream Sauce (left) and Tuna Mousse (right)

## *Tuna Mousse*

**The tangy top layer provides a good contrast to the creamy layer below and makes this a particularly eye-catching dish.**

**1 tbsp powdered gelatin**
**1 cup chicken stock**
**1 tsp lemon juice**
**½ pearl onion, grated**
**1 tbsp tomato sauce**
**1 tsp Worcestershire sauce**
**pinch of sugar**
**1 x 7 oz can tuna, drained and flaked**
**½ cup whipping cream, whipped**
**2 egg whites, beaten**

TOMATO LAYER
**1 x 5½ fl oz can tomato juice**
**¾ cup mayonnaise**
**1 tbsp anchovy paste**
**generous pinch of sugar**
**2 tsp powdered gelatin**
**5 tsp cold water**

Pour tomato juice into small bowl. Mix mayonnaise, anchovy paste and sugar. Add ¼ cup to tomato juice, reserve remainder. Beat well. Soften gelatin in cold water and dissolve over low heat, then stir into tomato-mayonnaise mixture. Pour into 4¼ cup mold, and set in refrigerator.

For the mousse, soften gelatin in stock, stir over low heat until dissolved, then pour into a bowl. Add lemon juice, onion, tomato sauce, Worcestershire sauce, sugar and tuna. Purée in blender until smooth, then return to bowl. Stir in the reserved mayonnaise, then fold in cream and egg whites. Pour carefully on top of first layer, which should be set, and return mold to refrigerator until firm. Unmold and serve with a lightly dressed lettuce and avocado salad.
Serves 8.

## *Monkfish with Mushrooms in Cream Sauce*

**Firm in texture, delicate in flavor, monkfish is ideal for a hot or cold first course.**

**1 lb 14 oz monkfish fillets**
**½ cup dry white wine**
**1 cup water**
**1 bay leaf**
**parsley sprig**
**½ small onion**
**6 peppercorns**
**½ tsp salt**
**2 cups sliced mushrooms**
**2 tbsp butter**
**3 tbsp sherry**
**⅓ cup heavy cream**
**2–3 tsp French mustard**
**potatoes mashed with butter and milk**
**grated Parmesan or Gruyère cheese**

WHITE SAUCE
**3 tbsp butter**
**⅓ cup flour**
**1 cup warm milk**
**1½ cups strained fish stock**

Put monkfish, wine, water, bay leaf, parsley, onion, peppercorns and salt in a saucepan and poach until just cooked through. Drain and cube fish. Fry mushrooms lightly in butter. Drain on absorbent paper towels.

Make a white sauce with butter, flour, milk and fish stock. Season to taste and then stir in fish, mushrooms, sherry, cream and mustard. Spoon into 6 scallop shells or individual baking dishes, surround with a border of creamed potatoes and sprinkle with cheese. Bake at 325°F for 25 minutes. Serves 6.

## Oyster and Cheese Molds

This is a convenient, store-cupboard hors d'oeuvre which will feed a large number of guests. Set in individual ramekins, unmold onto small plates and garnish with green onions. Serve with black pepper and Melba toast.

1 tbsp powdered gelatin
3 tbsp medium to sweet sherry
good ¾ cup seasoned chicken stock
1½ cups low-fat soft cheese
scant ½ cup thick mayonnaise
½ tsp Worcestershire sauce
2 green onions, finely chopped
pinch of sugar
1 lb canned or bottled smoked oysters
½ cup whipping cream, whipped
1 egg white, beaten

Soak gelatin in sherry. Heat chicken stock. Pour onto soaked gelatin and stir until dissolved. Beat together cheese, mayonnaise, Worcestershire sauce, green onions and sugar. Slowly beat in stock and gelatin mixture and chill until starting to set.

Drain oysters, dry well on absorbent paper towels and chop roughly. Stir into cheese mixture, then fold in cream and egg white. Pour into 10 rinsed ramekins and refrigerate for at least 4 hours. Run a knife round the edges to unmold. Serves 10.

## Avocado surprise

Set in individual ramekins, turned out and topped with lumpfish roe and sour cream, this is a super appetizer. The mixture is quite rich, so bear this in mind when planning the rest of the meal.

1 cup chicken stock
1 tbsp powdered gelatin
2 very large unbruised avocados
1 tbsp lemon juice
few drops of Tabasco
½ tsp Worcestershire sauce
pinch each of sugar and celery salt
ground black pepper
¼ cup mayonnaise
½ cup whipping cream, whipped
1 egg white
chilled lumpfish roe
sour cream
finely grated lemon zest

Pour chicken stock into a small saucepan, sprinkle in the gelatin, place over low heat and stir until dissolved without boiling. Using a silver fork, mash avocados with lemon juice. Add Tabasco, Worcestershire sauce, sugar, celery salt and a few grinds of pepper. Add to stock and purée in blender until smooth. Pour into a bowl. Stir in mayonnaise and fold in the cream. Beat the egg white until stiff, stir a little into the avocado mixture and then fold in the remainder.

Pour into 6 or 8 rinsed ramekins, cover with plastic wrap and chill for several hours until firm. Run a knife round the edges to unmold. With a teaspoon, scoop a small hollow in the top of each, and drop in a little lumpfish roe. Cover lumpfish roe with a spoonful of sour cream, and then sprinkle with a little lemon zest, or black pepper. Serve on the day it is made with hot toast. Serves 6–8.

## Haddock and Shrimp Mousse with Two Sauces

Visually, this is a stunning appetizer: a pale and delicate fish mousse, set in ramekins, unmolded and flanked by a ribbon of bright avocado sauce on one side, a pool of light tomato coulis on the other. The combination of flavors is superb, and a further plus is that the creamy textures are achieved without the usual lashings of cream. I have also eliminated egg yolks and used buttermilk, sour cream and egg whites to scale down the possibility of an overly rich beginning to a meal. There is quite a lot of preparation involved, but everything can be completed well in advance – the sauces in the morning, and the mousse even the day before.

good ½ lb haddock fillets
good ¾ cup water
2 onion slices
¼ cup white wine
salt
black peppercorns
1 bay leaf
2 tbsp butter
2 tbsp flour
⅔ cup haddock stock
½ cup milk
2 tsp powdered gelatin
¼ cup thick mayonnaise
good ⅓ cup sour cream
1 x 7 oz can shrimp
2 egg whites
lemon juice

TOMATO COULIS
2 tsp oil
1 tsp butter
1 onion, chopped
1 leek, sliced
good ½ lb tomatoes, skinned, seeded and chopped
¼ cup water
3 fresh thyme sprigs
salt and ground black pepper

1 bay leaf
½ tsp sugar
3 tbsp light cream

AVOCADO SAUCE
1 large, ripe avocado
½ tsp lemon juice
good ¾ cup buttermilk
generous pinch of salt
few drops of Worcestershire sauce
¼ cup mayonnaise
pinch of sugar

Poach the haddock gently in the water, with onion, wine, seasoning and bay leaf until just cooked. Cool in liquid. Reserve liquid and flake fish very finely. Make a velouté sauce with butter, flour, ½ cup poaching liquid and milk. When thickened, add to fish. Soak gelatin in remaining cooled poaching liquid, dissolve over low heat, and add to fish together with mayonnaise and sour cream. Rinse, dry and roughly chop shrimps, then fold half into mixture. Stiffly

beat egg whites with a pinch of salt and fold in. Adjust seasoning, add a dash of lemon juice, then spoon into 6 rinsed ramekins and chill.

To make the coulis, heat oil and butter and soften onion and leek. Add tomatoes and remaining ingredients, except cream. Cover and simmer gently for about 15 minutes until soft and thick. Cool. Remove thyme and bay leaf and purée in blender until smooth. Pour into a jug, stir in cream and chill.

For the avocado sauce, dice avocado and place in blender with remaining ingredients. Blend until smooth. If too thick, add a little milk or cream. Spoon into a jug and stir in remaining shrimps. Sink avocado seed in the middle (to preserve the color), cover and chill.

To serve, unmold ramekins onto serving plates. Pour a pool of avocado sauce on one side, tomato on the other. Garnish with a sprig of fennel or dill.
Serves 6.

## Salad Niçoise

This salad is usually served on its own, as a first course. It is a popular, somewhat eclectic affair, the ingredients depending on what's in season and on personal preference. It is often dressed just before being eaten, but I like to chill it for a while to give the flavors time to blend.

6–8 anchovy fillets
milk
7 oz green beans
½ large red Bell pepper
½ medium onion
2 medium tomatoes
¼ cucumber
1 x 7 oz can tuna in oil
black olives
hard-boiled eggs (optional)

DRESSING
¼ cup olive oil
1 tbsp tarragon vinegar
generous pinch of salt
generous pinch of paprika
1 large garlic clove, crushed
1 tsp capers, chopped
pinch of sugar
3 tbsp chopped parsley
6 fresh basil leaves, chopped

Soak anchovies in milk. Trim and slice beans, seed and dice red Bell pepper, and boil together until just tender. Slice onion into rings and skin and slice tomatoes. Pare and slice cucumber very thinly. Drain and flake tuna.

In a flattish bowl layer the beans, red Bell pepper, tuna, onion, tomato slices and cucumber to cover the entire top.

Make the dressing by beating all the ingredients together with a fork. Pour over salad. Top with drained anchovies, olives and hard-boiled eggs, if using. Cover and chill. Serve with hot French bread. Serves 4–5.

## Stuffed Mushrooms Gruyère

**A delicious appetizer for an elegant dinner.**

**4–6 large brown mushrooms**
**4 green onions, chopped**
**½ cup fine fresh wholewheat breadcrumbs**
**14 fresh rosemary needles, finely chopped**
**½ tsp Worcestershire sauce**
**3 tbsp thick mayonnaise**
**salt and ground black pepper**
**grated Gruyère cheese**
**paprika**
**3 tbsp butter**
**1 small garlic clove, crushed**

Remove mushroom stalks and scoop out a little of the center of each cap. Chop stalks and centers finely and mix with green onions, breadcrumbs, rosemary, Worcester-shire sauce, mayonnaise and a pinch of salt.

Oil a large baking sheet and arrange mushrooms, hollows up. Season with salt and ground pepper. Top with stuffing mixture and sprinkle with Gruyère cheese and paprika. Combine butter and garlic and put a pat on top of each mushroom. Bake at 350°F for 20 minutes, then serve with a spoonful of the juices over each mushroom, and buttered wholewheat bread. Serves 4–6.

### Hint

**To peel garlic cloves, pour boiling water over and leave to stand for 5 minutes. Skin will slip off easily.**

## Stuffed Eggplant

**Serve as an unusual first course with hot French bread.**

**2 medium eggplant**
**1 large tomato, skinned and chopped**
**½ small onion, finely chopped**
**¾ cup wholewheat breadcrumbs**
**3 tbsp garlic blender mayonnaise (page 69)**
**salt and ground black pepper**
**½ tsp dried basil**
**pinch of sugar**
**feta cheese**
**3 tbsp oil**
**black olives to garnish**

Boil eggplant in unsalted water for 8–10 minutes or until just softened. Cut in half and remove most of flesh, leaving shells intact. Chop the pulp coarsely and add tomato, onion, breadcrumbs, mayonnaise, seasoning, basil and sugar. Fill shells and sprinkle liberally with crumbled feta. Dribble the oil over the eggplant and bake, uncovered, at 325°F for 45 minutes. Leave to cool – the liquid will slowly be absorbed. Serve at room temperature garnished with black olives.
Serves 4.

## Avocados Stuffed with Mushrooms and Leeks

Stir-fried leeks and mushrooms, perfumed with rosemary, are marinated in sherry and soy sauce and then spooned into avocado halves. Assemble just before serving, but prepare the filling a few hours in advance. The following quantities are for 4 avocado halves, but can easily be doubled.

2 leeks
¼ cup oil
½ lb brown mushrooms, sliced
rosemary sprig
3 tbsp sweet sherry
1 tbsp soy sauce
ground black pepper
2 avocados, halved
parsley sprigs to garnish

Very finely shred the white parts only of the leeks – you should have about 1 cup – and add to the hot oil, together with mushrooms and rosemary. Stir-fry over fairly high heat for 1–2 minutes until just beginning to soften and brown.

Spoon into a bowl (including sprig of rosemary) and add sherry, soy sauce and a few grinds of pepper. Cover and cool.

Just before serving, remove rosemary and drain off most of the marinade. Enlarge cavities of halved avocados a little and spoon in filling. Top with a sprig of parsley, and serve with salt and black pepper.
Serves 4.

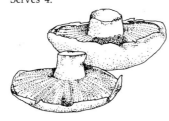

## Mushroom Pâté

Serve with crackers or hot toast.

4 tbsp butter
¾ lb brown mushrooms, sliced
1 small onion, chopped
1 garlic clove, crushed
pinch of dried thyme
5 tbsp butter, diced
5 tsp soy sauce
¼ cup sweet sherry
ground black pepper
pinch of sugar

Melt the butter and sauté mushrooms, onion, garlic and thyme. When brown and soft, reduce heat to low and add diced butter and remaining ingredients except sugar. Stir until melted, then remove from heat. Add sugar, cool slightly, then purée, leaving mixture somewhat chunky. Pot, cover with plastic wrap and chill for 24 hours.

## Oyster Pâté

Surely the simplest recipe in the book. This delicious pâté is rich, so it goes a long way.

1 x 8 oz can smoked oysters
1 tsp lemon juice
1 small onion slice, chopped
ground black pepper
7 tbsp butter, melted

Drain oysters and put into blender with remaining ingredients. Blend once or twice to chop coarsely, then pot and chill for about 4 hours. Serve with unbuttered wholewheat bread or hot toast.

### Variation
CLAM PÂTÉ
Use 1 x 11oz can clams instead of the oysters.

# Green Salad with Pears and Ricotta Balls

This is an unusual salad, interesting enough to be served as a first course, as part of a cold buffet, or with roast chicken. The ricotta balls, quickly made in a processor, and the pears, add an elegant touch.

NUTTY RICOTTA BALLS
¾ lb ricotta cheese
½ cup grated Cheddar cheese
1–2 green onions, chopped
generous pinch of onion salt
pinch of celery salt
few drops of Tabasco
½ tsp French mustard
½ tsp Worcestershire sauce
parsley sprigs
nuts (almonds, pecans, walnuts or hazels), finely chopped and toasted

DRESSING
5 tbsp vegetable oil
3 tbsp olive oil
1 small garlic clove, crushed
3 tbsp lemon juice
generous pinch of dry mustard
generous pinch of salt

SALAD
2 medium pears
good ½ lb broccoli spears
1 round lettuce
1 avocado

To make the ricotta balls, put all the ingredients, except nuts, into a processor fitted with the grinding blade. Process until thick and creamy and mixture forms a ball. Spoon into small dish and chill for several hours.

Put ingredients for dressing into large wooden salad bowl, and mix with a fork until creamy.

Peel and core pears and cut into eighths. Add to dressing, toss well and then cover and allow to stand for up to 2 hours.

Steam and chop broccoli. Just before serving, shred lettuce coarsely, and dice avocado. Add broccoli, lettuce and avocado to pears and toss well. Scoop out large teaspoons of chilled ricotta mixture and roll into 18–24 balls. Roll each ball in chopped nuts and place on top of salad.
Serves 6.

## Shrimp, Cucumber and Cheese Cream

**An unusual, cold and wobbly first course just right on a summer's evening before a special dinner.**

½ cucumber
1 cup water
scant ½ cup white wine
salt
1 lb peeled shrimp
⅓ cup powdered gelatin
¼ cup cold water
1⅓ cups low-fat soft cheese
scant ½ cup thick mayonnaise
3 tbsp chopped chives
1 tsp prepared mustard
1 tsp sugar
2 egg whites
½ cup whipping cream, whipped
3 tbsp mayonnaise
3 tbsp sour cream
few drops of Worcestershire
   sauce
pinch of paprika

Pare cucumber, chop into small cubes, then degorge (page 135). Bring water, wine and ½ tsp salt to boil. Add shrimp and cook for a few minutes until just tender, then drain, reserving the liquid. Sprinkle gelatin onto cold water, leave a few minutes to soften, then stir in 1 cup of the reserved hot liquid, and stir until gelatin has dissolved. Set aside. Mix cheese with scant cup mayonnaise, chives, mustard and sugar. Slowly stir in dissolved gelatin, then add rinsed and well-dried cucumber. Chop half the shrimp and stir into cheese mixture. Stiffly beat egg whites with a pinch of salt and fold in together with whipped cream. Pour into a rinsed ring mold or 8–10 individual ramekins and set in refrigerator. Mix remaining shrimp with 3 tbsp mayonnaise, sour cream, Worcestershire sauce and paprika and chill.

   To serve, turn out and either spoon shrimp mixture into the center of the ring mold, or top each ramekin with a spoonful.
Serve with Melba toast.
Serves 8–10.

Mushrooms with Spinach and Cheese (left) and Brown Mushrooms with Herb Butter (right)

## *Mushrooms with Spinach and Cheese*

**These delicious mushrooms may be served in several ways: either as first course in which case use large flat mushrooms, one per serving, or use medium-sized brown ones as an accompaniment to broiled steak. These mushrooms may also be served as a vegetarian meal with rice tossed with a knob of butter, toasted almonds and soy sauce.**

1 x 9 oz package frozen spinach
¾ lb brown mushrooms
3 tbsp oil
1 onion, chopped
1–2 garlic cloves, crushed
1⅓ cups low-fat soft cheese
generous pinch of ground
   nutmeg
generous pinch of dried dill
½ tsp salt
ground black pepper
1 egg, separated
7 tbsp grated Gruyère cheese

Thaw spinach completely and drain well in colander. (Frozen spinach takes a long time to thaw, so allow for this. It may be hurried along by immersing the whole package in cold water.) Remove stalks from mushroom caps and chop finely. Heat oil and lightly fry stalks, onion and garlic. Add spinach and toss a few minutes until mixture is absolutely dry and spinach is cooked. Set aside to cool.

   Mix cheese, seasonings and egg yolk into spinach mixture. Wipe mushroom caps and arrange on lightly oiled baking dish. Season. Beat egg white stiffly and fold into spinach mixture. Pile onto mushrooms to cover completely. Sprinkle with Gruyère and bake at 350°F for 25–30 minutes.
Serves 4.

## *Brown Mushrooms with Herb Butter*

**One of the easiest and most popular of hors d'oeuvres and the perfect way of treating large flat mushrooms. Slightly smaller brown mushrooms can be prepared in the same way, and are superb with broiled meat.**

6 large brown mushrooms
7 tbsp butter, softened
2 garlic cloves, crushed
6–8 fresh rosemary needles,
   finely chopped
1 tbsp chopped chives
1 tbsp chopped parsley
1 tsp soy sauce
salt and ground black pepper

Wipe mushrooms. Cut stalks off level with the caps, and chop finely. Arrange caps in a large baking dish. Cream butter with garlic, rosemary, chives, parsley and soy sauce. Divide this mixture into 6 large pats. Pile the chopped mushroom stalks on top of the caps and season very lightly. Top each mushroom with a pat of the herb butter.

   Preheat broiler and slide dish underneath. Broil for about 10 minutes until the mushrooms are soft and the butter melted. Serve with thin slices of buttered wholewheat bread.
Serves 6.

# Chilled Fresh Asparagus Creams

Canned asparagus is useful in salads but the flavor of fresh asparagus is unique. Made with the minimum of ingredients so as not to mask its delicate flavor, the set creams are unmolded onto small plates and served with mayonnaise.

¾ lb fresh asparagus
1½ cups salted water
light chicken stock
2 tsp powdered gelatin
¼ cup cold water
few drops of lemon juice
4 drops of Tabasco
2 egg whites
scant ½ cup whipping cream, whipped
mayonnaise

Rinse asparagus and remove the base of each stalk. In a wide, shallow saucepan bring the salted water to a boil, add asparagus in single layer and cook gently for 12 minutes, leaving lid of saucepan slightly tilted. Drain, reserving liquid. Make up reserved liquid to scant ¾ cup with light chicken stock if necessary. Chop asparagus, reserving 6 perfect tips. Purée chopped asparagus and the liquid in a blender until smooth, then press through a strainer into a bowl. You should have about 1¼ cup purée.

Soften gelatin in ¼ cup cold water and dissolve over low heat. Stir into purée, add lemon juice and Tabasco, then cool, or chill, until mixture thickens. Beat egg whites with a pinch of salt and fold into mixture together with cream. Adjust seasoning. Pour into 6 rinsed ramekins and allow to set in refrigerator. To serve, run a knife round the edges and unmold onto individual plates. Spread a thin layer of mayonnaise over the tops and place one asparagus tip in the center of each. If available, place a red oak lettuce leaf at the side, simply for color.
Serves 6.

Individual Smoked Salmon Cheesecakes (left) and Chicken Liver Pâté (right)

## *Individual Smoked Salmon Cheesecakes*

This light, savory cheesecake may be set in individual ramekins or on a cracker crust. Serve with lemon wedges and hot toast.

FILLING
**1–2 green onions**
**1⅓ cups low-fat soft cheese**
**¼ lb smoked salmon, finely chopped**
**6 tbsp plain yogurt**
**3 tbsp thick mayonnaise**
**generous pinch of finely grated lemon zest**
**ground black pepper**
**2 tsp powdered gelatin**
**5 tsp cold water**
**2 egg whites, beaten**
**¼ cup whipping cream, whipped**

CRUST
**¼ lb savory cheese crackers, crushed**
**¼ cup melted butter**

Chop green onions and finely chop a little of the green tops. Mix cheese with salmon, green onions, yogurt, mayonnaise, lemon zest and pepper. Soften gelatin in the cold water and dissolve over low heat. Stir gelatin into mixture and fold in egg whites and cream. Pour into individual ramekins, cover and chill for at least 4 hours.

Before serving, grind a little black pepper over each and garnish with lemon zest.

To make the crust, mix crushed crackers with butter and press onto base of greased 8-in pie dish. Chill. Make filling as described above, pour onto crust, cover and chill for at least 4 hours. Serve sliced in wedges sprinkled with a little ground black pepper.
Serves 6–8.

## *Chicken Liver Pâté*

I thought for a long time before including this recipe, because pâtés on this theme have become standard snack-fare with wholewheat bread. This is, however, such a delicious version that even jaded palates might well be tempted once again.

**½ cup butter**
**½ tsp dried thyme**
**½ tsp dried marjoram**
**1 onion, chopped**
**1 lb chicken livers**
**½ tsp salt**
**2 garlic cloves, chopped**
**generous pinch of ground nutmeg**
**3 tbsp brandy**
**⅓ cup sweet sherry**
**clarified butter (see below)**

In a large saucepan melt butter with thyme and marjoram. Fry onion until softened, then add washed, trimmed and sliced chicken livers. Don't overcook, remove from heat when just done, smelling nicely and the gravy beginning to look like gravy. Cool slightly, then spoon into container of blender.

Add remaining ingredients, except clarified butter, and blend until smooth. Pot and pour a little clarified butter over. Mixture will be very soft, but firms up in refrigerator. Chill overnight. Serve with bread, toast fingers or Melba toast. Makes just under 1 lb.

### *To clarify butter*
Cut butter into dice and allow to melt over low heat without browning, skimming off any surface scum. Remove from heat and allow to stand – the yellow liquid which rises to the top is the clarified butter. Cool and strain over pâté.

Leeks with Rosemary Mayonnaise

## Leeks with Rosemary Mayonnaise

**Buy young, fresh leeks for this unusual hors d'oeuvre.**

**8 leeks**
**1 cup salted chicken stock**
**2 bay leaves**
**2 x 3-in fresh rosemary sprigs**
**paprika to garnish**

ROSEMARY MAYONNAISE
**1 egg**
**4 tsp lemon juice**
**½ tsp salt**
**¾ cup oil**
**1 tsp sugar**
**3 tsp Dijon mustard**
**¼ cup sour cream**

Cut off roots and most of the tops of the leeks, leaving not more than 1 in of the green leaves. Remove outside layer. Make a shallow cut down length of leek so that the layers may be opened out slightly. Wash very well to remove grit. Put stock, bay leaves and rosemary sprigs into large skillet with a lid. Add leeks, bring to a boil and simmer, covered, for about 7–10 minutes or until just cooked. Cool in liquid, then drain and chill, reserving rosemary.

To make the mayonnaise, place egg, lemon juice, salt, 3 tbsp oil, sugar and mustard into a blender. Strip needles from the reserved cooked rosemary sprigs and add. Blend well, then with motor running, add remaining oil in a slow steady stream. Tip into small bowl, stir in sour cream, cover and chill for at least 2 hours.

To serve, arrange chilled leeks on serving plates – 2 each should be enough, depending on size. Spoon some mayonnaise down the center of each serving, and dust with paprika.
Serves 4.

## Green Bean Salad with Feta Cheese

**A favorite bean salad, served as a Greek-style first course, dressed with a herby olive oil dressing and studded with olives and feta cheese. Use the youngest and slimmest beans you can find, and assemble the salad several hours in advance.**

**1–1¼ lb young green beans**
**2 bay leaves**
**10 black olives, sliced**
**1 onion, sliced into rings**
**1 red bell pepper, seeded and sliced**
**feta cheese**

DRESSING
**¼ cup vegetable oil**
**¼ cup olive oil**
**1½ tsp dried oregano**
**5 tsp lemon juice**
**½ tsp celery salt**
**1 tsp thin honey**
**2 garlic cloves, crushed**

First mix ingredients for dressing, cover and stand a few hours for flavor to develop. Shake well before using.

Trim the beans. Leave them whole if very small, otherwise halve. Poach lightly in a little salted water with the bay leaves. If you leave the lid of the saucepan slightly ajar while cooking, you'll retain the bright color. When just tender, drain well and spoon into a large shallow serving dish. Remove bay leaves and add olives, onion and red bell pepper.

Pour dressing over, cool, cover and chill for about 4 hours. Sprinkle generously with feta cheese before serving with chunks of crusty white bread.
Serves 4–6.

Asparagus with Lemon Mayonnaise served with French Loaf with Fresh Herb Butter

## Asparagus with Lemon Mayonnaise

**A timeless old favorite. When asparagus is not in season, substitute slender, young leeks.**

**¾ lb fresh asparagus**
**paprika or chives to garnish**

LEMON MAYONNAISE
**1 large egg or 2 yolks**
**5 tsp fresh lemon juice**
**1 tsp sugar**
**½ tsp salt**
**scant 1 cup oil**
**1 garlic clove, crushed**
**finely grated zest of ½ lemon**
**sour cream or whipped cream**

To prepare asparagus, rinse gently, then remove bases of stalks. Bring some salted water to a boil in a large shallow saucepan, add asparagus in a single layer and simmer,

uncovered, until just tender. Drain and chill.

For the mayonnaise, put egg, lemon juice, sugar, salt and 3 tbsp oil into blender. Blend to mix thoroughly, then with the motor running, pour in remaining oil in a slow, steady stream. Spoon into a small bowl and stir in garlic and lemon zest. Cover and chill for several hours. To thin down before serving, stir in a little sour cream or fold in a few spoonfuls of cream.

Arrange 3–4 asparagus spears on each plate and spoon a ribbon of mayonnaise across each serving. Dust with paprika or sprinkle with snipped chives.
Serves 6–8.

## French Loaf with Fresh Herb Butter

**A welcome change from the ubiquitous garlic bread.**

**1 large or 2 small French loaves**
**1 cup plus 2 tbsp softened butter**
**4 thyme sprigs, chopped**
**6 sage leaves, chopped**
**1 oregano sprig, chopped**
**ground black pepper**
**2 tbsp chopped parsley**
**1 medium onion, grated**
**1 tsp onion salt**
**1 tsp prepared mustard**

Slice French loaves in ½-in slices to the base, but not right through. Combine remaining ingredients and butter generously between the slices. Reshape, wrap in foil, leaving the top exposed, and bake at 350°F for 15 minutes. Enough for 30–40 slices.

## Tuna Pâté

**A tuna pâté with a difference.**

**6 anchovy fillets**
**¼ cup milk**
**1 x 7 oz can tuna in oil**
**½ cup melted butter**
**2 tsp lemon juice**
**pinch of sugar**
**3 tbsp finely chopped parsley**
**3 tbsp finely chopped chives**
**3 tbsp thick sour cream**

Soak anchovy fillets in milk for 1 hour, then drain. Place in blender with tuna (plus the oil), melted butter, lemon juice and sugar. Blend until smooth, then stir in remaining ingredients. Pot and chill.

Serve at room temperature with Melba toast or unbuttered wholewheat or dark rye bread. Serves about 10 as a snack.

# Blue Cheese Mousse

Not everybody likes blue cheese. Used in quantity, it can be very strong and strangely odiferous, rather like old tennis shoes. Used with discretion, however, it adds an interesting tang to a creamy mousse. It really depends on personal taste and the type of cheese used, so just taste as you go.

½ lb low-fat soft cheese
crumbled blue cheese, starting
    with 2 tbsp
scant ½ cup mayonnaise
½ tsp Worcestershire sauce
½ tsp paprika
generous pinch of garlic salt
generous pinch of sugar
1 tbsp powdered gelatin
½ cup chicken stock
½ cup whipping cream, whipped
1 egg white, beaten
3 tbsp finely chopped chives

Cream low-fat cheese, blue cheese, mayonnaise, Worcestershire sauce, paprika, garlic salt and sugar. Soak gelatin in stock, dissolve over low heat, then beat into cheese mixture. Leave until mixture thickens, then fold in cream, egg white and chives. Pour into rinsed mold and chill until set. To unmold, run a knife round the edge and give a gentle shake. Garnish with watercress, parsley, or walnuts. Serve at the end of a meal with savory crackers.
Serves 12–14.

## Note

Roquefort, the most famous blue-veined cheese, comes from an arid mountain region in France. Here, sheep feed on dry grass and wild herbs and produce a unique, sweet milk from which the cheese is made. Its distinctive flavor develops while the cheese is left to mature inside the limestone caves found in this area.

Potted Roquefort

## *Potted Cheese with Herbs*

Such a simple recipe, but so useful. Use on wholewheat sandwiches, on savory crackers, or spread liberally on lightly buttered toast and cook under the broiler until bubbling.

scant ½ cup milk
4 tbsp butter
¾–1 lb Cheddar cheese, grated
2 eggs, beaten
generous pinch each of dried
    sage, dry mustard and salt
ground black pepper
1 small garlic clove, peeled
pinch each of sugar and dried
    thyme

Heat milk and butter in a smallish, heavy saucepan. Add cheese and eggs. Stir over low heat until cheese melts and mixture thickens.

Remove from stove and cool slightly, then pour into blender. Add remaining ingredients and blend until smooth. Spoon into storage container and chill for at least a day before using.
Makes about ¾ lb.

### *Variation*

Heat 2 tsp each butter and oil in a small saucepan and add 1 finely chopped onion and 1 small, skinned and chopped tomato. Cover and sweat over low heat until softened. Beat 2 eggs together with ½ tsp dry mustard. Add to saucepan together with 1 cup finely grated Gouda cheese. Season with salt and black pepper and cook over low heat, stirring, until mixture thickens and eggs are cooked. Cool and refrigerate.
**Makes about ½ lb.**

## *Potted Roquefort*

A splendid addition to the cheese board, either before or after the dessert.

6 oz blue cheese
1 tsp Worcestershire sauce
4 tsp brandy
1 tsp onion salt
½ cup smooth cottage cheese
scant ½ cup heavy cream
1 tbsp finely chopped parsley
generous pinch of sugar
walnuts to garnish

Grate cheese and mash with remaining ingredients, except walnuts, until smooth. Put into storage container and chill for 12 hours. To serve, form into a square and press halved walnuts all over. Serve with savory crackers.
Makes about ½ lb.

## *Cream Cheese and Cheddar Roll*

1⅓ cups cream cheese
2 cups very finely grated
    Cheddar cheese
½ tsp Worcestershire sauce
few drops of Tabasco
1 tbsp brandy
½ tsp French mustard
1 tsp finely grated onion
a little softened butter (optional)
chopped pecan nuts or walnuts

Using a wooden spoon, work all ingredients, except nuts, together until smooth. Roll into a sausage shape (mixture will be fairly soft but firms up in refrigerator), wrap in waxed paper and chill overnight. Before serving, roll in nuts until coated.
Makes 20–24 small slices.

## Avocado Soup

Not as quick as some avocado soups, but it's reliable and very good, and manages to be smoothly rich without the addition of either egg yolks or cream. May be served either hot or chilled.

2 tbsp butter
¼ cup flour
1½ cups hot chicken stock
1½ cups warmed milk
salt and pepper
1 very large or 2 medium, ripe but unbruised avocados
2 tsp lemon juice
4 parsley sprigs
1 small green onion, chopped
pinch of sugar
avocado balls and paprika to garnish

Melt butter in saucepan, stir in flour and when absorbed remove from heat and slowly stir in stock and milk. Return to heat and stir until thick and smooth – use a wire whisk to avoid lumps. Season and remove. Mash peeled avocado with lemon juice and add to white sauce together with parsley, green onion and sugar. Pour into blender and purée until smooth.

To reheat, pour into top of double saucepan and stir over simmering water. On no account must the soup boil or even bubble. Check seasoning and serve in individual, heated bowls, garnished with a few avocado balls and a dusting of paprika for color. Alternatively chill and serve cold. Serves 4–6.

### Hint
If this soup is to be refrigerated sink avocado seed into soup. This helps to preserve the color.

## Gourmet Mushroom Soup

The perennial favorite, but with a difference – here half the mushrooms are cooked and puréed, the rest simmered in the resulting thick broth, finished off with cream and sherry and garnished with fried onion rings.

3 tbsp oil
1 tbsp butter
1 onion, chopped
2 leeks, sliced
1 fresh rosemary sprig
4 cups thinly sliced brown mushrooms
¼ cup flour
3 cups chicken stock
salt and ground black pepper
pinch of ground mace
1 cup milk
1 tbsp soy sauce
pinch of sugar
3 tbsp sherry
¼ cup whipped cream
fried onion rings to garnish

Heat oil and butter, add onion and leeks and allow to soften without browning. Add rosemary and half the mushrooms. Fry gently until soft, then remove rosemary and stir in flour. When well mixed add chicken stock slowly, stirring. Season lightly with salt, pepper and mace. Cover and simmer for 15 minutes. Cool for 10 minutes, then purée until smooth. Return to saucepan, add remaining mushrooms, milk, soy sauce and sugar.

Cover and simmer for 10 minutes, then add sherry and finally swirl in whipped cream. Serve at once garnished with fried onion rings. Serves 6.

## Spiced Pumpkin Soup

A surprisingly lovely soup, smooth and thick, which uses basic ingredients. Serve in individual bowls, top with whipped cream and a sprinkling of paprika, and wait for the compliments.

1 lb peeled firm pumpkin, cubed
3 tbsp oil
1 tbsp butter
1 large onion, chopped
2 medium potatoes, peeled and
  cubed
2 carrots, diced
1 tsp ground ginger
1 tsp ground cinnamon
4¼ cups chicken stock
1 cup milk
1 tsp honey
½ tsp paprika
salt
whipped cream and paprika to
  garnish

Add pumpkin to heated oil and butter, together with onion, potatoes, carrots, ginger and cinnamon. Toss together over low heat for about 5 minutes, then add stock, milk, honey, paprika and salt to taste.

Bring to a boil, half-cover and simmer until vegetables are soft. Cool a little, then purée until smooth. Adjust seasoning, then reheat over low heat, stirring, and serve as suggested.
Serves 6–8.

## Cauliflower and Watercress Soup with Blue Cheese Cream

Quite a mouthful, and better than the usual Crème Dubarry. This subtly flavored vegetable soup, flecked with watercress and topped with savory whipped cream is very easy to make and grand enough for any dinner party. If you can't find watercress, it may be omitted – but it does add a bit of color and interest. For a chunkier soup, remove some cauliflower before puréeing soup, then return and reheat gently.

3 tbsp oil
1 tbsp butter
2 onions, chopped
1–1¼ lb cauliflower
1 bunch watercress
1 large potato, peeled and cubed
4¼ cups chicken stock
1 bay leaf
2 cups milk (skimmed milk may be used)
salt and ground black pepper
pinch of sugar
watercress to garnish

SAVORY CREAM
½ cup heavy cream
½ tsp Worcestershire sauce
blue cheese

Make savory cream in advance and refrigerate. Whip cream with Worcestershire sauce and cheese – start with a 1-in cube and then add more to taste. When thick, cover and chill.

Heat oil and butter in a large saucepan and gently sauté onions. Break cauliflower into flowerets, wash and add to saucepan. Strip leaves from watercress, wash, then add together with potato. When softened, add stock, bay leaf, milk, seasoning and sugar. The liquid should just cover the vegetables. Half-cover the saucepan and simmer until soft. Remove bay leaf and cool slightly. Purée in blender until smooth. Reheat gently.

To serve, spoon soup into serving bowls and top each serving with a dollop of cream and a sprig of watercress.
Serves 6–8.

## Quick Minestrone with Pesto

This very simple version of the famous Italian soup is just right for Sunday suppers. A spoonful of pesto stirred into each bowl gives the soup a deliciously different taste. Serve with hot garlic bread.

¼ cup oil
2 onions, chopped
2 large carrots, diced
2 celery stalks, sliced
1 leek, chopped
2 garlic cloves, crushed
5 cups shredded cabbage
3 tomatoes, skinned and chopped
3 tbsp tomato paste
¼ lb small pasta shells
2 tbsp chopped parsley
5 oz green beans, chopped
7 cups water or stock
1 tsp dried oregano
salt and ground black pepper
pinch of sugar
2 bay leaves
pesto (page 31)

Heat oil in a large saucepan and sauté onions, carrots, celery, leek and garlic. When softened, add remaining ingredients, except pesto. Bring to a boil, then cover and simmer for about 1 hour. Remove bay leaves.

If possible, make soup in advance, and reheat for the best flavor. Have the pesto at room temperature and add 1 tsp to each serving.
Serves 8.

### Note
If desired, a small triangle of toast may be floated on the soup, and topped with a spoonful of pesto.

## Zucchini and Green Pepper Soup

A most delicate and delicious soup, which contains neither potatoes, egg yolks nor cream. It is lower in calories than most smooth soups, and yet the texture is beautifully creamy.

3 tbsp oil
1 large green Bell pepper, seeded and diced
1 small onion, chopped
2 leeks, sliced
about 1lb zucchini
1 bay leaf
3 cups chicken stock
few parsley sprigs
½ tsp salt
3 tbsp skimmed milk powder
½ cup milk

Heat oil in a large saucepan and add green bell pepper, onion and leeks. Cover saucepan and sweat over low heat until softened. Add trimmed, pared and sliced zucchini and toss to mix, then add bay leaf, stock, parsley and salt. Cover and simmer for about 20 minutes until vegetables are soft.

Blend milk powder with milk, add to soup, then purée in blender. Adjust seasoning and reheat without boiling, or cool and chill. Serve garnished with green Bell pepper and sliced zucchini.
Serves 4–6.

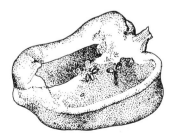

## Hake and Mussel Soup

A hearty and delicious soup, just right for an informal supper and great served with Anchovy French bread.

3 tbsp oil
1 tbsp butter
1 large onion, chopped
1 garlic clove, crushed
3 tomatoes, skinned and chopped
2 carrots, finely diced
2 potatoes, peeled and diced
¼ cup chopped parsley
¾–1 lb fresh or frozen hake fillets
4¼ cups fish stock (see below)
1 bay leaf
1 tsp dried dill
salt and ground black pepper
pinch of sugar
1 x 10 oz can mussels
¼ cup sherry

Heat oil and butter in a large saucepan and soften onion and garlic. Add tomatoes, carrots, potatoes and parsley. When vegetables are softened, place fish on top, then add stock, bay leaf, dill, seasoning and sugar. Cover and simmer for about 20 minutes until cooked. When cool enough to handle, remove fish and discard skin and bones, if any, then flake it and return to saucepan. Reheat without boiling, adding mussels plus their liquid and sherry. Serves 6 generously.

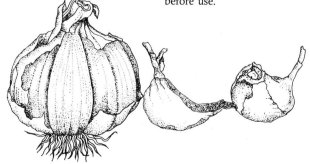

## Fish Stock

1¾–2 lb fish trimmings
1 onion, sliced
a few parsley sprigs
1 bay leaf
salt
1 small carrot
6 black peppercorns
⅔ cup white wine
4¼ cups water

Combine all the ingredients and simmer for 45 minutes. Strain before use.

## Anchovy French Bread

good 1 cup unsalted butter
1 x 2 oz can anchovies
pinch of paprika
¼ cup finely chopped parsley
a few drops of lemon juice
1 French loaf

Mash butter with remaining ingredients, except bread. Slice bread to base, but not right through, in ¾-in slices, and spread generously with anchovy butter. Wrap in foil, leaving top exposed. Bake at 350°F for 15–20 minutes.

### Hint
To remove excess saltiness, soak anchovies in milk before using.

## Lentil and Vegetable Soup

This is a nourishing, speedy and meatless soup. Low in cost, it is a meal in itself served with wholewheat bread and cheese and perfect for Sunday suppers. Use red lentils, which cook to a pulp very quickly. Do not soak them, simply rinse them.

¼ cup oil
1 large onion, chopped
1–2 garlic cloves, crushed
½ tsp dried thyme
2 large carrots, coarsely grated
good 1 cup red lentils
7 cups stock or water with 1 tbsp Marmite
1½ oz parsley, chopped
1 bay leaf
3 cups shredded cabbage
1 tbsp tomato paste
1 tsp each salt and sugar
1 tsp Worcestershire sauce

Heat the oil in a large saucepan and add onion, garlic, thyme and carrots. Stir-fry for a few minutes and then add remaining ingredients. Bring to a boil, then cover and simmer for 20 minutes, stirring once or twice. For best flavor, allow to cool and then reheat before serving. Remove bay leaf and adjust seasoning. Serve with 1 tsp pesto (below) stirred into each serving, and Cheddar thins.
Serves 6.

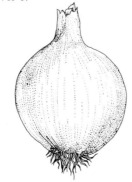

## Cheddar Thins

Crisp, savory biscuits which go well with most soups.

2 cups coarsely grated Cheddar cheese
¼ cup butter
2 cups flour
½ tsp salt
1 tsp dry mustard
paprika or sesame seeds

Cream cheese and butter. Add flour sifted with salt and mustard. Knead well until smooth. Roll into two 1½-in diameter sausages and wrap in waxed paper. Chill for 2–3 hours. Slice into ¼-in thick rounds.

Arrange on lightly oiled cookie sheet and sprinkle with paprika or sesame seeds. Bake at 350°F for about 12 minutes. Allow to crisp for a few seconds before removing to a cake rack to cool. Makes 60.

## Traditional Pesto

¼ lb fresh basil leaves
1½ oz parsley sprigs
2 garlic cloves, chopped
¼ cup chopped walnuts or pine nuts
⅓ cup grated Parmesan cheese
1 tbsp butter, softened (optional)
about ¼ cup olive oil
salt and ground black pepper

Using the grinding blade, process all the ingredients except the oil and seasoning. With the motor running, slowly add oil in a steady stream to make a thick green purée. Season, then spoon into jars, run a thin film of oil over the top and refrigerate.

## Carrot and Orange Soup

A cold, creamy, surprising soup with a lovely color.

3 tbsp oil
a knob of butter
6–8 carrots, pared and diced
1 large onion, sliced
2 medium potatoes, cubed
4¼ cups chicken stock
2 cups milk
grated zest of 1 small orange
salt
½ tsp paprika
1 bay leaf
4 parsley sprigs
fresh orange juice (optional)
1 cup light cream or milk
whipped cream
thin strips of orange zest
snipped chives

Heat oil and butter in large saucepan and add carrots, onions and potatoes. Allow to soften without browning, then add stock, milk, orange zest, salt, paprika, bay leaf and parsley. Half-cover saucepan and simmer until vegetables are soft. Cool, remove bay leaf, and purée in blender until smooth. The addition of freshly squeezed orange juice at this stage is optional – it will sharpen the flavor somewhat, and up to ½ cup may be added.

Stir in cream, or milk ( or ½ cup of each), adjust seasoning, then chill thoroughly. Serve in cold bowls, garnished with whipped cream, thin strips of orange and snipped chives.
Serves 8.

# *Chilled Zucchini and Cucumber Soup*

**Delicate in both flavor and color and lightly spiked with mint.**

**3 tbsp oil**
**1 tbsp butter**
**14 oz zucchini, peeled and sliced**
**1 onion, chopped**
**½ large cucumber, peeled and diced**
**1 large potato, peeled and diced**
**3 cups chicken stock**
**1 cup milk**
**2 bay leaves**
**finely grated zest of 1 small lemon**
**a few parsley sprigs**
**salt and ground black pepper**
**pinch of sugar**
**10 fresh mint leaves**

Heat oil and butter in a large saucepan and add zucchini, onion and cucumber. Allow to soften without browning. Add potato, stock, milk, bay leaves, lemon zest, parsley, seasonings and sugar.

Half-cover and simmer for about 25 minutes until soft. Cool, remove bay leaves, and add mint leaves. Purée in a blender until smooth. Adjust seasoning and chill thoroughly.

Serve in chilled soup bowls, garnished with lightly whipped cream and finely grated zucchini. Serves 6–8.

# *Iced Celery Soup*

**Madame de Pompadour, it is said, used to drink hot celery soup to rouse her passions. That's why I feel it's safer to serve this soup cold.**

**3 tbsp oil**
**knob of butter**
**5 celery stalks chopped**
**1 large onion or 4 leeks, chopped**
**2 large potatoes, peeled and cubed**
**3 tbsp parsley, chopped**
**3 cups seasoned chicken stock**
**1 cup milk**
**generous pinch of celery salt**
**1 bay leaf**
**½ tsp dried basil**
**pinch of sugar**
**½ cup light cream**

Heat oil and butter in a large saucepan and add celery, onion or leeks, potatoes and parsley. Sauté gently for 5 minutes, tossing now and then. Add remaining ingredients, except cream, cover saucepan, tilt lid slightly, and simmer gently for about 20 minutes until vegetables are soft.

Cool soup slightly, remove bay leaf and purée in blender until smooth. Pour into container, stir in cream, and chill well before serving in chilled bowls. Serves 8.

## *Hint*

To serve hot, return soup to saucepan after puréeing. Reheat gently and swirl in cream. Stir until very hot, without boiling.

## Tomato Salad with Sour Cream and Blue Cheese or Basil

Very good with curry or broiled meats.

½ large onion, thinly sliced
   into rings
3 large, firm tomatoes, thinly
   sliced
salt and ground black pepper
sugar
scant ½ cup sour cream
knob of blue cheese
1 tsp brandy
snipped chives

Blanch onion rings by pouring boiling water over, leaving for 5 minutes and then draining. Spread half tomato slices over bottom of smallish, shallow salad bowl. Cover with half the onion slices. Sprinkle with salt, pepper and sugar. Repeat tomato and onion layers and season.

   Beat cream and cheese together until cream stiffens and cheese is thoroughly broken up. Stir in brandy. Taste and add more blue cheese, if desired. Alternatively, omit blue cheese and add about 8 chopped fresh basil leaves to the sour cream and brandy. Spoon over tomato-onion slices, sprinkle with chives and chill for 30 minutes. Don't leave this standing for too long because it will weep. Serves 4.

### Hint
Blue cheese adds a tasty tang to a green bean salad. Combine 14 oz cooked beans with chopped, blanched onion and red Bell pepper. Season and add grated blue cheese to taste. Mix French dressing (page 47) with 5 tsp sour cream. Toss with hot vegetables, cool, then cover and chill.

Chinese Cabbage and Fennel Salad with Sherry Dressing

## Chinese Cabbage and Fennel Salad with Sherry Dressing

A marvelous mixture of raw salad ingredients – particularly good with pork.

**about 1 lb Chinese cabbage, shredded**
**9 oz zucchini scrubbed and thinly sliced**
**2 leeks, thinly shredded**
**2½ cups mung bean sprouts**
**1 bulb fennel, thinly sliced**
**toasted almonds to garnish (optional)**

DRESSING
**4 tbsp oil**
**1 tsp lemon juice**
**3 tbsp sherry**
**generous pinch of ground ginger**
**pinch of sugar**
**7 tsp soy sauce**

Put cabbage into a large bowl and add zucchini, leeks and sprouts. Blanch fennel in boiling water for 2 minutes, drain and add to rest of salad.

Mix oil, lemon juice, sherry, ginger and sugar and pour over vegetables, tossing until glistening. Cover and leave for 1–2 hours. Just before serving, add soy sauce and toss well. Garnish with toasted almonds, if desired.
Serves 6.

### Note
The bulbous Florentine fennel is the one used in cooking, and is not to be confused with wild fennel. Trim the root end and top, remove the outer layer, and scrub the bulb.

## Cheese and Cucumber Mold

**Surround with marinated mushrooms and serve as an eye-catching salad at a cold buffet.**

**1 medium cucumber**
**1½ cups low-fat soft cheese**
**½ cup mayonnaise**
**½ cup sour cream**
**1 tsp sugar**
**4 tsp powdered gelatin**
**½ cup chicken stock**
**generous pinch of celery salt**
**½ tsp dried dill**
**3 tbsp chopped chives**
**¼ cup finely chopped parsley**
**2 egg whites, stiffly beaten**

Peel, slice, seed and chop cucumber finely, reserving a chunk to slice into thin rings for the garnish.

Beat together low-fat cheese, mayonnaise, sour cream and sugar. Sprinkle gelatin over stock to soften, then stir over low heat to dissolve gelatin. Cool slightly and beat into cheese mixture. Add celery salt and dill. Stir in cucumber, chives and parsley; then fold in egg whites. Pour into a rinsed soufflé dish and set in refrigerator. Unmold when firm and garnish with reserved cucumber.
Serves 8.

### Hint
To make marinated mushrooms, heat 3 tbsp oil and 2 tbsp butter and fry 2½ cups small, white button mushrooms. When brown and soft, remove with slotted spoon to serving dish. To pan juices add 1 medium onion, grated, 1–2 crushed garlic cloves, scant 1 cup white wine, ½ tsp each paprika, salt and sugar. Simmer, stirring, for 2 minutes. Add 2 tsp basil. Pour over mushrooms, cool, cover and chill.

# Green Bean, Cucumber, Feta and Nut Salad

Easy to prepare in advance, this attractive, special-occasion salad should be served in a large, shallow dish. It is particularly good with broiled or barbecued chicken or garlicky lamb.

1–1¼ lb young, slender green
   beans
2 large fresh rosemary sprigs
⅓ cucumber, cut in julienne
salt and ground black pepper
feta cheese
pecan nuts

DRESSING
5 tsp lemon juice
½ tsp prepared mustard
generous pinch of salt
1 garlic clove
2 parsley sprigs
1 green onion, chopped
scant ½ cup oil

Trim and halve beans and cook, with rosemary, in a minimum amount of water. Leave pan half-covered to retain the bright color, and don't overcook. Arrange beans in salad bowl, add cucumber. Finely chop a little of the rosemary and add to beans together with seasoning.

Blend all the ingredients for the dressing in a blender, pour over vegetables, toss to coat and then leave, covered, to marinate for a few hours. Just before serving, top generously with crumbled feta and sprinkle with chopped pecan nuts. Serves 6–8.

## Hints
Feta is a salty cheese and it is advisable to rinse and pat dry before using.

The flavor of pecan nuts is enhanced by toasting them lightly in the oven.

## Zucchini Salad with Sprouts, Apples and Almonds

A crunchy, nutritious raw salad, good as part of a cold buffet.

good ½ lb zucchini, peeled and coarsely grated
½ lb lentil sprouts
2 Granny Smith apples, peeled and coarsely grated
2 tbsp seedless raisins
toasted, flaked almonds

DRESSING
scant ½ cup oil
¼ cup lemon juice
1 tbsp soy sauce
1 garlic clove, halved
2 tsp honey
1 pearl onion, quartered
3 tbsp mayonnaise
a few parsley sprigs

Mix zucchini with sprouts, apples and raisins.

Put all ingredients for dressing into blender and blend until creamy. Toss vegetables with dressing, spoon into salad bowl, cover with plastic wrap and chill for several hours. Scatter almonds over top of salad just before serving.
Serves 6.

### Hint
Growing your own sprouts is easy. Buy a perforated top for a jar (or use cheesecloth and a rubber band) and mung beans, lentils, alfalfa and so on from your nearest health food shop. Rinse and soak 1½ cups in the jar overnight. Next day drain and place jar in a cupboard at an angle so that all the water will run off. Rinse and drain sprouts twice a day. Once sprouted, rinse, dry well and refrigerate.

## Tomato Salad with Basil and Italian Cheese

The simplest of salads, brought to life with fresh basil. Serve as a side dish with pasta, or add black olives and anchovies and serve as a light first course.

4 firm, medium-sized tomatoes
1 onion, thinly sliced into rings
5 tsp finely chopped fresh basil (firmly packed to measure)
ground black pepper
sugar
mozzarella, coarsely grated

DRESSING
3 tbsp oil (garlic, preferably)
2 tsp lemon juice
pinch each of salt, sugar and dry mustard

Plunge tomatoes into boiling water, leave for a few minutes, then slip off skins and slice thinly. Pour boiling water over onion slices, stand for 5 minutes, then drain. Arrange tomatoes and onions on flat salad dish and sprinkle with basil. Grind over a little pepper and sprinkle with a little sugar to bring out the flavor. Cover thinly with grated cheese. If preparing in advance, cover and leave.

Mix together ingredients for dressing and pour over salad 15 minutes before serving. Do not toss.
Serves 4–6.

Brown Rice Salad with Mushrooms

## Brown Rice Salad with Mushrooms

Specially good with cold chicken. I like unpolished rice for this salad, but quick-cooking, white rice can be substituted, in which case simply adjust the cooking time, and reduce stock to 1½ pints.

1⅔ cups brown rice
½ tsp salt
3¼ cups chicken stock
1 tsp dried tarragon
3 tbsp oil
2 tbsp butter
about ⅔ lb brown mushrooms, sliced
1 green Bell pepper, seeded and diced
5 tsp soy sauce
ground black pepper
4 tbsp finely chopped parsley
6 green onions, chopped

Put rice, salt, stock and tarragon into a saucepan, bring to a boil, cover, turn heat to very low and leave for 50 minutes without looking.

Meanwhile prepare mushrooms: heat oil and butter and add mushrooms and green Bell pepper. Sauté until just softened, remove from heat, add soy sauce and pepper to taste, then cover and stand until rice is cooked. Spoon rice into large bowl – the grains should be separate and dry. Using a fork, add mushroom mixture, including all the juices, and toss. Add parsley and green onions, then cover and cool, or chill until required.
Serves 8.

### Note

Wipe cultivated mushrooms clean with a damp cloth, or carefully wash under running water, with the gill side down. Wipe dry and use immediately. Do not soak or wash mushrooms before storing.

## Greek Salad

Perfect with roast lamb, or Stifado (page 77), or served as a first course, in which case include a handful of crisply fried croûtons.

2 garlic cloves
¼ cup olive oil
1 tbsp lemon juice
½ tsp salt
ground black pepper
feta cheese
half a small lettuce, coarsely shredded
12–18 pitted black olives, sliced
1 large tomato, chopped
¼ cucumber
1 green Bell pepper
1 medium onion, thinly sliced into rings
pinch of sugar
croûtons (optional)

Crush garlic directly into wooden

salad bowl. Add oil. Using a wooden spoon, stir in lemon juice, salt and pepper. Add as much crumbled feta as you like, cover and stand for an hour or so. Just before serving add lettuce, olives, tomato, and peeled, seeded and diced cucumber.

Slice green pepper into thin strips and discard seeds. Place in a bowl with onion and sugar, cover with boiling water and stand for a few minutes. Drain, add to salad and toss well. Add croûtons at this stage if desired.
Serves 4–6.

Green Salad with Herb Croûtons

## *Green Salad with Herb Croûtons*

A crisp, green salad that is slightly more interesting than the usual tossed salad. Most of the preparation can be done in advance.

1 small head lettuce
½ small bunch young spinach
1 large avocado, cubed
4 green onions, chopped
1 garlic clove, crushed
½ tsp salt
1 tbsp lemon juice
½ tsp Worcestershire sauce
¼ cup oil
sliced hard-boiled egg to
  garnish

CROÛTONS
2 thick slices stale white bread
3 tbsp oil
2 tbsp butter

1 tsp mixed dried herbs
onion salt

Wash and shred lettuce and spinach – have these two in roughly equal quantities. Add avocado and green onions. Into a wooden salad bowl put garlic, salt, lemon juice and Worcestershire sauce. Stir in oil, add greens and toss. Top with herb croûtons and toss again. Garnish with sliced hard-boiled egg.

To make croûtons, remove crusts from bread and cut into small cubes. Heat oil, butter and dried herbs and fry bread cubes until brown. Drain on absorbent paper towels and sprinkle with onion salt.

To make in advance, prepare and chill greens, except avocado. Have dressing standing ready in salad bowl. Make croûtons and set aside. Combine just before dinner, and garnish with hard-boiled egg. Serves 6.

## *Broccoli Salad with Creamy Curry Dressing*

A chunky, colorful salad which looks particularly attractive served in one of those shallow, pizza-type earthenware dishes. It makes an eye-catching addition to any cold buffet.

about 1¼ lb broccoli
salt and ground black pepper
1 red Bell pepper, seeded
2 leeks, thinly sliced
½–1 tsp curry powder
½–1 tsp turmeric
2 tsp boiling water
½ cup thick mayonnaise
½ cup buttermilk
toasted flaked almonds

Cut away lower tough ends of broccoli stalks. Chop stems

coarsely and break off flowerets. Poach stems in a little boiling water until softened. Add flowerets and cook until just tender, keeping lid of saucepan tilted (this retains the bright color). When just cooked, drain, if necessary, spoon into salad bowl and season.

Cut pepper into thin strips. Pour boiling water over leeks and pepper to blanch, stand for a few minutes, drain and spoon on top of broccoli. Put curry powder and turmeric in a cup, pour over the boiling water and stand for 5 minutes, then stir into mayonnaise mixed with buttermilk. Pour over vegetables and sprinkle generously with almonds. May be chilled for an hour or two before serving. Serves 6.

# Green Salad with Walnuts

A crisp and crunchy salad with a light, creamy dressing.

good ½ lb lettuce, shredded
good ½ lb young spinach
½ cucumber, peeled and diced
1 apple, peeled and diced
1 celery stalk, thinly sliced
½ cup walnuts, chopped

DRESSING
1½ oz blue cheese
¼ cup oil
½ cup buttermilk
a few drops of Worcestershire
    sauce

Make dressing first. Crumble cheese into a bowl and mash with a fork. Slowly mix in oil. When this becomes a smooth paste, stir in buttermilk and Worcestershire sauce. Beat well with a rotary whisk, cover and chill for 1–2 hours.

Put lettuce and spinach into salad bowl. Add cucumber, apple and celery. Toss to mix and then pour dressing over. Sprinkle with walnuts, and serve.
Serves 4–6.

## Variation

GREEN SALAD WITH YOGURT
DRESSING
A light, refreshing salad to serve with curry.

DRESSING
good ¾ cup drinking yogurt
3 tbsp oil
1 tsp lemon juice
generous pinch of paprika
½ medium onion, thinly sliced
¼ cup chopped parsley
1 tsp sugar
1 garlic clove crushed with
    generous pinch of salt

Put dressing ingredients into a wooden salad bowl, stir well, then cover and leave for about 2 hours. When ready to serve, add green salad leaves and toss well.
Serves 4–6.

## Chinese Green Salad with Ginger and Almonds

A combination of crisp green leaves, ginger and soy sauce, this salad is marvelous with pork dishes, or may even be served as a light first course.

1¾ lb Chinese cabbage, shredded
good ½ lb zucchini, scrubbed and thinly sliced
2 leeks, thinly sliced
2 knobs preserved ginger in syrup, cut in slivers
5 tsp soy sauce
5 tsp ginger syrup
5 tsp oil
1 tsp lemon juice
halved, toasted almonds

Toss cabbage, zucchini, leeks and

ginger in a large bowl. Mix soy sauce and ginger syrup, add to vegetables and mix well. Mix oil with lemon juice and add. Toss until glistening, then cover securely and stand for about 2–3 hours.

Spoon into a salad bowl, and top with almonds.
Serves 6–8.

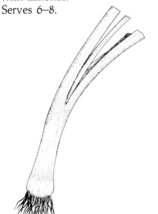

## Spinach, Mushroom and Blue Cheese Salad

A fresh, raw salad with a lovely tang.

1 bunch young spinach
½ bunch green onions, chopped
¼ lb mushrooms, sliced

DRESSING
2 x 1-in cubes blue cheese (or more to taste)
1 garlic clove, crushed
scant ⅓ cup oil (half olive, if liked)
3 tbsp tarragon or garlic vinegar
1 tsp Worcestershire sauce
salt
ground black pepper
pinch of sugar

Begin with the dressing. Grate cheese coarsely into wooden salad bowl. Add remaining ingredients, stir to mix and allow to stand for at least 30 minutes.

Wash spinach, discard ribs and stems, then dry and shred – you should have just under 6 cups. Add to dressing together with green onions and mushrooms. Toss well, then cover and leave for 15 minutes, to allow flavors to blend, before serving.
Serves 6.

### Variation
HERB DRESSING
An alternative dressing may be made with fresh basil.

Blend scant ½ cup oil, 5 tsp lemon juice, generous pinch of salt, ½ tsp sugar, 1 tsp Dijon mustard, few parsley sprigs, 1–2 chopped garlic cloves, 12 fresh basil leaves. Pour into a jar, cover and leave for 1 hour. Shake well before using.

## Mushroom Bean Salad with Sherry Dressing

Choose slim, young green beans to make this salad, which goes particularly well with steak or chicken.

1 cup seasoned chicken stock
1 tsp dried marjoram
good ½ lb green beans, trimmed and halved
1 onion, sliced into rings
scant ½ lb mushrooms, sliced
knob of butter
hard-boiled eggs, marjoram sprigs or toasted almonds to garnish

DRESSING
3 tbsp oil
3 tbsp sweet sherry
1 tbsp soy sauce
pinch of salt

Put stock into a saucepan, rub marjoram to crush, and add. Bring to boil, then add beans, onion, mushrooms and butter. Cook, partially covered, until just tender, tossing once or twice. Using a slotted spoon, remove to shallow salad bowl.

Mix ingredients for dressing and pour over warm vegetables. Cool, cover and chill for about 4 hours. Garnish just before serving. Serves 4–6.

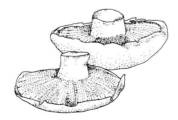

## Broccoli and Mushroom Salad with Creamy Cheese Dressing

A colorful and nourishing salad to set off a spread at a cold buffet. The combination of lightly cooked broccoli with raw mushrooms is delicious, but green beans, red Bell peppers and/or cauliflower would make good alternatives.

1–1¼ lb broccoli
salt and ground black pepper
about ¾ lb white or brown mushrooms, wiped and sliced
2 green onions
1½ cups low-fat soft cheese
scant ¾ cup buttermilk or plain drinking yogurt
¼ cup thick mayonnaise
¼ cup chopped parsley
1–2 tsp honey
generous pinch of celery salt
1–2 dill pickles, chopped
paprika
chopped walnuts or toasted almonds

Trim broccoli and slice lengthwise. Poach in a little boiling water until just tender. Drain, chop coarsely and arrange in large, shallow bowl. Season, then add mushrooms. Chop onions, including a little of the tops, and combine with the remaining ingredients, except paprika and nuts, using a wooden spoon, not a blender. Pour over vegetables, mixing very lightly to coat thoroughly. Dust with paprika and top with nuts. Cover and set aside for an hour or two, or chill until required. Serve at room temperature.
Serves 6–8.

## Mushroom Salad

Soaked in a little sherry-flavored dressing, these mushrooms can be served as a super, low-calorie side dish, tossed with green leaves and extra dressing to make a special salad, or enriched with a little sour cream or yogurt and then piled into avocado halves as a delicate starter.

about ¾ lb button mushrooms, wiped and thinly sliced
6 slim green onions, finely chopped

MARINADE
3 tbsp olive oil
3 tbsp vegetable oil
¼ cup sherry
1 tbsp soy sauce
pinch of sugar
ground black pepper

Spoon mushrooms into a large, shallow salad bowl. Add green onions. Mix ingredients for marinade, pour over mushrooms, toss to moisten and then cover and chill, preferably overnight.
Serves 6–8 as a starter or will fill 8–10 avocado halves.

## Pineapple Rice Salad

scant 1 cup long-grain white rice
2 cups salted water
1 x 9 oz can pineapple pieces in natural juice
scant ⅓ cup oil
½ tsp dry mustard
1 tbsp soy sauce
1 green Bell pepper, seeded and finely chopped
1 celery stalk, thinly sliced
¼ cup seedless raisins

Put rice into saucepan, add water and bring to a boil. Cover and simmer on very low heat for about 20 minutes, until cooked.
Meanwhile, make the dressing. Drain pineapple and reserve ¼ cup of the juice. Mix oil, mustard, soy sauce and pineapple juice. Tip cooked rice into bowl and immediately fork in the dressing. Add green pepper, celery and raisins. Chop pineapple and add. Allow to cool, then cover and chill for a few hours.
Serves 6–8.

Mushroom Salad

## Bulgar Salad with Tomatoes and Black Olives

Bulgar wheat is used extensively in the Middle East. The grains are first soaked and then toasted, after which they need only be soaked in water. It makes a delicious and unusual salad and can also be served as a light first course, with cheese or with hummus and pitta bread.

1½ cups bulgar wheat
6 small green onions, finely
  chopped
2 tbsp finely chopped parsley
2 tbsp finely chopped fresh mint
2 medium tomatoes, chopped
black olives, sliced
lettuce, mint and sliced
  cucumber to garnish

DRESSING
¼ cup vegetable oil
¼ cup olive oil
3 tbsp lemon juice
1 garlic clove, crushed
salt and ground black pepper
½ tsp dried oregano

Mix ingredients for dressing first and stand for several hours to blend flavors.

Soak bulgar wheat in water to cover generously for about 1 hour. Drain in colander, and squeeze out excess moisture with hands. Put into a large bowl and add green onions, parsley and mint. Pour over prepared dressing, toss, cover and stand 30 minutes. Adjust seasoning and then fold in tomatoes and olives. Serve garnished with lettuce, mint and sliced cucumber.
Serves 6.

## Broccoli, Leek and Carrot Salad with Orange Dressing

A colorful salad, with a light and subtle dressing.

1 lb broccoli flowerets
3 leeks
5 carrots, cut in julienne
salt and ground black pepper

DRESSING
scant ½ cup oil
scant ½ cup fresh orange juice
generous pinch of finely grated
    orange zest
generous pinch of salt
½ tsp prepared mustard
½ tsp honey
1 tsp finely chopped parsley

Trim broccoli and divide thinly lengthwise. Wash and slice leeks,

white parts only. Cook broccoli, leeks and carrots in a minimum amount of boiling water in a large saucepan until tender-crisp. Drain if necessary and spoon into large, shallow salad bowl. Season.

Mix ingredients for dressing and pour over hot salad ingredients, using just enough dressing to moisten vegetables thoroughly. Allow to cool, tossing gently once or twice. Cover and stand for about 1 hour before serving.
Serves 8.

### Hint
**Vegetables such as broccoli and green beans, especially when served as a salad, should be bright green and crisp. Keep the lid of the saucepan tilted to retain the color.**

## Stir-fried Green Bean Salad with Pecan Nuts

**Use the most slender, youngest French beans you can find for this super salad, which is particularly good to serve with beef or tongue.**

1–1¼ lb green beans
¼ cup oil
2 garlic cloves, crushed
1 tbsp soy sauce
¼ cup sherry
½ tsp dried basil
½ cup pecan nuts, coarsely
    chopped

Trim beans and halve if necessary. Heat oil in a large skillet and stir-fry beans and garlic for about 5 minutes. Reduce heat and add soy sauce, sherry and basil. Cover and cook over very low heat, stirring occasionally, until just tender.

Spoon into shallow salad bowl, including juices, and toss in pecans. Cool, cover and stand for about 1 hour before serving.
Serves 4–6.

### Hint
**To retain the freshness of shelled nuts, put them in the freezer immediately after purchasing.**

Green Bean, Red Bell Pepper and Anchovy Salad

## Green Bean, Red Bell Pepper and Anchovy Salad

This bright, robust salad goes particularly well with pasta dishes but may also be served as a light first course. It is important not to overcook the vegetables – the beans should retain their cheerful color and the pepper and onion rings be blanched only briefly to take the edge off their bite.

1 lb young green beans
1 red Bell pepper
1 onion, thinly sliced
1 x 2 oz can rolled fillets of anchovy with capers

DRESSING
¼ cup vegetable oil
5 tsp olive oil
5 tsp lemon juice
generous pinch of salt
½ tsp sugar
½ tsp dried tarragon

Trim and halve the beans, or if very slender, leave them whole. Cook in a minimum amount of salted water until just tender – leave lid of saucepan ajar to retain color. Drain in a colander. Don't be tempted to refresh under cold water as they'll absorb the dressing better if hot. While beans are cooking, seed and cut Bell pepper into thin strips. Pour boiling water over pepper and onion, stand for 2 minutes, then drain. Spoon vegetables into a shallow salad dish.

Mix ingredients for dressing and pour over hot vegetables. When cool, cover and chill several hours to allow dressing to be absorbed. Soak anchovies in milk for 15 minutes to remove excess salt and arrange on top of salad just before serving. Serves 4–6.

## Chinese Rice Salad with Almonds

A super combination of different salad ingredients, flavors and textures. I prefer using brown rice but white may be substituted.

scant 1 cup brown rice
3½ cups lentil sprouts
1 x 8 oz can water chestnuts, drained and sliced
2 celery stalks, finely chopped
4–6 green onions, chopped
1 x 9 oz can pineapple rings in natural juice
½ cup toasted flaked almonds

DRESSING
¼ cup oil
5 tsp soy sauce
1 knob ginger root, peeled and grated
1 tsp sugar
2 tsp lemon juice

First mix together the dressing ingredients, then boil rice as usual until fluffy and dry. Toss dressing with rice while still hot. Add lentil sprouts, water chestnuts, celery and green onions. Drain pineapple and reserve about ½ cup of the juice. Pat dry and cube 4 rings of pineapple and add to rice mixture. Moisten with reserved pineapple juice, then cover and chill for a few hours or overnight.

To serve, pile onto serving dish and top with almonds.
Serves 8.

(Clockwise) Creamy French Dressing with Herbs, Blender Mayonnaise, Green Mayonnaise with Fresh Herbs and French Dressing with Wine and Herbs

## Green Mayonnaise with Fresh Herbs

Gives a colorful lift to cold chicken, fish, and chilled appetizers such as asparagus or leeks.

6 spinach leaves
small handful of chopped parsley
4 fresh tarragon sprigs
4 small fresh marjoram sprigs
10 basil leaves
1 cup mayonnaise

Boil spinach, parsley, tarragon, marjoram and basil rapidly for 2 minutes in a small saucepan. Drain well, pat dry and chop finely, discarding marjoram stems. Add to mayonnaise and blend briefly. Chill well to allow flavor to develop before using.
Makes about 1 cup.

## Blender Mayonnaise

Made in seconds, this mayonnaise is easily doubled if larger quantities are required.

1 extra large egg or 2 yolks (for a thicker consistency)
½ tsp salt
½ tsp dry mustard
5 tsp tarragon vinegar or lemon juice
1 cup oil
1 tsp sugar
1 garlic clove, chopped

Put egg, salt, mustard, vinegar, 5 tsp oil, sugar and garlic into a blender. Blend well and then, with motor running, slowly pour in remaining oil through the hole in the lid. You should have a smooth, creamy mayonnaise.
For a lighter mayonnaise, stir in a little sour cream, yogurt or buttermilk.
Makes about 1¼ cups.

## French Dressing with Wine and Herbs

A nice change from ordinary vinaigrette and good with most green salads.

½ cup oil
¼ good red wine
1 tbsp lemon juice
generous pinch of salt
1 tsp sugar
1 tbsp chopped mixed fresh herbs (sage, thyme, basil, marjoram)
¼ cup chopped parsley

Put all the ingredients into a screw-top jar, shake and stand briefly before using – if left too long the fresh herbs could turn bitter. Makes about ¾ cup or enough for 1 very large salad.

## Creamy French Dressing with Herbs

The addition of wine and buttermilk makes a lovely, light dressing that is lower in calories than most. Use on any green salad, but before adding, toss the salad ingredients with a dash of oil first so that the dressing will cling to the leaves.

½ cup each oil, dry white wine and buttermilk
1 tsp honey
½ tsp dried oregano
½ tsp dried tarragon
2 garlic cloves, crushed
generous pinch of celery salt

Shake all the ingredients in a screw-top jar and leave to stand for at least 1 hour before using. Use when freshly made, as it does not keep well.
Makes about 1½ cups.

# Chicken and Prawn Paella

The following is a scaled-down version of an authentic paella, using easily available ingredients.

½ tsp saffron threads
1¾ lb chicken wings or
    drumsticks
3 tbsp vegetable oil
3 tbsp olive oil
2 onions, chopped
2 garlic cloves, crushed
1 red Bell pepper, seeded and
    diced
scant 1 cup long-grain white rice
about 4¼ cups hot chicken stock
scant ½ cup white wine
1 x 14 oz can chopped tomatoes
salt and ground black pepper
2½ cups pink peeled frozen
    shrimp
5 oz Dublin Bay prawns with
    shells
knob of butter
a few drops of lemon juice
generous pinch of paprika
1 x 8 oz can mussels in brine
12 black olives, sliced
1½ cups green peas (optional)

Soak saffron in 3 tbsp hot water for 1 hour. If using chicken wings, trim off tips. Heat oils in large skillet and brown chicken well. Remove. To pan juices add onion, garlic and pepper and stir until softened. Add rice and toss until glistening. Add 2½ cups stock and the wine and, when boiling, add tomatoes plus juice, and saffron. Pour into your largest baking dish, add chicken and seasoning, then cover and bake at 325°F for 1 hour. Remove. The rice should be tender and the liquid absorbed. Add another 1 cup stock and bake for 30 minutes or until chicken is very tender.

Meanwhile cook peeled shrimp according to package directions. Fry large prawns with shells in butter with lemon juice and paprika. Drain and rinse mussels. Add shelled shrimp, mussels, olives (and peas, if using) to rice mixture, and arrange fried prawns on the top. If mixture seems dry, add more stock. Cover and heat through for about 30 minutes.
Serves 6.

## Squid Casserole with Mushrooms

about 1 lb squid
3 tbsp oil
1 tbsp butter
1 onion, chopped
2 garlic cloves, crushed
1 red Bell pepper, seeded and diced
good ¼ lb mushrooms, wiped and sliced
2 large beef tomatoes, skinned and chopped
¼ cup sherry
1 tbsp soy sauce
ground black pepper
pinch of sugar
beurre manié or 1 tbsp cornstarch mixed with little sour cream

Dry squid and slice if necessary. Heat oil and butter, add squid and toss for a few minutes until it stiffens and turns white, then remove to baking dish. Add a little more oil to the pan, and lower heat. Add onion and allow to soften before adding garlic, red pepper, mushrooms, tomatoes, sherry, soy sauce, pepper and sugar. Stir briefly, until just bubbling and juicy, and then pour over squid.

Cover and bake at 325°F for about 1 hour 15 minutes, until squid is tender and a good gravy has formed. Thicken with beurre manié or cornstarch mixture and return to oven, uncovered, for 15 minutes. Serve on rice with a green salad. Serves 4.

## Oriental Squid

1¾ lb squid
¼ cup oil
3 tbsp whisky
1 large bunch green onions, chopped
1 onion, chopped
2 garlic cloves, crushed
about ¾ lb brown mushrooms, wiped and sliced
⅓ cup flour
2 cups chicken stock
⅔ cup white wine
3 tbsp soy sauce
small knob ginger root, peeled and grated
a few drops of lemon juice

Slice squid into thin rings, pat dry and fry in hot oil in large saucepan for a few minutes or until just stiffening and turning white. Flame with warmed whisky, remove from pan with slotted spoon and set aside.

To pan add a dash of oil if necessary and add green onions, onion, garlic and mushrooms. Toss for a few minutes until glistening, then sprinkle in flour and slowly add stock, wine, soy sauce, ginger, lemon juice and squid. Cover and simmer very slowly for approximately 50 minutes, stirring occasionally. Adjust seasoning, and serve on a bed of rice, with peas and a crisp salad.
Serves 6.

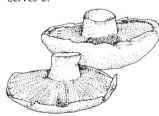

Lobster Salad

## Lobster Salad

**This is a salad for a special summer luncheon: lobster tails piled with diced lobster flesh, doused with a dash of vermouth and then tossed with a creamy dressing lightly flavored with tarragon. Surround with rice and raw mushroom salad (page 43) and add the prettiest of garnishes: red leaf lettuce, cherry tomatoes, sprays of tarragon.**

Allow one cooked lobster per serving. Place on its back and cut down the middle. Squeeze tail to snap covering membranes and then snip them off. Carefully pull out alimentary canal which runs down the length of the lobster. Remove flesh from body, tail and legs, discarding body and head and all soft matter and entrails. Keep the tail and flatten gently to maintain

its shape. Rinse flesh and tail and pat dry. Dice flesh. Each lobster should provide about ½ cup. Put into glass bowl and pour over 2 tsp dry vermouth per lobster. Cover and chill for about 2 hours. Fold mayonnaise dressing (see below) into each serving of chilled lobster flesh, pile into reserved tails and serve as suggested.

MAYONNAISE DRESSING
**1½ tsp dried tarragon**
**4 tsp boiling water**
**scant ½ cup thick mayonnaise**
**¼ cup sour cream**
**½ tsp Dijon mustard**
**pinch of sugar**

Place tarragon in a cup, pour over boiling water, cover and allow to steep for about 1 hour. Strain the flavored liquid into mayonnaise and stir in sour cream, mustard and sugar.
Makes enough for 4 small salads.

## Seafood Risotto

**Serving seafood on its own can be expensive. The solution is to mix it with other ingredients, as in the following recipe in which shrimps are combined with rice, cooked Italian-style. This is a simple, easily prepared dish, wide open to variations, with but one imperative – a risotto must include Parmesan cheese.**

**3 tbsp oil**
**butter**
**1 large onion, chopped**
**2 garlic cloves, crushed**
**about ¾ lb mushrooms, wiped and sliced**
**1¼ cups long-grain white rice**
**2⅓ cups hot chicken stock**
**scant ½ cup white wine**
**½ tsp turmeric**
**salt and ground black pepper**

**1 x 14 oz can shrimps in brine, drained and rinsed**
**grated Parmesan cheese**

Heat oil and 2 tbsp butter in a large skillet. Add onion and garlic and fry gently until softened. Add rice and mushrooms and toss until coated with oil. Slowly add heated stock, half the wine, turmeric, salt and pepper. Cover and simmer for 25–30 minutes on very low heat. Add remaining wine, the shrimps, Parmesan cheese and a knob of butter. Using a fork, toss until well mixed and heated through. Serve with peas, or a tossed salad, and extra Parmesan to sprinkle on each serving.
Serves 4.

Seafood Sauce for Pasta

## Seafood Sauce for Pasta

A great dish for informal entertaining. Add a salad and grated Parmesan for sprinkling, and if you want to stretch it beyond 6 servings, simply increase the amount of pasta.

**1 lb 14 oz filleted firm white fish**
**1½ cups water**
**2 bay leaves**
**salt**
**2 tsp lemon juice**
**14 oz squid**
**¼ cup oil**
**2 onions, chopped**
**1 green Bell pepper, seeded and diced**
**2 garlic cloves, crushed**
**¼ cup flour**
**scant ½ cup white wine**
**14 oz tomatoes, skinned and chopped**
**½ tsp each salt and paprika**
**5 tsp tomato paste**
**½ tsp dried oregano**
**½ tsp dried basil**
**1 tsp sugar**
**2 lb cooked mussels in shells**
**about ¾ lb ribbon noodles**

Place fish fillets flat in a large pan. Add water, bay leaves, a little salt and lemon juice. Poach until just cooked, then leave to cool in liquid. Remove skin, any bones and dark flesh, and flake. Strain stock and reserve.

Slice squid into thin rings. Heat oil and sauté onion, green bell pepper and garlic. Add squid and toss over fairly low heat just until it stiffens. Sprinkle in flour, stir to mix, then add 1 cup reserved fish stock, wine, tomatoes and remaining ingredients, except mussels and noodles. Bring to a boil, then cover and simmer very slowly, stirring occasionally, for about 45 minutes or until sauce is thick and squid tender. Add flaked fish and a little more stock. Cover and simmer slowly for 10–15 minutes while you boil the pasta.

Adjust seasoning (it could need another pinch of sugar), then spoon into a large baking dish. Rinse mussels and place round edge, then put in oven at 325°F just to heat through very briefly.

To cook the pasta, boil the noodles in plenty of salted water until just done. Drain and toss with a little oil to keep the strands separate.
Serves 6–8.

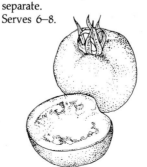

## Clam Sauce

**1 tbsp vegetable oil**
**1 tbsp olive oil**
**1 onion, chopped**
**1 celery stalk, finely chopped**
**2 garlic cloves, crushed**
**1 x 14 oz can tomatoes, chopped**
**¼ cup dry vermouth**
**salt and ground black pepper**
**generous pinch of dried oregano**
**generous pinch of dried basil**
**¼ cup chopped parsley**
**1 x 1¼ lb can clams in water, drained**

Heat oil in large skillet and sauté onion, celery and garlic. When soft, add tomatoes plus their juice, and remaining ingredients, except clams. Cover and simmer gently for 20 minutes. Add clams and heat through. Serve on pasta with grated Parmesan cheese.
Serves 4.

## Mussel Quiche

PROCESSOR PASTRY
**1½ cups flour**
**generous pinch of salt**
**about 7 tbsp butter, diced**
**1 tsp lemon juice**
**¼ cup cold water**

FILLING
**4 tsp oil**
**2 slim leeks, finely chopped**
**3 eggs**
**1 cup milk**
**½ cup light cream**
**generous pinch of freshly grated nutmeg**
**½ tsp salt**
**1 tsp flour**
**1 x 8 oz can mussels in brine, drained and coarsely chopped**
**paprika**

To make pastry, use metal blade of processor and mix flour, salt and butter until well blended. With motor running, slowly add lemon juice and water through feed tube, and continue to blend until mixture forms a ball. Wrap and chill for 1 hour, then roll out and line a 10-in diameter, deep, fluted flan pan. Cover pastry with waxed paper and fill to the brim with dried beans. Preheat oven to 400°F and heat a large cookie sheet. Place flan pan on cookie sheet and bake blind for 10 minutes. Remove paper and beans and bake for 5 minutes longer.

For the filling, heat oil and add leeks. Cover and sweat slowly until soft. Drain on absorbent paper towels. Beat eggs, milk, cream, nutmeg and salt. Brush base of pastry crust with 1 tsp flour. Arrange leeks and mussels on base. Carefully pour egg mixture over and dust with paprika. Place pan on cookie sheet and bake for 35–40 minutes until just set.
Serves 6–8.

## Fish and Shrimp Casserole

**Simply the quickest of fishy dishes using a firm fish, a can of soup and a can of shrimps, all baked together, then topped with a buttery crumble.**

**1¾ lb filleted fish**
**salt and ground black pepper**
**lemon juice**
**1 x 7 oz can shrimps in brine**
**1 x 15 oz can asparagus soup**
**¼ cup dry vermouth**
**¼ cup heavy cream or sour cream**

TOPPING
**2 tbsp butter**
**1½ cups fine, stale white breadcrumbs**
**3 tbsp grated Parmesan cheese**

Cut fish into 4 equal pieces, dry well and arrange close together in buttered baking dish. Season, then dribble each piece with a little lemon juice. Drain and rinse shrimps and scatter over fish. Stir soup with vermouth and cream or sour cream until smooth, pour over fish and bake, uncovered, at 350°F for about 35 minutes or until fish is just cooked through.

Meanwhile, make topping. Melt butter in small skillet. Add breadcrumbs and toss over medium heat until lightly browned and crisp. Mix in Parmesan, sprinkle over fish and return to oven for 5 minutes to heat through. Serve with baby potatoes and brightly coloured vegetables such as broccoli and glazed baby carrots, or, more simply, with lemon-flavored rice and a green salad.
Serves 4.

## Hake, Cheese and Asparagus Casserole

A simple old favorite which is given airs by topping with puff pastry fleurons before serving.

**4 x 7 oz hake fillets**
**salt and ground black pepper**
**lemon juice**
**1 x 14 oz can asparagus spears**
**4–6 green onions, finely**
  **chopped**

SAUCE
**milk**
**3 tbsp butter**
**¼ cup flour**
**1 tsp dry mustard**
**salt and pepper**
**1½ cups coarsely grated**
  **Cheddar cheese**
**3 tbsp sherry**

FLEURONS
**puff pastry**
**1 egg, beaten**
**paprika**

Arrange fish in greased 12 x 8-in baking dish. Season and sprinkle each piece with a few drops lemon juice. Drain asparagus and reserve liquid. Dot fish with asparagus spears and green onions.

To make the sauce, make up asparagus liquid to 2 cups with milk. Melt butter and stir in flour and mustard. Remove from heat and slowly add the 2 cups of liquid. Return to cooker and cook, stirring, until sauce is smooth and thick. Season, stir in cheese and sherry and pour over fish. Bake, uncovered, at 400°F for about 30 minutes or until fish is cooked through. Top with fleurons before serving, or simply sprinkle with a little grated Parmesan cheese before baking.

To make fleurons, cut puff pastry into small crescents or rounds. Brush with beaten egg, dust with paprika and bake at 400°F on moistened cookie sheet for 10–15 minutes until risen and lightly browned.
Serves 4–5.

## Fish Fillets in Cream Sauce

The light creamy sauce used in this recipe enhances the delicate flavor of fresh succulent fish. Serve the fillets on a pool of sauce, or pour it over and sprinkle with very finely grated lemon zest.

**4 x 7 oz pieces of firm white fish**

POACHING LIQUID
**1½ cups water**
**1 small onion, chopped**
**few parsley sprigs**
**scant ½ cup white wine**
**salt and a few black peppercorns**

CREAM SAUCE
**3 tbsp butter**
**¼ cup flour**
**1½ cups reserved poaching liquid**
**1 egg yolk**
**1½ cups heavy cream**
**2 tsp lemon juice**
**3 tbsp finely chopped parsley**
**salt and pepper**

Bring ingredients for poaching liquid to a boil in a large pan and simmer for 5 minutes. Add fish fillets, cover and simmer until just cooked. Carefully remove to serving platter, cover with waxed paper and keep warm. Strain stock.

To make the sauce, melt butter, add flour and cook for 1 minute. Slowly add hot reserved stock and simmer, stirring, for a few minutes. Beat egg yolk and cream, add a little of the hot sauce, then return to saucepan and heat through, stirring, without boiling, until thickened. Remove from heat, add lemon juice and parsley, adjust seasoning, pour over fish and serve immediately. Braised fennel makes a good accompaniment.
Serves 4.

### Hint
Having bought your fish, unwrap it as soon as you get home. Spread out on large plate, salt it, and keep in coldest part of refrigerator. Never re-freeze thawed fish.

## Crumbed Baked Fish

**This is the easiest and most convenient way of "frying" fish.**

**1¾lb skinned, filleted fish
salt and ground black pepper
½ cup mayonnaise
1½ cups cornflake crumbs**

If using frozen fish, thaw, skin and dry very well with absorbent paper towels. Season, then coat both sides with mayonnaise. Roll in crushed cornflakes and chill for at least 1 hour to set crumbs.

To bake, cover bottom of cookie sheet with a shallow layer of oil. Preheat oven to 350°F and heat cookie sheet until hot. Turn fillets once in hot oil and then bake for about 20 minutes or until cooked. Serve with lemon wedges and Sauce Tartare.
Serves 4.

## Sauce Tartare

**1 cup mayonnaise
1 tsp finely chopped pickle
½ tsp chopped capers
1 tsp chopped chives
2 tsp chopped parsley
½ tsp Dijon mustard
pinch of sugar
hard-boiled white of egg,
  shredded (optional)**

Combine ingredients and chill. Makes about ½ cup.

## Baked Fish with Mushrooms and Buttermilk

**In this dish, floured fish fillets are baked in a savory vegetable sauce enriched with a little buttermilk, instead of cream.**

**4 x 6 oz skinned fish fillets
¼ cup flour
½ tsp each salt and paprika
¼ cup oil
1 onion, chopped
1 red Bell pepper, seeded and
  diced
¾ lb white or brown
  mushrooms, wiped and sliced
1 tbsp soy sauce
ground black pepper
about ½ cup buttermilk
1 x 8 oz can mussels (optional)**

Coat fish with mixture of flour, salt and paprika, and arrange in lightly greased baking dish to fit. Heat oil and sauté onion, red bell pepper and mushrooms. When soft, season with soy sauce and pepper. Stir in enough buttermilk to moisten, then pour evenly over fish. Bake, uncovered, at 350°F for 20–25 minutes or until fish is cooked through. If using mussels, drain and rinse and add to the dish 5 minutes before serving.
Serves 4.

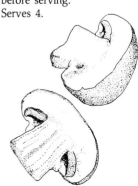

## Greek-Style Fillets of Hake

In this casserole, fish is baked in a robustly flavored sauce. The result is high on color, low in cost. Serve with rice and a salad topped with feta.

1 lb 14 oz filleted hake
2 large onions
3 tbsp vegetable oil
3 tbsp olive oil
2 garlic cloves, crushed
½ lb eggplant, cubed
1 green Bell pepper, seeded and diced
¾ lb tomatoes, skinned and chopped
¼ cup chopped parsley
½–1 tsp dried oregano
scant ¾ cup white wine
salt and ground black pepper
pinch of sugar
black olives

If using a pack of frozen fillets, thaw in milk. Dry well and place in a large baking dish in a single layer. Season lightly. Slice onions into thin rings. Heat oils in a large saucepan and sauté onions, garlic, eggplant and Bell pepper for a few minutes.

Add tomatoes, parsley, oregano, wine, seasoning and sugar. Cover and simmer for 20 minutes stirring occasionally. The mixture should be thick and juicy. Pour over fish and bake, uncovered, at 325°F for 35–40 minutes until fish is cooked. Add a handful of black olives 5 minutes before end of baking time.
Serves 4.

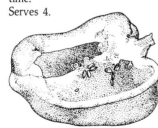

## Low-Calorie Fish Dish

No breading and frying, no eggs, no cream – this fish is poached and blanketed with a light, delicately flavored sauce.

2¼ lb filleted firm white fish
good ¾ cup water
a few onion slices
scant ½ cup white wine
salt
2 bay leaves
thinly sliced orange to garnish

SAUCE
¼ cup oil
1 large onion, finely chopped
¼ cup flour
1¼ cups reserved poaching liquid
1 cup fresh orange juice
¼ cup chopped parsley
1 tsp French mustard
1–2 tsp sugar
scant ½ cup buttermilk
pinch of salt

Remove skin from fish, slice into portions and place in large pan. Add water, onion, wine, salt and bay leaves, bring to boil and simmer gently until just cooked. Drain and arrange in baking dish to fit in single layer. Reserve 1¼ cups of the poaching liquid.

Heat oil and sauté onion. Sprinkle in flour, then slowly stir in reserved liquid and orange juice. When sauce thickens, add remaining ingredients and simmer briefly. Adjust seasoning, pour over fish and heat through, uncovered, at 350°F for about 10 minutes or until just beginning to bubble. Garnish with thinly sliced orange.

Serve with baby potatoes and steamed broccoli.
Serves 6.

## Whole Barbecued Fish

This is a basic recipe, using simple ingredients. If you have fresh herbs at hand, tuck them inside the fish to add interest but be circumspect, for the fresh fish flavor should not be masked. Succulence is the aim, and the marinade will take care of that.

The fire must be very deep and very low, and the fish should not be salted until near the end of the cooking period.

3¾–4½ lb hake or bass, gutted and scaled

MARINADE
½ cup white wine
½ cup oil
2 garlic cloves, crushed
1 tsp dry mustard
1 tsp paprika
2 tsp Worcestershire sauce
1 large onion, coarsely grated
¼ cup chopped parsley
1½–2 tsp dried dill

Mix ingredients for marinade. Place fish in a large glass or earthenware dish, pour marinade over, spooning some into the cavity, and leave for 2 hours, turning a few times.

Oil the grid well before barbecuing, and cook the fish very slowly for about 45 minutes, basting often and turning grid regularly. Any remaining marinade may be spooned over each serving. Serve with Barbecued Mushrooms (below).
Serves about 6.

## Barbecued Mushrooms

Large, brown mushrooms make a splendid accompaniment.

Brush with melted butter spiked with crushed garlic, or alternatively brush with rosemary-flavored oil, and barbecue on the grid until cooked.

## Broiled Golden-Topped Cod

Deliciously juicy, these butter-brushed fillets are broiled and then finished off with a soufflé topping which melts to a rich golden-brown.

4 x 9 oz skinless cod fillets
1 tsp salt
4 tsp flour
½ tsp dried dill
2 tbsp butter, melted
1 tbsp lemon juice
½ cup thick mayonnaise
½ cup grated Cheddar cheese
1 tsp French mustard
1 egg white, stiffly beaten

Dust fish with a mixture of salt, flour and dill. Place in ovenproof dish to fit and brush top with butter mixed with lemon juice. Broil until top turns white (this takes only a few minutes) then turn carefully.

Mix mayonnaise, cheese and mustard and fold in egg white. Spread over fish pieces and broil until golden brown. Do not position too close to the broiler, as the mayonnaise mixture scorches easily. Serve with baby potatoes and beans or a salad.
Serves 4.

### Note
When broiling the mayonnaise-topped fish, watch carefully, and remove as soon as it melts and turns color.

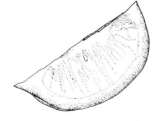

## Baked Fish with Almonds

There's no frying with this dish, and it's very easy to assemble. Any firm fish will do, as long as it's filleted and skinless.

3 tbsp oil
2 tbsp butter
2 garlic cloves, crushed
4 x ¼ lb fish fillets
salt
paprika
4 tsp soy sauce
finely chopped parsley
1 onion, coarsely grated
⅓ cup almonds, flaked

Preheat oven to 350°F. Melt oil and butter in a baking dish. Add garlic and put in oven to heat. Remove when hot and turn fish once in buttery mixture. Sprinkle each piece lightly with salt and paprika and spoon 1 tsp soy sauce over each. Sprinkle with a little parsley and onion. Finally, top each piece with 2 tbsp almonds. Bake, uncovered, for about 25 minutes until cooked, basting once or twice.

Pour buttery juices over each portion and serve with Orange Carrots (page 131), a green salad and boiled baby potatoes.
Serves 4.

Fish with Cucumber Cream Sauce

## Fish with Cucumber Cream Sauce

**Any firm fish fillets can be used for this dish, and they may be broiled, poached or baked, with the sauce served over the top or underneath.**

**1 lb 5 oz filleted firm white fish**
**fresh dill or cucumber twists to garnish**

SAUCE
**cucumber**
**1 tbsp butter**
**½ tsp dried dill**
**2 tsp flour**
**1 cup fish stock (page 60)**
**2 egg yolks**
**2 tsp chopped capers**
**1 tbsp sherry**
**2 tbsp sour cream or fresh cream**
**salt and ground black pepper**

Broil, poach or bake fish as desired.
To make the sauce, peel and cube enough cucumber to make up ¾ cup, discarding the seeds. Heat butter, add cucumber, sprinkle in dill and sauté gently until softened, shaking pan occasionally. Sprinkle in flour, then stir in stock. Beat together egg yolks, capers, sherry and sour cream or cream and add to pan. Stir until thickened. Adjust seasoning and, if desired, sharpen with a dash of lemon juice.
Garnish the dish with fresh dill, if available, or thin twists of cucumber and serve with rice tossed with fried mushrooms. Serves 3-4.

### Hint
**You can use frozen fish steaks but thaw them in milk for that fresh-from-the-sea flavor, and be sure to dry them well before baking.**

## Hake Baked in Cucumber Sauce

**A simple, yet tasty, budget fish dish.**

**1¾ lb skinned hake fillets**
**milk**
**salt and ground black pepper**
**2 tbsp butter**
**2 tsp oil**
**6 green onions, chopped**
**½ large cucumber, peeled and diced**
**½ tsp dried dill**
**2 tbsp finely chopped parsley**
**generous pinch of celery salt**
**¼ cup flour**
**grated Cheddar or Gruyère cheese**

Place fish in shallow oven dish and pour over 1 cup milk. Season and bake at 350°F until just done. Remove fish to lightly buttered baking dish and add enough milk to poaching liquid to give you 2 cups. Set aside. In a smallish saucepan heat butter and oil. Add green onions and toss until coated, then add cucumber (you should have ½lb). Add dill, parsley and celery salt. Cover and cook for about 10 minutes on a low heat, shaking saucepan occasionally until vegetables are soft. Sprinkle in flour and slowly stir in the 2 cups milk. When sauce is thick, check seasoning – it might need a pinch of salt, a dash of lemon juice or a little sugar – and pour over the fish.
Sprinkle with a little grated cheese and bake until just heated through and cheese has started to melt.
Serves 4.

Poor Man's Thermidor

## Cod with Mushrooms and Sour Cream

**The fish cooks slowly in the juices from the onions and mushrooms, and the result is both delicate and delicious.**

2¼ lb cod
3 tbsp flour
½ tsp salt
½ tsp paprika
2 tbsp butter
3 tbsp oil
1 large onion, chopped
about ¾ lb mushrooms, wiped
  and sliced
2 tsp soy sauce
⅔–¾ cup sour cream
5 tsp sherry
grated Parmesan or mozzarella
  cheese

Skin and fillet fish so that you have two good pieces, totalling about 1¾lb. Mix flour, salt and paprika and dust fish on both sides. Arrange in lightly buttered dish to fit really closely, but without actually overlapping.

Heat butter and oil and soften onion and mushrooms. When just beginning to shrink, remove from heat, add soy sauce and pour over fish. Combine sour cream and sherry in the warm pan, then dribble over fish, sprinkle with chosen cheese and bake, uncovered, at 350°F for about 40 minutes. Serve with buttered rice and peas, or a salad and new potatoes.
Serves 4.

### Hint

**If commercially sour cream is unobtainable, fresh cream may be soured by adding a dash of vinegar or a little lemon juice. This cream will, however, be higher in calories than the cultured product.**

## Poor Man's Thermidor

**This is the sort of dish that looks so inviting in a beautiful casserole set on a hot tray at an informal party: chunks of firm, poached fish in a creamy mushroom and cheese sauce accompanied by a bowl of saffron rice and a green salad, this is one of the nicest of fork suppers.**

4 x 7 oz chunks of poached,
  filleted firm white fish
3 tbsp butter
6 tbsp flour
1½ pints hot milk
salt and pepper
3 tbsp oil
1 onion, finely chopped
about ¾ lb white mushrooms,
  wiped and sliced
scant ½ cup tomato paste
1–2 tsp French mustard
1 cup grated Cheddar cheese
4 tsp brandy

The fish should be in neat pieces, with all bones and skin carefully removed. Melt butter, stir in flour, remove from heat and slowly add hot milk. Return to heat and cook until smooth and thickened. Season and set aside. Heat oil in skillet, add onion and mushrooms and fry gently until soft, then increase heat to remove any moisture. Add to white sauce together with tomato paste, mustard, cheese, brandy and the fish. Adjust seasoning.

Turn mixture into a buttered 12 x 8-in casserole, cover and heat through at 325°F for about 30 minutes, then serve as suggested.
Serves 6.

## Salmon in Pastry

1 x 14 oz can pink salmon
½ cup sour cream
1 celery stalk, finely chopped
3 tbsp chopped parsley
¼ cup finely chopped green
    onions
3 hard-boiled eggs, chopped
salt and ground black pepper
1 tsp lemon juice
14 oz puff pastry
1 egg, beaten

SAUCE
⅔ cup sour cream
scant ½ cup thick mayonnaise
½ tsp finely grated lemon zest
2 tsp lemon juice
pinch of sugar

Drain and flake salmon, discarding skin and bones. Mix with sour cream, celery, parsley, green onions, hard-boiled eggs, seasoning and lemon juice. Roll pastry out lightly on floured board into a long rectangle and divide in two, making one piece about 9 x 7 in and the other slightly larger. Spoon salmon filling onto smaller piece, moisten edges of pastry and cover with the second piece. Seal edges, and scallop to make a raised edge. Brush with beaten egg, prick top, and decorate with any pastry trimmings. Lift carefully onto a large, moistened cookie sheet and bake at 400°F for 35 minutes until puffed and golden brown. Transfer to warmed platter, or allow to cool. Serve with the sauce and a salad.

Combine all the ingredients for the sauce. If serving the pie hot, heat sauce gently in top of double saucepan. To serve cold, simply stir ingredients until blended. Serves 6.

## Rainbow Trout with Vermouth and Almonds

**A sophisticated way of treating trout: baked in vermouth and butter, topped with toasted almonds and garnished with slices of lemon. Serve this splendid dish with tiny potatoes and the simplest of salads.**

6 rainbow trout
¼ cup flour
1 tsp salt
½ tsp paprika
scant ½ cup butter
2 tsp finely grated lemon zest
4 pearl onions, grated
¼ cup snipped chives
1 cup dry vermouth
blanched, flaked almonds

Clean trout. Wipe with a damp cloth and pat dry. Dust trout with flour mixed with salt and paprika and place side by side in 1 or 2 buttered baking dishes. Cream butter with lemon zest, onions and chives. Divide into 12 portions. Place one portion inside the cavity of each fish and spread the rest over the top. Pour the vermouth over. Cover and bake at 350°F for about 25 minutes or until just cooked. Brown almonds in the oven at the same time and remove when lightly toasted.

To serve, top each trout generously with almonds and spoon juices over each serving. Serves 6.

# Chicken Chow

Serving Chinese food to guests
is tricky, because of last-minute
stir-frying. Therefore I've
worked out a Chinese-type dish
which can be assembled and
semi-cooked in advance. This
breaks all the rules, of course,
but it's a good and useful recipe.

1 small chicken
water
a few parsley sprigs
1 bay leaf
1 onion, halved
salt
1 small cucumber, peeled and
    diced
5 green onions, chopped, or 2
    leeks, thinly sliced
about ½ lb mushrooms, thinly
    sliced
3 cups mung bean sprouts
1 large green Bell pepper,
    seeded and thinly shredded
2 celery stalks, thinly sliced
¼ cup oil
¼ cup soy sauce
¼ cup flour
¼ cup sherry
toasted almonds

Poach chicken in plenty of water
with herbs, onion and salt. Strip
flesh from bones and dice enough
to give you 1–1¼ lb. Reserve
1½ cups stock.

Mix together cucumber, green
onions or leeks, mushrooms,
sprouts, green Bell pepper and
celery. Heat oil in large Chinese
wok or in heavy skillet and sauté
vegetables briskly over high heat
for 2–3 minutes, turning constantly
with a wooden spoon. Spoon into
large baking dish, add cubed
chicken and toss.

Beat together reserved stock,
soy sauce, flour and sherry and
pour over chicken mixture. At this
stage you can leave it for a while,
covered, in a cool place.

To serve, preheat oven to
400°F and bake, uncovered for
20 minutes, stirring once after
10 minutes. Spoon onto brown rice
in Chinese bowls and sprinkle with
almonds.
Serves 6–8.

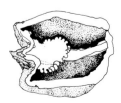

## Crunchy Rice and Chicken Salad

The crunchy rice adds an interesting texture to this salad, which is quite different from the usual chicken mayonnaise.

¼ cup oil
5 tsp lemon juice
1 tbsp honey
2 cups hot, cooked brown rice
2 celery stalks, chopped
1 leek, finely sliced
¼ cup chopped parsley
½ cucumber, peeled and cubed
scant 2 cups mung bean sprouts
salt and ground black pepper
1 chicken
parsley sprigs
1 bay leaf
1 onion, halved
1 x 12 oz can pineapple rings in natural juices
1 cup thick mayonnaise

2 tsp soy sauce
½–1 tsp tsp ground ginger
toasted almonds

Mix oil, lemon juice and honey and fork into hot rice. Add celery, leek, parsley, cucumber and sprouts. Adjust seasoning, cover and chill.

Poach chicken in plenty of water with parsley, bay leaf, onion and salt. Cool chicken in liquid, then strip flesh from bones, and dice, discarding skin. Drain pineapple and reserve juice. Chop 3–4 rings into small pieces and add to chicken. Mix mayonnaise with soy sauce, ginger and a little of the reserved pineapple juice to taste. Toss this dressing with chicken and pineapple, cover and chill.

To serve, make a border of rice, spoon chicken into center and sprinkle with almonds.
Serves 6–8.

## Chicken Baked with Soy Sauce and Sherry

Another aromatic and quickly prepared chicken dish. Serve this one with a salad and baked potatoes topped with a creamy mushroom sauce.

2¼ lb chicken pieces
oil for frying
1 large onion, coarsely grated
3 garlic cloves, crushed
1 knob gingerroot, peeled and grated
3 tbsp oil
¼ cup soy sauce
¼ cup sweet sherry
1 tsp curry powder

Cut chicken breasts in half, if large, and remove excess fat from thighs. Brown on both sides in a little oil, then transfer to baking dish in single layer, close together and skin-side down. Sprinkle over onion, garlic and ginger. Mix remaining ingredients together and pour over chicken. Do not season. Bake at 350°F for 45 minutes, then reduce heat to 325°F, turn chicken and continue baking for about 30 minutes until well browned and tender. Serve with the juices spooned over each serving.
Serves 5–6.

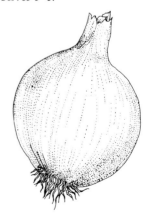

# Deviled Chicken

Another quick and easy recipe. Serve this tangy chicken with baked potatoes and sour cream and a salad. As the chicken bakes at a low temperature, don't use large potatoes as they won't cook through – I simply roll small to medium ones in oil, place in a baking dish, and by the time the chicken is ready they should be done too.

2¼ lb chicken pieces
salt and pepper
oil
¼ cup chutney
¼ cup tomato sauce
2 tsp Worcestershire sauce
1 tsp curry powder
1 tsp prepared mustard
1 large onion, coarsely grated
2 garlic cloves, crushed
butter

Cut chicken breasts in half if large and remove excess fat from thighs. Season lightly and place, skin-side up, in a shallow baking dish brushed with oil. Mix together the chutney, tomato sauce, Worcestershire sauce, curry powder, mustard, onion and garlic. Spread over chicken.

Bake, uncovered, at 325°F for 1 hour. Dot with butter and continue baking until chicken is cooked through and a deep, rich color.
Serves 4 generously.

# Spicy Chicken Curry

3 tbsp oil
2¾ lb chicken pieces
salt and ground black pepper
2 large onions, chopped
2 garlic cloves, crushed
2 large apples, peeled and diced
1 knob gingerroot, peeled and grated
¼ cup flour
1 tbsp curry powder (or to taste)
1 tsp turmeric
1 tsp ground cinnamon
1 tsp ground coriander
½ tsp ground cumin
2 cups seasoned chicken stock
⅓ cup golden raisins
1 tbsp honey
5 tsp tomato paste
5 tsp fruit chutney
finely grated zest of ½ lemon
2 bay leaves

Heat oil in saucepan and brown chicken on both sides. Transfer to large baking dish and season. Add a little more oil to saucepan if necessary and sauté onions, garlic, apples and ginger. When softened, sprinkle in flour, curry powder and spices. Slowly add stock and stir until boiling. Stir in golden raisins, honey, tomato paste, chutney and lemon zest. Spoon over chicken, tuck in bay leaves, cover and bake at 325°F for about 1 hour 30 minutes or until tender.

If desired, enrich gravy with a little cream or sour cream, or sharpen with lemon juice or yogurt, and serve with rice and a tomato and onion salad.
Serves 6.

# Chicken with Mushrooms and Sour Cream

A simple, satisfying casserole which never seems to lose its appeal. In this dish the mushrooms are not fried beforehand, which means that the chicken cooks gently in the juices.

2¼ lb chicken pieces
1 tsp paprika
¼ cup oil
salt and ground black pepper
1 large onion, chopped
2 garlic cloves, crushed
¼ cup flour
1 cup hot chicken stock
about ¾ lb brown mushrooms, wiped and sliced
⅓ cup sour cream
5 tsp sweet sherry
4 tsp soy sauce

Trim off any bits of fat from chicken pieces. Dust with paprika. Heat oil and fry chicken on both sides until lightly browned. Remove to baking dish to fit closely in a single layer, skin-side up, and season lightly. To pan juices add onion and garlic and sauté lightly. Stir in flour and slowly add hot stock. When thickened, remove from heat and add mushrooms, sour cream, sherry and soy sauce. Pour over chicken and bake, uncovered, at 325°F for 1 hour 20 minutes, or until tender, and gravy is thick and nut-brown. Serve with Oriental Rice (see below).
Serves 5–6.

# Oriental Rice

scant 1 cup long-grain rice
2 cups water or stock
½ tsp salt
¼ cup finely chopped parsley
4 green onions, chopped
5 tsp soy sauce
3 tbsp toasted flaked almonds
knob of butter

Put rice into saucepan with water and salt and bring to a boil. Cover and cook on low heat until dry and fluffy. Fork in remaining ingredients and turn into heated serving dish.
Serves 5–6.

## *Chicken Breasts Duxelle with Whisky Cream Sauce*

These breasts are stuffed, flamed in whisky, poached, then covered in a creamy sauce and topped with toasted almonds. Duxelle is the French name for a simple mixture of mushrooms, green onions and herbs fried in butter, used to enhance a variety of sauces, soups and stuffings.

**4 x ¼ lb filleted, skinless chicken breasts**
**1 tbsp oil**
**salt and ground black pepper**
**1 tbsp whisky, warmed**
**¼ cup white wine**
**¼ cup water**
**chicken stock or water**

DUXELLE
**good ¼ lb brown mushrooms, very finely chopped**
**3 tbsp butter**
**6 green onions, chopped**
**1 small carrot, diced**
**1 tsp finely chopped fresh rosemary needles**
**salt and ground black pepper**

SAUCE
**2 tbsp butter**
**3 tbsp flour**
**1 cup reserved chicken stock**
**⅔ cup light cream, sour cream, or half and half**
**1 tsp French mustard**
**2 tsp whisky**
**1 egg yolk**
**pinch of sugar (if using sour cream)**
**toasted flaked almonds**

Begin with the duxelle: squeeze mushrooms in absorbent paper towels until very dry. Heat butter, and fry mushrooms, green onions, carrot and herbs over medium heat for about 15 minutes, turning with wooden spoon, until dry and shrunken and richly browned. Remove from heat and season. Set aside.

Either cut pockets in chicken breasts by slicing horizontally, but not right through, and opening out, or flatten gently with a mallet. Be careful not to tear the flesh.

Divide duxelle equally between the four breasts. Either stuff pocket or spoon down length of one side of breast and fold over, then pinch to close. It is not necessary to tie or skewer them. Heat oil and seal breasts on both sides without browning, turning once, carefully, with a spatula. Season breasts, and then flame with whisky. Add wine and water. Cover and poach over low heat for about 20 minutes or until just gender. Do not boil rapidly, or overcook, or they will toughen. Remove breasts to small baking dish to fit fairly snugly, and make up pan juices to 1 cup with stock or water.

To make sauce, melt butter, stir in flour, cook 1 minute then slowly add hot stock and stir until thickened. Mix together cream/ sour cream, mustard, whisky, egg yolk and pinch of sugar. Pour on a little of the hot sauce, stir to mix, then return to saucepan and heat, stirring, until thickened. Do not boil. Pour over chicken and sprinkle generously with toasted almonds.

Cover and heat through at 325°F for 20–30 minutes. Serve with rice tossed with stir-fried, grated zucchini and a green salad. Serves 4.

## Chicken Breasts with Tarragon and Mustard Cream Sauce

These breast fillets are coated with a creamy velouté sauce with just a hint of tarragon.

1 tbsp oil
4 x ¼ lb filleted, skinless chicken breasts
¼ cup white wine
chicken stock
salt and ground black pepper
2 tbsp butter
1 tsp dried tarragon
2 tsp flour
1 cup reserved chicken stock
1 egg yolk
scant ½ cup light or sour cream
1 tsp French mustard
paprika

Heat oil and seal breasts quickly on both sides – don't allow to brown. Add wine and stock, cover and poach gently for about 20 minutes or until cooked. Transfer to warm platter, season and keep warm. Measure pan juices and make up 1 cup with hot chicken stock.

Make a velouté sauce by melting butter with tarragon. Stir in flour and cook for a few seconds without browning. Remove from heat and gradually stir in stock, then simmer, stirring, until thickened. Mix together egg yolk, cream and mustard. Pour sauce through a small strainer (to strain out tarragon) into the egg mixture, then return to saucepan and stir over low heat to cook egg without boiling. Adjust seasoning, pour over breasts, and sprinkle with paprika.
Serves 4.

## Chicken Niblets

These spicy chicken wings make a delicious party snack or can be served as a main course with rice tossed with fried mushrooms. An added bonus is that they can be prepared in advance.

16 chicken wings
8 tbsp butter
4 tsp soy sauce
1 cup flour
1 tsp garlic salt
1 tsp curry powder
½ tsp ground ginger
½ tsp paprika
½ tsp ground coriander
oil for baking

Slice tips off chicken wings and separate each wing at the joint with poultry shears, being careful not to cut through the bone. This will give you 32 neat little pieces. Melt butter and add soy sauce. Mix flour with remaining dry ingredients.

Using a pastry brush, brush each joint with butter and soy sauce mixture, then roll in seasoned flour. Chill thoroughly – all day if you like. To bake, cover base of one very large or two medium, shallow baking dishes with a thin layer of oil. Place in oven for a few minutes to heat, then arrange chicken in a single layer, closely but not overlapping. Cover and bake at 325°F for 1 hour, then uncover and bake for further 10 minutes.
Serves 8.

*The following are all variations on the crumbed chicken theme. These are singularly useful recipes because they can, or rather must, be prepared in advance and then baked just before dinner, without any need for constant attention or basting. Serve with baked potatoes, sour cream and a salad for a complete meal.*

## Sesame Chicken

3 tbsp sesame seeds
1 cup finely crushed toasted
  breadcrumbs
½ tsp celery salt
½ tsp dried thyme
1 tsp ground coriander
5 tsp soy sauce
good ⅓ cup thick mayonnaise
2 garlic cloves, crushed
about 2¾ lb chicken pieces
oil for baking

Mix sesame seeds, breadcrumbs, celery salt, thyme and coriander on a large plate. Mix soy sauce, mayonnaise and garlic. Remove wing tips from chicken pieces and cut breasts in half if large. Using a pastry brush, brush chicken with mayonnaise mixture, then coat with crumb mixture – there will be enough for quite a thick coating. Chill for at least 2 hours.

To bake, heat a thin film of oil in a large baking dish. Turn chicken once in hot oil and arrange skin-side down. Bake, uncovered, at 400°F for 15 minutes. Reduce heat to 325°F and bake for 30 minutes. Turn pieces over and continue baking for about 20 minutes more until crisp, golden brown and tender.
Serves 6.

## Mustard-Baked Chicken with Honey and Almonds

**Coated with a buttery mustard mixture and then baked until richly browned, this is a quick chicken dish with a delicious flavor.**

1 lb 14 oz–2 lb chicken pieces,
  preferably thighs
3 tbsp butter, softened
1 tbsp honey
5 tsp French mustard
½ tsp salt
¼ cup fine, fresh white
  breadcrumbs
1 tsp lemon juice
chopped, toasted almonds

Remove excess fat from thighs and arrange on plate, skin-side up. Cream butter with remaining ingredients, except almonds. Cover top of each piece of chicken thickly with butter mixture, and refrigerate for several hours.

To bake, place chicken pieces in lightly oiled baking dish. Bake at 325°F for 30 minutes. Baste well, then bake until tender and well-browned, about 60 minutes more, basting twice. Add a little water to dish if necessary to prevent scorching and to keep chicken moist. Sprinkle almonds over each piece 10 minutes before end of baking period, and baste before returning to oven.

To serve, spoon succulent juices over each serving, or pour into a saucepan and use to make a light gravy.
Serves 4–5.

### Hint
**To blanch almonds, place in a small saucepan, cover with cold water and just bring to a boil. When cool enough to handle, the skins should slip off easily.**

# Crumbed Chicken with Tarragon and Garlic

This chicken dish is enhanced by garlic mayonnaise, which should be made at least a few hours in advance, and chilled.

8 x ¼ lb chicken thighs
1 cup fine cereal or toasted breadcrumbs
½ tsp garlic salt
½ tsp salt
1½–2 tsp dried tarragon

GARLIC BLENDER MAYONNAISE
1 egg
½ tsp salt
scant 1 cup oil
5 tsp tarragon vinegar
½ tsp sugar
4 garlic cloves, peeled

First make the mayonnaise: Put egg, salt, 3 tbsp oil, vinegar, sugar and garlic into blender and blend well, then, with motor running, slowly add remaining oil through the hole in the top. Chill.

Remove any fat from thighs and coat thoroughly with mayonnaise – you'll need about two-thirds of the batch. Mix remaining ingredients on a large plate, coat chicken in crumbs, then chill for at least 1 hour to set.

To bake, heat a little oil in a baking dish and arrange chicken quite closely. Cover and bake at 325°F for 1 hour, then uncover and bake 15 minutes longer. Serve with spinach and blue cheese salad. Serves 8.

# Crumbed Parmesan Chicken Wings

16 x 2½ oz chicken wings
½ cup mayonnaise
3–4 garlic cloves, crushed
1 tsp Worcestershire sauce
1 cup fine, toasted breadcrumbs
⅓ cup finely grated Parmesan cheese
1 tsp salt
ground black pepper
2 tsp dried oregano
oil for baking

Remove and discard wing-tips. Using poultry scissors and cutting between bones at the top, divide wings in half. Mix mayonnaise, garlic and Worcestershire sauce on large plate. Mix remaining ingredients, except oil, on another large plate.

Using a pastry brush, coat chicken wings with mayonnaise mixture, then roll in crumb mixture, coating well. Chill for at least 1 hour to set crumbs.

To bake, cover bases of two large baking dishes with a thin layer of oil and place in 325°F oven until hot. Turn wings once in hot oil and then bake, uncovered, for about 45 minutes, or until brown and crisp.

Serve as a cocktail snack or for a light supper, with baked potatoes or rolls and a salad.
Serves 4 as supper or 16 as a snack.

## Hint
Toasted breadcrumbs may be bought at some supermarkets. To make your own, place thin slices of bread, crusts removed, on a cookie sheet and place in a low oven until golden brown and crisp. Place in a plastic bag and crush with a rolling pin until the desired consistency is reached.

## Stuffed Roast Chicken with Herbs

The following is possibly my favorite way of treating roast chicken. The addition of just a few simple ingredients adds a wonderful flavor, and the smell as it roasts brings everyone to the kitchen.

2 tbsp butter
3 tbsp oil
2 garlic cloves, crushed
1 small onion, grated
½ tsp each dried thyme, basil
   and oregano
1 tbsp soy sauce
1 x 4½ lb chicken
salt and ground black pepper
2 small fresh rosemary sprigs
1½ cups chicken stock or water

STUFFING
2⅓ cups cooked rice
1 small onion, chopped
3 tbsp chopped parsley
generous pinch of salt
¼ cup chopped toasted walnuts
   or brazil nuts
3 tbsp reserved herb-butter
   mixture

Heat butter and oil until just melted. Add garlic, onion, dried herbs and soy sauce. Mix well, reserving 3 tbsp to add to the stuffing ingredients.

Wipe chicken inside and out and dry well. Remove all fat and nick out oil gland in parson's nose. Combine all ingredients for stuffing, stuff body cavity, then truss. Season lightly and brush with remaining herb-butter mixture — there should be just enough to coat it lightly all over.

Place chicken on rack in roasting pan. Add rosemary and stock or water to pan. Roast at 325°F for about 2 hours 45 minutes, basting a few times. Cover top loosely with a tent of foil, shiny-side up, when it has browned sufficiently, and add more stock or water to roasting pan whenever necessary.

When done, remove to serving platter and leave in warming drawer for about 15 minutes. Make a gravy from juices, and serve with roast potatoes and colorful vegetables. Serves 6.

## Chicken Breasts in Curry-Cream Sauce

**A smooth sauce blankets the chicken in this dish which can be assembled beforehand and baked when required. Served with Orange Golden Raisin Rice (right) it's an easy but elegant version of curried chicken.**

**¼ cup oil**
**1 tbsp butter**
**2 onions, finely chopped**
**2 tsp curry powder (or more to taste)**
**1 tsp each ground ginger, ground cinnamon, ground cumin, ground coriander and turmeric**
**8 x ¼ lb filleted, skinless chicken breasts**
**salt and ground black pepper**
**scant ½ cup water**
**¼ cup cornstarch**

**1 cup chicken stock**
**good ¾ cup sour cream**
**¼ cup sherry**
**toasted almonds**
**paprika**

Heat oil and butter in large, heavy skillet. Add onions and allow to soften over low heat without browning. Stir in curry powder and all spices, and when well mixed turn heat down low and arrange breasts on top. Season, add water, cover and cook gently until tender, turning after 15 minutes. When done, transfer to baking dish to fit closely.

Whisk together cornstarch, stock, cream and sherry and add to pan juices, which should measure about 1 cup. Stir until thickened, season, pour over chicken and bake, uncovered, at 325°F for 30–40 minutes. Sprinkle with toasted almonds and paprika and serve.
Serves 8.

## Orange Golden Raisin Rice

**good ¾ cup quick-cooking rice**
**1 cup fresh orange juice, strained**
**1 cup water**
**1 cinnamon stick**
**¼ cup golden raisins**
**½ tsp salt**
**1 tsp finely grated lemon or orange zest**
**chopped parsley**

Put all the ingredients, except parsley, into a saucepan. Bring to a boil, stir once, then cover and simmer on lowest heat for 25–30 minutes, without looking or stirring. Remove cinnamon stick and fork in parsley.
Serves 6.

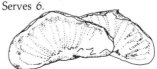

## The Shah's Chicken Curry

The Shah liked mild and aromatic curries.

1¼ lb chicken pieces
1 tbsp butter
1 tbsp oil
2 cinnamon sticks
2 large onions, chopped
2 garlic cloves, crushed
2 bay leaves
1 knob gingerroot, peeled and grated
2 tsp curry powder
½ tsp ground cumin
¼ cup flour
2 cups hot seasoned chicken stock
2 tomatoes, chopped
1 tsp honey
½ tsp salt
2 tsp lemon juice
⅓ cup golden raisins

scant ½ cup buttermilk
coriander leaves to garnish

Remove any fat from chicken and cut breasts in half if large. Heat butter and oil, add cinnamon sticks and brown chicken on both sides. If necessary, do chicken in batches, but leave cinnamon sticks in skillet. As chicken browns, transfer pieces to baking dish.

To pan juices and cinnamon sticks add onions, garlic, bay leaves, gingerroot, curry powder and cumin and toss together for a minute over low heat. Sprinkle in flour, stir to mix, then slowly stir in stock. Add tomatoes, honey, salt, lemon juice and golden raisins. Bring to a boil, stirring, then pour over the chicken. Bake, covered, at 325°F for about 1½ hours, by which time chicken should be tender and sauce nicely thickened. Remove cinnamon sticks and bay leaves. Swirl in buttermilk (do not stir) and return to low oven for

5 minutes to heat through without boiling.

Garnish with a sprinkling of chopped coriander and serve with Spiced Rice and little bowls of coconut, chutney, sliced bananas and toasted almonds.
Serves 4–6.

## Spiced Rice

2 tbsp butter
1 tbsp oil
⅔ cup white long-grain rice
1 onion, chopped
1 tsp masala paste
½ tsp turmeric
4 whole cloves
1½ pints hot chicken stock
¼ cup golden raisins
4 cardamom pods, split
1 cinnamon stick
2 bay leaves
8 peppercorns

Heat butter and oil and add rice, onion, masala, turmeric and cloves. Fry lightly, stirring with a fork. Slowly add hot stock and then remaining ingredients. Cover pot with a dish towel and then with a lid, and simmer very gently for about 25 minutes until liquid has been absorbed. Discard spices.
Serves 6–8.

# Chicken Casserole

A simple, tasty casserole using everyday ingredients.

1 tbsp oil
2 large onions, chopped
2 garlic cloves, crushed
2 carrots, finely diced
2¼ lb chicken pieces
salt and ground black pepper
1 x 14 oz can tomato soup
½ cup water
¼ cup sherry
1 tbsp honey
5 tsp Worcestershire sauce
2 tbsp chopped parsley
1 tbsp brown vinegar
1 tsp prepared mustard
½ tsp dried oregano
generous pinch of cinnamon
sour cream and snipped chives
    to garnish

Heat oil in large skillet and sauté onions, garlic and carrots. Transfer to large baking dish. Add a little oil to skillet if necessary and brown chicken lightly on both sides. Arrange on top of vegetables and season lightly.

Pour off any fat remaining in pan and add remaining ingredients, except sour cream and chives. Mix well and pour over chicken. Cover and bake at 325°F for about 1 hour 30 minutes until tender. For a thicker gravy, bake uncovered for a further 15 minutes. Swirl in a few spoonfuls of sour cream and sprinkle with chives. Serve with rice.
Serves 4–6.

## Hints
Keep peeled cloves of garlic on hand by storing them in a jar of oil in the refrigerator. Use the flavored oil for salad dressings.

Cartons of sour cream and cottage cheese are best stored upside-down in the refrigerator.

## Duck with Orange Liqueur Sauce

**This duck is first roasted then carved and simmered in the orange-flavored sauce.**

1 x 4½ lb duck (weighed with
    giblets and neck)
salt and ground black pepper
1 onion, peeled
½ unpeeled orange, quartered
1 tsp ground ginger
⅔ cup orange liqueur
1 cup fresh orange juice
2 cups giblet stock
peel of ½ orange, cut into thin
    strips
3 tbsp cornstarch
1 tbsp soy sauce

Wipe duck inside and out. Nick out point of gland in tail, squeeze the little glands on either side, and remove loose fat in body cavity and at neck end. Season body cavity and stuff with whole onion and orange quarters. Rub duck with ginger and 1 tsp salt, truss, and prick well all over. Place breast side up on rack in roasting pan and roast at 400°F for 30 minutes. Pour off fat and add a little water to roasting pan. Prick duck again all over, pour over ¼ cup orange liqueur, reduce heat to 350°F and roast for 1 hour. Pour over another ¼ cup orange liqueur, prick well, add more water to roasting pan if necessary and continue roasting for about an hour until tender and browned. To test, prick between leg and thigh-juices should run clear. Set duck aside while making sauce.

Heat orange juice, giblet stock and peel. Boil 5 minutes, then add ⅓ cup orange liqueur mixed with cornstarch and soy sauce. Boil until thickened, then adjust seasoning — if it needs salt add a little more soy sauce.

Carve duck into neat pieces and arrange in baking dish. Pour sauce over and bake, uncovered, at 325°F for 30 minutes until hot and bubbling. Serve with boiled baby potatoes, peas and carrots. Serves 4.

# Almond Chicken Salad

Quite different from the usual chicken mayonnaise, this salad uses filleted chicken breasts, lightly poached and drenched with a creamy buttermilk dressing. Serve with Brown Rice Salad with Mushrooms (page 38).

6 x ¼ lb filleted, skinless
   chicken breasts
oil
¼ cup water
¼ cup sherry
1 small onion
2 bay leaves
1 tsp salt
paprika and toasted, flaked
   almonds to garnish

BUTTERMILK-LEMON DRESSING
1 cup buttermilk
⅔ cup heavy cream
¼ cup reserved stock
3 egg yolks
very generous pinch of finely
   grated lemon zest
generous pinch of salt

Seal breasts on both sides with a little oil in a large skillet – do not allow to brown. Add water, sherry, onion, bay leaves and salt, cover and simmer for about 20 minutes. Cool in the stock, remove chicken and slice lengthwise into long, thin strips. Reserve stock. Mix ingredients for dressing in the top of a double saucepan, beat until smooth, then stir over simmering water until mixture is slightly thickened and coats back of spoon. Adjust seasoning and then pour, while warm, over chicken. When cool, cover and refrigerate. Just before serving, sprinkle with paprika and toasted, flaked almonds.
Serves 6.

# Coronation Turkey

A succulent and moist day-after-Christmas salad using left-over turkey breast, a little jellied turkey stock, and a creamy dressing.

1–1¼ lb turkey breast
1 cup jellied stock
toasted almonds

CURRY DRESSINC
1 tbsp butter
1 tbsp oil
1 small onion, chopped
1 tbsp curry powder
½ tsp ground cinnamon
½ tsp ground ginger
⅔ cup turkey stock
1 tbsp tomato paste
3 tbsp fruit chutney
1 cup mayonnaise
scant ⅓ cup sour cream
pinch of sugar

First make the dressing: in a small saucepan heat butter and oil and lightly fry onion. Stir in curry powder and spices, cook for 1 minute, then add stock, tomato paste and chutney. Simmer, covered, for 5 minutes, then strain into a bowl, pressing through with the back of a spoon. Cool, then stir in mayonnaise, sour cream and a pinch of sugar. Cover and chill to blend flavors.

To assemble, arrange turkey strips on flat platter, dot with jellied stock and toss lightly. Pour over about 1 cup dressing and top with almonds. Serve at once, or lightly chilled, with brown rice tossed with French Dressing (page 47), chopped green onions and celery.
Serves 6.

## Hint
Avoid weeping when chopping onions by chilling them thoroughly in the refrigerator beforehand.

# Casserole of Steak, Wine and Mushrooms

This is a robustly flavored dish which should be made in advance, left to cool, and then reheated for best results. It is important to use a good cut, rump or Porterhouse, and a reasonably good red wine.

3 tbsp oil
knob of butter
6 x 7 oz thick slices steak
prepared mustard
2 onions, chopped
2 garlic cloves, crushed
¼ cup flour
1 cup red wine
1 cup stock
½ tsp each dried thyme, basil
    and oregano
½ cup tomato paste
salt and ground black pepper
pinch of sugar
about ¾ lb brown mushrooms,
    sliced
chopped parsley to garnish

Heat oil and butter in skillet and brown steaks quickly on both sides. Transfer to baking dish in single layer, and spread each steak with a little prepared mustard. In same skillet, soften onions and garlic over low heat. Sprinkle in flour and slowly stir in wine, stock, herbs, tomato paste, seasoning and sugar. Bring to a boil, stirring, and when thickened pour over steak, cover securely and bake at 325°F for 1¼ hours.

Lightly sauté mushrooms in a little oil. Add to steak, cover and bake another 30 minutes. Cool, and if necessary, skim fat. Reheat at 325°F until hot and bubbling. Sprinkle with parsley and serve with small glazed onions, baked potatoes and a green vegetable. Serves 6.

## Hint
On informal occasions, serve the casserole with buttered noodles and a green bean salad. Toss young, cooked beans with sliced onion, red Bell pepper and vinaigrette dressing. Fry breadcrumbs until crisp in oil with a clove of crushed garlic, and then mix with grated Gruyère cheese. Just before serving, sprinkle crumb mixture over beans.

Stifado

## *Stifado*

This is a highly flavored, peasant-type Greek stew for which I like to use beef shank for added succulence.

¼ cup flour
2 tsp salt
1 tsp paprika
1 tsp dried oregano
3 tbsp oil
2¼ lb best quality beef shank cut in slices, 1 in thick
24 pearl onions, peeled
1 cup beef stock
3 tbsp tomato paste
1 tbsp brown sugar
2 garlic cloves, crushed
2 bay leaves
1 cinnamon stick
3 whole cloves
⅔ cup red wine
scant ½ cup sour cream

Mix flour, salt, paprika andoregano and coat shank on both sides, reserving any that remains. Heat oil and brown meat lightly on both sides. Remove to baking dish in single layer. Brown onions in same skillet, adding a little more oil if necessary. Transfer to baking dish with meat when golden brown. Drain off any fat from pan, then add stock, tomato paste, sugar, garlic, bay leaves, cinnamon, cloves and red wine mixed with remaining flour mixture. Bring to a boil and pour over meat. Check that spices are lying in the gravy and not on the shank. Cover and bake at 325°F for 1½ hours or until tender. Cool. Remove bay leaves, cloves and cinnamon 40 minutes before serving. The gravy should be fairly thick and quite generous in quantity, but if not add scant ½ cup stock before reheating at 325°F. Before serving swirl in sour cream, and garnish with parsley.
Serves 4–5.

## *Aromatic Beef Curry*

A beef stew of a different kind is the following aromatic curry.

2 tbsp butter
3 tbsp oil
2 large onions, sliced
2 tart apples, peeled and diced
1 tbsp curry powder
2 garlic cloves, crushed
1 tsp each turmeric, ground cinnamon and cumin
1¾ lb boneless chuck steak, cubed
1½ tsp salt
¼ cup mild fruit chutney
5 tsp brown vinegar
1 tbsp brown sugar
good ¾ cup tomato paste
1 cup water
2 bay leaves
3 tbsp shredded coconut
⅓ cup golden raisins
light cream (optional)

Heat butter and oil and fry onions and apples. Add curry powder, garlic, spices and beef. When browned, turn off heat and stir in remaining ingredients, except golden raisins. Spoon into a large baking dish and bake, covered, at 325°F for 1½ hours. Add more water or stock if necessary, and the golden raisins. Cover and bake for further 30 minutes or until very tender. If using, swirl in cream just before serving.
Serves 6.

## Roast Rump with Chasseur-Style Sauce

1 x 5½ lb boneless beef rump
2 garlic cloves, peeled and
    thinly sliced
2 tsp salt
2 tsp dry mustard
2 tsp brown sugar
1 tsp dried oregano
1 tsp dried sage
3 tbsp flour

SAUCE
3 tbsp oil
about ½ lb mushrooms, wiped
    and sliced
1 onion, chopped
3 tbsp flour
scant ½ cup white wine
1 cup chicken stock
1 tbsp tomato paste
½ tsp salt
½ tsp sugar

1 tsp Worcestershire sauce
¼ cup sour cream

Make deep slits in the joint and insert garlic. Mix dry ingredients and rub all over meat. Allow to stand for 4 hours. Place on rack over a little water and roast at 325° F for about 2¼ hours for medium rare. No need to baste, but after 1½ hours cover loosely with a tent of foil, shiny-side out, to stop further browning. When cooked to your liking, transfer to warming oven, and stand while making sauce.

Heat oil and fry mushrooms and onion. When softened add flour, cook for a minute, stirring, then add remaining ingredients, except sour cream. Simmer, uncovered, for 10–15 minutes until thick. Stir in sour cream. Serve with robust sauce and Casserole of Potatoes and Onions.
Serves about 10.

## Casserole of Potatoes and Onions

**This old-fashioned dish of potatoes layered with onions and baked in stock is easy to assemble and good with almost any main course.**

1 lb 5 oz potatoes, scrubbed and
    thinly sliced
2 onions, thinly sliced
2 garlic cloves, crushed
½ tsp mixed dried herbs
salt and ground black pepper
3 tbsp butter
1½ cups stock
paprika

Cover base of deep, 8-in pie dish with half the potatoes, there is no need to grease the dish. Cover with onions, garlic and herbs. Season. Dot with half the butter, then cover with remaining potatoes.

Dot with remaining butter. Pour stock over, using chicken if serving with white meat or fish, or beef stock for red meat (1 bouillon cube dissolved in a good ½ pint hot water does very well). Dust top with paprika and bake, uncovered, at 350°F for about 1 hour, until potatoes are soft and succulent. Serves 5–6.

### Note

**If meat is being cooked at 325°F, bake potato and onion casserole at the same temperature, but increase the baking time by 30 minutes.**

## Roast Sirloin with Herb Butter

A splendid way of preparing steaks for a special meal, this tenderized sirloin is brushed with a savory butter before roasting, and may be carved into thick steaks (if preferred) rather than thin slices. There is no need to bother with gravy, either, as the buttery juices are simply spooned over each serving. A bowl of sour cream flavored with horseradish, mustard, or green peppercorns makes an excellent accompaniment.

2¾–3 lb rolled sirloin
buttermilk

HERB BUTTER
3 tbsp butter
2 garlic cloves, crushed
1 tsp dry mustard
1½ tbsp parsley, chopped
¼ cup chopped chives
½ tsp dried thyme
½ tsp dried oregano
1 tsp salt

Remove strings, any fat, and the thin outer skin, and put joint in a glass or earthenware dish to fit. Pour over enough buttermilk to coat generously, and marinate in refrigerator for 12–24 hours. Dry very well with absorbent paper towels. Open out, or if necessary butterfly the sirloin by cutting in half horizontally, three-quarters of the way through, and then folding open like a book. Score inside quite deeply, in a diamond pattern.

Cream butter with remaining ingredients and spread two-thirds over scored meat. Roll up and spread remaining butter mixture over the top. (It is not always necessary to tie up again, it depends on the way in which it has been cut.) Place flat in roasting pan and roast at 325°F for about 1 hour. Switch off oven and leave for 15 minutes before carving. Serve with Baked Fried Potatoes (page 132) and a salad.
Serves 6–8.

## Meatball Stroganoff

Serve these meatballs in a mushroom sauce on ribbon noodles with a green salad.

1–1¼ lb lean ground beef (or a mixture of pork, veal and beef)
1 cup fresh breadcrumbs (see note)
1 onion, grated
1 garlic clove, crushed
½ tsp dried thyme
1 egg, beaten
generous pinch of salt
2 tsp soy sauce
3 tbsp oil

SAUCE
1 onion chopped
about ¾ lb brown mushrooms, wiped and sliced
3 tbsp flour
1 cup beef stock
scant ½ cup thick sour cream
1 tbsp soy sauce

Mix ground meat with bread-crumbs, onion, garlic, thyme, egg, salt and soy sauce and form into about 16 small balls. Heat oil in large skillet and fry meatballs over low heat until browned on all sides. Remove. In pan juices, sauté onion and mushrooms. When mushrooms are browned and have drawn juices, sprinkle in flour. Slowly stir in stock and when thickened, add cream and soy sauce. Return meatballs and simmer, half-covered, until cooked through.
Serves 4 generously.

### Note
**Cut thick slices of day-old bread, remove crusts, then cube. Reduce to crumbs in a food processor or blender.**

## Oven-Baked Spicy Steak

18 oz–1 lb 5 oz good quality steaks
oil
salt and ground black pepper
2 onions, chopped
2 garlic cloves, crushed
¼ cup tomato sauce
4 tsp Worcestershire sauce
3 tbsp chutney
1 tsp brown sugar
1 tsp prepared mustard
good ¼ cup red wine

Beat steaks well with a mallet and brown on both sides in a little oil. Transfer to shallow baking dish, and season. Add a little more oil to skillet if necessary, and sauté onions and garlic. Remove pan from heat, and stir in remaining ingredients. Mix well, pour over steak, and bake, uncovered, at 325°F for about 1 hour or until tender. Serve with a crisp salad and baked potatoes with sour cream. Serves 3–4.

### Hint
**Baked potatoes are always a good accompaniment to steak. Normally, however, they are baked in a hot oven, whereas meaty casseroles are often baked at 325°F. This problem can be overcome by starting the potatoes off ahead, at 400°F and then allowing them to finish baking at the lower temperature with the meat dish.**

# Steak au Poivre Vert

4 x 6 oz thick slices fillet steak
oil for frying
5 tsp brandy
salt
knob of butter
4–6 green onions, chopped
1 tbsp green peppercorns,
   rinsed and drained
¾–1 cup light cream or sour
   cream (or half and half)
2 tsp Dijon mustard
pinch of sugar

Smear base of a heavy skillet with
just a very little oil and fry steak
until done to your liking, turning
once, without piercing. Stand back
and flame with warmed brandy,
shaking pan until flame dies. Salt
lightly, transfer to platter and keep
warm. Add knob of butter to pan
and sauté green onions. When
softened, add peppercorns, cream

or sour cream, mustard and sugar.
Stir until just heated and well
blended, then add any steak juices
that escaped while it was standing.
Mix well, pour over steak and
serve at once.
Serves 4.

## Hint
Use a pair of tongs to turn
steaks or chops. If the meat is
pierced, natural juices will be
lost.

# Piquant Porterhouse

A rather classy stew. Even
though this steak is not broiled,
a top quality cut, such as rump
or Porterhouse, should still be
used.

3 tbsp oil
4 x ¼ lb Porterhouse steaks
1 large onion, chopped
1–2 garlic cloves, crushed
generous pinch of dried oregano
pinch of thyme
3 tbsp flour
scant ½ cup port
scant ½ cup tomato sauce
2 tsp Worcestershire sauce
1 tsp prepared mustard
1 tbsp brown sugar
1 tbsp brown vinegar
2 whole cloves
salt and ground black pepper
light cream (optional)

Heat oil in large, heavy skillet and

quickly brown steaks on both sides.
Remove and set aside. Lower heat
and add onion, garlic and herbs.
When onion is softened, mix flour
with port and add to pan together
with steaks and remaining
ingredients. Stir to mix, bring to a
boil, then turn heat down to very
low. Cover and simmer for about
40 minutes, turning once. When
steak is tender and gravy thick,
remove cloves. Stir the cream into
the gravy if desired. Serve with
noodles and a crisp salad.
Serves 4,

## Ground Beef Roll

Mozzarella cheese and canned chili tomatoes give ordinary meat loaf a new look and an Italian flavor.

1–1¼ lb lean ground beef
½ tsp salt
1 onion, coarsely grated
2 garlic cloves, crushed
½ cup fine, fresh wholewheat breadcrumbs
1 egg, lightly beaten
½ tsp dried thyme
½ tsp dried oregano
1 tbsp Worcestershire sauce
¼ cup chopped parsley
1 x 14 oz can chili tomatoes
mozzarella cheese

Mix all ingredients well, except chili tomatoes and mozzarella. Press ground beef mixture out on a sheet of waxed paper into a rectangle measuring 12 x 8 in.

Spread with half chili tomatoes and sprinkle with 1 cup coarsely grated mozzarella. With the help of the paper, roll up from the long edge, like a jelly roll. Place, seam-side down, on an oiled jelly roll pan a little larger than the meat roll. Bake at 325°F for 30 minutes. Remove from oven and spread remaining chili tomatoes over the top, and then arrange thin slices of mozzarella, side by side, to cover the top completely. Return to oven and bake for 30 minutes more.

Serve in thick slices with baked potatoes and sour cream, a mushroom gravy, or simply with mash and vegetables.
Serves 6.

## Marinated Steak with Mustard Butter

Use small T-bone, rump or fillet steaks for this succulent dish.

2 lb steak, sliced

MUSTARD BUTTER
4 tbsp butter
3 tbsp chopped chives
1 tbsp French mustard
few drops of lemon juice
pinch of sugar

MARINADE
¼ cup red wine
5 tsp soy sauce
1 medium onion, grated
3 tbsp oil
1 tsp dried oregano
2 garlic cloves, crushed

First make mustard butter: Cream all ingredients together, form into a roll, wrap in waxed paper and chill.

Arrange steaks in glass dish in single layer. Mix ingredients for marinade and pour over steak. Leave for 3–4 hours, turning occasionally. To cook, don't wipe steaks dry. Fry in heavy, ungreased skillet, and pour over any remaining marinade when browned. Do not season.

Serve with a slice of mustard butter on each steak.
Serves 4–6.

## Roast Fillet of Beef with Mushrooms and Wine

2¼ lb beef fillet
2 garlic cloves, slivered
1 tsp dry mustard
½ tsp paprika
3 tbsp oil
salt and ground black pepper
1 onion, chopped
½ lb mushrooms, wiped and sliced
6 thyme sprigs, chopped
½ cup red wine
½ tsp salt
½ tsp sugar
sour cream (optional)

Spike meat all over with garlic. Rub with mustard and paprika and brown gently on all sides in hot oil. Transfer to small roasting pan that is a little larger than the meat, and season lightly.

In the same pan, fry onion, mushrooms and thyme. When beginning to brown, remove from heat and add wine, salt and sugar. Pour over fillet and roast at 325°F for about 1 hour 10 minutes for rare. Remove meat to serving platter and stand in warm place for 5 minutes.

Serve the gravy thickened, reduced, or with the addition of a little sour cream.
Serves 6–8.

### Hint
**The only really accurate method of judging whether meat is done is to use a thermometer, as so many factors affect the amount of cooking time required.**

## Marinated T-Bone Steaks with Herbs

**It's the marinade that makes this dish special, so don't be tempted to make any sauces.**

2¾ lb T-bone steaks

MARINADE
3 tbsp oil
3 tbsp lemon juice
2 tsp French mustard
3 tbsp chopped mixed fresh herbs

Mix marinade ingredients and spoon on both sides of steak. Leave about 4 hours, turning occasionally. Pan-fry in relays, if necessary adding the merest little dashes of water or white wine to the pan if browning too fast. Season as you turn.
Serves 3–4.

## Fillet Steak with Port and Mustard

4 x 5 oz fillet steaks
1 tbsp butter
2 tsp oil
salt and ground black pepper
¼ cup light cream

MARINADE
¼ cup port
2 tsp French mustard
2 tsp Worcestershire sauce
2–3 garlic cloves, crushed

Mix marinade ingredients. Pour over steaks and leave for 5–6 hours, turning once. Melt butter and oil in a heavy skillet. Pat steaks dry, reserving marinade. Brown steaks and season lightly. Remove to warmed dish. To pan add reserved marinade and the cream. Swirl around quickly, pour over steaks and serve immediately.
Serves 4.

## Roast Sirloin with Green Peppercorn Sauce

This recipe is for a small sirloin, on the bone. Choose a piece with a good undercut of fillet and give it the following careful treatment. To ensure tenderness, the joint is first marinated and then roasted at a low temperature. It should be rare on the inside and darkly browned on the outside due to the soy-mustard baste. It is given a further lift with the tangy sour cream sauce.

1 x 2¼ lb piece sirloin on the
   bone
2 tsp dry mustard
2 garlic cloves, crushed
1 tbsp soy sauce
1 tbsp oil

1 fresh rosemary sprig
salt and ground black pepper

MARINADE
¼ cup oil
¼ cup lemon juice
scant ½ cup red wine
1 small onion, chopped
2 bay leaves

SOUR CREAM SAUCE
1 cup sour cream
1 egg yolk plus ½ tsp cornstarch
   or 2 egg yolks
2 tsp green peppercorns,
   drained and rinsed
1 tsp French mustard
2 tsp brandy
pinch of salt
pinch of sugar

Remove any excess fat from meat and place in glass dish. Mix oil, lemon juice and wine and pour over meat. Add onion and bay leaves. Marinate for a few hours at room temperature if kitchen is cool,

otherwise place in refrigerator. Turn occasionally.

To roast, pat meat dry. Mix mustard, garlic, soy sauce and oil and brush all over meat. Place on rack in roasting pan, put rosemary on top, and pour a little water in at the side to prevent scorching. Roast at 325°F for 1½ hours, adding a little more water as necessary. Season lightly towards end of roasting period. Turn off the oven and let stand for 10–15 minutes to allow juices to settle.

Put all sauce ingredients into a small saucepan and heat slowly, stirring with a balloon whisk to mix, and then a wooden spoon. Stir until mixture thickens, but do not allow to boil. Serve sauce separately.

Carve joint upper side downwards, towards the bone, in thin slices. Cut fillet separately. Serves 4.

## Marinade for Steak on the Barbecue

3 tbsp fruit chutney
3 tbsp tomato sauce
5 tsp Worcestershire sauce
1 tsp prepared mustard
1 tsp brown sugar
2 tsp brown vinegar
1 onion, chopped
2 garlic cloves, crushed

Arrange 1½ lb rump steak in non-metallic dish. Mix ingredients for marinade, pour over steak and leave for 6 hours, turning twice. Makes about scant ½ cup.

# Frosted Meat Loaf

**The potato "frosting" and a home-made tomato sauce or mushroom gravy add to the appearance and flavor of this meat loaf variation.**

½ cup milk
1 egg
⅔ cup quick-cooking
    porridge oats
3 tbsp oil
2 onions, chopped
1–1¼ lb ground beef
1 tbsp Worcestershire sauce
3 tbsp tomato sauce
¼ cup chopped parsley
1 medium carrot, coarsely
    grated
1 tsp salt
1 tsp mixed dried herbs

FROSTING
**6 medium potatoes, boiled and
    mashed**
scant ½ cup milk, heated
**1 tbsp butter
1 egg yolk
salt and pepper**

Beat milk with egg, add porridge oats and leave to soak for 10 minutes. Heat oil and fry onions until lightly browned. Mix remaining ingredients, then add fried onion and milk mixture. Combine thoroughly and pack firmly into an oiled 10 x 3 x 2½-in loaf pan. Bake at 350°F for 1 hour. Stand for about 10 minutes or until juices are absorbed, then unmold onto a flat, warmed serving dish.

Beat mashed potato with hot milk, butter and egg yolk until fluffy and creamy. Season, then swirl over the entire loaf, top and sides, and return to the oven at the same temperature for 15–20 minutes. Serve with a green vegetable and maybe pumpkin baked in the oven at the same time. Serves 6.

## *Casseroled Rump with Port*

A type of ragoût with a full-bodied flavor, which is excellent served peasant-style with hot bread or noodles, a salad and a good burgundy. It should be made well in advance, cooled and refrigerated to allow the flavors to mature.

1 x 1¾ lb piece of rump steak, well-trimmed
oil
knob of butter
salt and ground black pepper
1 large onion, chopped
1 green Bell pepper, seeded and diced
about ½ lb brown mushrooms, wiped and sliced
¼ cup flour
good ¾ cup port
good ¾ cup seasoned beef stock
pinch of sugar
2 whole cloves
2 garlic cloves, crushed
½ tsp dried oregano

Cut rump into biggish pieces, about 2 x 3-in, and brown briefly over high heat in a large heavy skillet just slicked with oil. Remove steak to baking dish, arrange in single layer, and season. To skillet add a little more oil and a knob of butter and fry onion, green Bell pepper and mushrooms. When softened and beginning to smell good, spoon over steak.

To pan juices, add flour and stir until nut-brown. Slowly add port, stock, sugar and cloves. Stir well, and when hot and thick, pour over steak. Cover and bake at 325°F for 30 minutes. Add garlic and oregano and bake for another 30 minutes. Remove and cool.

Refrigerate all day, but remove in time for dish to reach room temperature. Reheat, uncovered, at 325°F for about 50 minutes, by which time gravy will be thickened and slightly reduced. Remove cloves before serving as suggested, or with baby potatoes, spinach and zucchini.
Serves 4.

## Fillet Steak with Sherry and Cream

**So quick, and so good.**

1 lb 5 oz fillet steak
ground black pepper
crushed garlic
1 tbsp oil
1 tsp butter
salt
½ cup light cream or sour cream
1 tsp French mustard (or more to taste)
5 tsp sweet sherry
pinch of sugar if using sour cream

If the fillet is in one piece, slice into 4 and cut horizontally three-quarters of the way through the middle and open out like a book. Sprinkle each piece with pepper and garlic. Heat oil and butter in heavy skillet and brown steak quickly on both sides. Salt as you turn. Mix light cream or sour cream with remaining ingredients, then pour over steaks when nearly done, and simmer until very hot, stirring gently. Allow sauce to reduce and thicken slightly.

Spoon steaks onto serving dish, pour sauce over and serve at once, with baby potatoes and a simple tossed salad.
Serves 4.

## Braised Top Round of Beef

**This lean boneless cut needs to be spiked with herb butter before being slowly simmered in a richly flavored stock. Vegetables are added towards the end of the cooking period and served round the meat.**

1 x 3 lb top round of beef
3 tbsp butter
2 garlic cloves, crushed
1 tsp mixed dried herbs
1 tsp salt
1 tsp dry mustard
½ tsp paprika
3 tbsp oil
2 onions, chopped
1 cup beef stock, heated
½ cup red wine
½ cup tomato paste
2 bay leaves
2 tsp Worcestershire sauce
2 tsp brown sugar
baby potatoes and baby carrots

Trim off any loose bits of sinew or fat from joint. Cream butter with garlic and herbs and place in freezer to harden. Make small slits in joint and stuff with slices of the herb butter. Rub outside of meat with salt, mustard and paprika. Heat oil in a large saucepan and brown meat and onions over low heat. Add stock, wine, tomato paste, bay leaves, Worcestershire sauce and sugar. Bring to a slow boil and then cover and simmer very gently for about 2 hours, or until meat is tender, turning twice. Add prepared vegetables and simmer until cooked.

Remove meat to large serving platter and surround with potatoes and carrots. Thicken gravy with a mixture of flour and water. Ladle a few spoonfuls over the joint and serve the remainder separately.
Serves 6.

## Tipsy Steak

**One of the nicest ways of doing steak – flamed with brandy and then smothered in butter and sherry.**

**2 tbsp butter**
**1 garlic clove, crushed**
**1 tbsp chopped chives**
**½ tsp Worcestershire sauce**
**4 x 6 oz rump or fillet steaks**
**paprika**
**5 tsp brandy, warmed**
**salt and ground black pepper**
**¼ cup sherry**

Cream together butter, garlic, chives and Worcestershire sauce. Allow to stand for several hours.

Brush heavy skillet with a little oil (or use a non-stick pan) and heat. Sprinkle steaks on both sides with paprika, and then fry on both sides until done to taste. Pour over brandy and flame, while you stand

well clear. Remove steaks to heated platter and season lightly.

To skillet, add sherry and the butter mixture. Stir until melted, then pour over steaks and serve at once.
Serves 4.

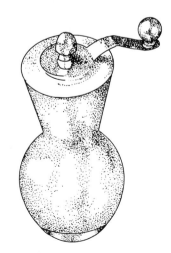

## Easy Fillet Steaks

**This useful recipe meets the challenge of serving slices of rare fillet without any last-minute frying.**

**1 lb 5 oz – 1¾ lb fillet steak**
**oil for frying**
**salt and ground black pepper**

SAVORY BUTTER
**scant ½ cup butter, softened**
**½ tsp French mustard**
**2 garlic cloves, crushed**
**1 tbsp chopped chives**
**1 tbsp chopped fresh oregano or
a generous pinch of dried**
**½ tsp Worcestershire sauce**

First make the savory butter: cream butter with remaining ingredients. Roll into a sausage shape, wrap in waxed paper and chill.

Cut fillet into ¾-in slices, then

sear steaks over high heat in a heavy skillet smeared with oil, for about 15 seconds per side. Be careful not to pierce when turning. Remove to ovenproof serving platter and leave, covered loosely.

Fifteen minutes before serving, season steaks lightly, and top each slice with a round of herb butter. Bake at 425°F for about 10 minutes, but the time does depend on the thickness of the meat and the degree of rareness required. Remove and leave in warming oven for 5 minutes for juices to settle. Serve with the buttery juices spooned over and baby potatoes.
Serves 4–6.

# Chinese Stroganoff

In this dish – a combination of Russian Beef Stroganoff and Chinese steamed beef – everything is cooked together without any previous frying, which means that not only is it simple to prepare, but also none of the flavor is lost.

2¼ lb fillet of beef
1 large onion, coarsely grated
2 garlic cloves, crushed
about ¾ lb mushrooms, sliced
1¼ cups chicken stock
¼ cup soy sauce
¼ cup dry white wine
2 tbsp cornstarch
1 tsp dry mustard
3 tbsp oil
good ¾ cup sour cream

Slice fillet into thin strips across the grain. Divide between two medium, or one large, shallow baking dish, arranging in a single layer. Add onion, garlic and mushrooms. Beat together stock, soy sauce, wine, cornstarch, mustard and oil. Pour over meat and mushrooms, stir gently to moisten, then cover and stand for 3 hours.

Uncover and bake at 350°F for about 35 minutes, or until meat is cooked and gravy thick and brown. Swirl in cream and return to oven for 5 minutes to heat through. Serve with Chinese-Style Noodles (below).
Serves 8.

# Chinese-Style Noodles

9 oz very small ring noodles
scant ½ cup oil
2 bunches green onions, chopped
2 green Bell peppers, seeded and diced
2 knobs gingerroot, peeled and grated
1 lb 14 oz can bean sprouts, rinsed and drained
4–5 tbsp soy sauce

Boil noodles in plenty of salted water. Heat oil in a large, deep saucepan. Add green onions, green pepper and ginger and stir-fry until tender-crisp. Drain noodles and toss with a spoon of oil. Add to vegetables and, keeping the heat low, fork in the sprouts and soy sauce to taste. Serve immediately.
Serves 8.

## Bobotie

I like ground beef for this dish. Lamb can too often be fatty, unless it's left-over leg, which, no matter what you do to it, will always taste like left-over leg. The following version is smooth and moist and a favorite in our house. It's even good cold. Traditionally, this Dutch dish should also include a handful of quartered almonds, although I don't think they make any difference to the flavor.

1 fairly thick slice bread (white or brown)
1½ cups milk
3 tbsp oil
1 tbsp butter
2 onions, sliced
2 garlic cloves, crushed
5 tsp curry powder
2 tsp salt
2 tbsp fruit chutney
1 tbsp smooth apricot jam
1 tbsp Worcestershire sauce
1 tsp turmeric
5 tsp brown vinegar
2¼ lb ground beef
⅓ cup golden raisins
3 eggs
pinch of salt
pinch of turmeric
bay leaves

Remove crusts and soak bread in milk. Heat oil and butter in large pan and fry onions and garlic. When onions are soft, add curry powder, salt, chutney, jam, Worcestershire sauce, turmeric and vinegar and mix well. Drain, mash bread and reserve milk. Add bread to pan together with ground beef and golden raisins. Cook over low heat, stirring, and when meat begins to turn brown, remove from heat. Add 1 beaten egg, mix well, then spoon into a greased, 12 x 6-in baking dish and level the top.

Beat remaining eggs with reserved milk, you should have 1¼ cups, and the salt and turmeric. Pour over meat mixture and put a few bay leaves on top. Stand dish in a larger pan of water (this is important to prevent drying out) and bake, uncovered, at 350°F, for 1 hour or until set. Serve with rice, coconut, chutney, nuts and bananas.
Serves 8.

## Biriani with Lentils

Biriani is a Malay dish usually prepared with rice and mutton. This is a simple variation, spicy rather than hot.

3 tbsp oil
1 large onion, sliced
2 garlic cloves, crushed
1 fat cinnamon stick
2 bay leaves
4 cardamom pods, split
½ tsp ground cumin
2 tsp ground coriander
1 knob gingerroot, peeled and crushed
2 tsp biriani paste
1¾ lb ground beef
1½ cups brown lentils, soaked overnight
2 tsp lemon juice
1 tsp salt
2⅔ cups stock
3 tbsp tomato paste
pinch of sugar

Heat oil in large saucepan and add onion and garlic. When browned add all the spices and stir for a minute or two, then add ground beef. Keep stirring, and when meat is no longer pink, add drained lentils and remaining ingredients. Cover and simmer very gently for 45 minutes, then remove bay leaves, cinnamon and cardamom pods. Raise the heat and simmer uncovered for about 5 minutes until excess liquid has evaporated. Adjust seasoning and serve with Spiced Yellow Rice or Spiced Raisins (see right).
Serves 8.

## Spiced Yellow Rice

1⅓ cups rinsed brown rice
4¼ cups water
1 tsp salt
1 tsp sugar
½ tsp turmeric
generous pinch of ground cloves
oil
good ⅓ cup seedless raisins

Put all ingredients except raisins into large saucepan, bring to a boil, then cover and simmer until rice is tender. Rinse, then steam in colander with raisins until dry and fluffy.
Serves about 8.

## Spiced Raisins

scant 2 cups seedless raisins
1 tbsp ground cinnamon
scant ½ cup brown vinegar
scant ½ cup water
¼ cup brown sugar
generous pinch of ground cloves
½ tsp ground ginger
2 bay leaves

Simmer all the ingredients in a covered saucepan for 30 minutes. Spoon into a bowl and cool. Remove bay leaves before serving.

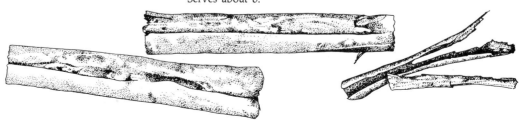

## Stuffed Eggplants with Ground Beef and Feta

A favorite way of serving ground beef, simmered in red wine, piled into eggplant cases, baked and topped with feta cheese. This dish can be assembled in advance and set aside until an hour before serving. Serve simply with a green salad and crusty bread.

4 x ¼ lb small, firm eggplants
salt
3 tbsp oil
1 onion, finely chopped
1 green Bell pepper, seeded and
   diced
good ½ lb lean ground beef or
   lamb
1–2 garlic cloves, crushed
1 tsp dried oregano
scant ½ cup red wine
scant ½ cup water
3 tbsp tomato paste
salt and ground black pepper
pinch of sugar
2 bay leaves
feta cheese

SAUCE
1 cup beef stock
3 tbsp tomato paste
pinch of sugar

Cut stem end from eggplants, slice in half, scoop out and dice flesh finely, leaving cases about ¾ in thick. Sprinkle cases with salt and stand while making stuffing.

Heat oil and fry onion and green pepper. Add meat and stir until no longer pink. Add garlic, eggplant flesh, oregano, wine, water, tomato paste, seasoning, sugar and bay leaves. Cover and simmer for 20 minutes, or until mixture is succulent and thick. Cool, then remove bay leaves.

Rinse eggplant cases and pat dry using absorbent paper towels. Arrange in a 12 x 8-in baking dish and fill cases with meat mixture. Mix ingredients for sauce, pour around eggplants and bake, covered, at 350°F for 45 minutes, by which time cases should be soft. Sprinkle generously with crumbled feta cheese to cover tops, and return to oven for another 15 minutes. Spoon sauce over each serving.
Serves 4.

Stuffed Leg of Lamb

## Glazed Leg of Lamb

4 garlic cloves, thinly sliced
1 thick slice wholewheat bread, crumbled
¼ cup seedless raisins
½ tsp dried thyme
1 tsp dried marjoram
½ tsp salt
3¾–4½ lb leg of lamb
flour
1 tbsp oil
2 onions, chopped
salt and ground black pepper
½ cup water
2 tsp brown vinegar

GLAZE
3 tbsp smooth apricot jam
5 tsp lemon juice
3 tbsp brown sugar
5 tsp Worcestershire sauce
3 tbsp tomato sauce

Mix garlic with bread, raisins, herbs and salt. Make several incisions in leg and lard with crumb mixture, then dredge on all sides with a little flour. Heat oil in roasting pan and soften onions. Add leg and brown lightly on all sides. Remove from heat, season, then add water and vinegar. Bake, covered, at 325°F for about 2 hours, until nearly done.

Heat ingredients for glaze. Dribble half of it over the leg, then pour remainder over 15 minutes later. Bake for a further 15 minutes, then place on serving platter and stand in warm place for a short while before carving. If necessary simply add a little stock to pan to make gravy, or thicken if preferred. Serves 6.

## Stuffed Leg of Lamb

1 x 3¾ lb boned leg of lamb
2 garlic cloves, crushed
½ tsp dried oregano
1 tsp salt
½ tsp dried thyme
½ tsp paprika
¼ cup flour
2 cups water

STUFFING
4 tsp oil
1 tsp butter
2 onions, chopped
bare ½ cup mushrooms, wiped and sliced
1 green Bell pepper, seeded and diced
½ cup toasted, flaked almonds
3 cups cooked rice
2 tsp soy sauce

Make the stuffing by heating butter and oil and frying half the onion, all the mushrooms, green pepper and almonds. Keep stirring, and remove when nicely browned. Add rice and soy sauce and toss well.

Open out leg of lamb and make the surface area larger and flatter by scoring it a bit. Sprinkle with garlic, oregano and ½ tsp salt. Stuff with rice mixture and tie securely.

Mix thyme, paprika, ½ tsp salt and flour, rub all over lamb and place on rack in roasting pan, adding water and remaining onion at the side. Roast at 325°F for 2 hours, basting a few times with pan juices, then cover loosely with foil and leave in oven for another hour, adding water or stock to roasting pan as necessary. Leave in warming oven for 10 minutes, then make gravy from pan juices before carving meat.
Serves 6–8.

Casserole of Lamb and Mushroom

## Casserole of Lamb and Mushrooms

Any lean lamb may be used in this casserole, but lamb shanks are my choice because they have a few bones, which add to the flavor, and very little fat, and become very tender with slow simmering.

3 tbsp oil
2¼ lb lamb shanks cut in
   1-in slices
salt and ground black pepper
1 large onion, chopped
2 garlic cloves, crushed
bare ¾ lb mushrooms, wiped
   and sliced
1 fresh rosemary sprig, chopped
butter
3 tbsp flour
1 cup seasoned stock
scant ½ cup red wine
1 tsp Worcestershire sauce

3 tbsp tomato paste
1 bay leaf

Heat oil and brown lamb slices on both sides, then remove to baking dish and season. To pan juices add onion, garlic, mushrooms and rosemary. Fry over low heat until soft and beginning to brown, then combine with meat in baking dish. Add a knob of butter to pan, if necessary, then stir in flour. Cook 1 minute, stirring, then slowly add stock and wine. When thickened add Worcestershire sauce, tomato paste, bay leaf and a good pinch of sugar. Stir well and then pour over meat and mushrooms. Cover and bake at 350°F for 1 hour.

   Remove from oven and stir to mix meat with the gravy. Reduce heat to 325°F and continue baking, covered, until meat is very tender. Adjust seasoning, remove bay leaf, and ladle over portions of rice. Serves 4.

## Leg of Lamb in Beer

**This is a super combination, resulting in a succulent, tasty joint – and it's perfect food when entertaining as it needs little attention.**

1 x 4½ lb leg of lamb
2–3 garlic cloves, thinly sliced
1 x 4-in fresh rosemary sprig
salt and ground black pepper
1 tbsp prepared mustard
2 carrots, diced
2 onions, chopped
2 bay leaves
¼ cup chopped parsley
1½ cups beer
1 tsp brown sugar

Lard lamb with garlic and rosemary needles. Season, then spread mustard over top. Place in roasting pan and roast at 400°F for 30 minutes. Pour off any accumulated fat and add carrots, onions, bay leaves, parsley, beer and sugar.

   Reduce heat to 325°F and continue roasting, basting occasionally. After 1½–2 hours add a little water or stock to ensure about 2 cups for gravy. After roasting for 2½ hours, the lamb should be tender and a good color, and the gravy chunky and no longer tasting of beer.

   Allow to rest for 20 minutes in the warming oven before carving. Don't thicken the gravy, but serve separately or pour over the joint. Mint sauce is an optional extra with lamb prepared in this way. Serves 8.

# Spicy Lamb Curry

This is based on a traditional Malay curry, not hot, but full of interesting flavors.

3 tbsp oil
2–3 large onions
3 garlic cloves, crushed
1 tbsp curry powder
2 tsp turmeric
2 tsp ground coriander
1 tsp ground cumin
1 cinnamon stick
1 knob gingerroot, peeled and crushed in garlic press
4 cardamom pods, split
2 bay leaves
3 whole cloves
2¼–2¾ lb shoulder of lamb, sliced
3 tomatoes, skinned and chopped
2 tsp salt
1 tsp sugar
¾ cup hot water or stock

Heat oil in large saucepan and brown onions. Add garlic, curry powder, turmeric, coriander, cumin, cinnamon, ginger, cardamom pods, bay leaves and cloves and fry for a few minutes, stirring and taking care not to scorch. Remove most of the fat from the lamb but do not slice off the bone. Add to pan and when coated with curry mixture add tomatoes and remaining ingredients.

Cover and simmer very slowly, stirring occasionally, for about 1½ hours, or until tender. You shouldn't need to add more liquid, or have to thicken the rich gravy. Remove whole spices and serve with rice and sambals (see below). Serves 4–5.

## Note
Sambals are the little side dishes served with curries and range from diced paw-paw to poppadoms, but the simplest (and most popular) are: shredded coconut, chutney, cucumber in yogurt or sour cream, sliced bananas, and sweet fruit relishes.

# Lamb with Eggplant and Yogurt

This hearty casserole is ripe with vegetables and has a full-bodied flavor. Because of its Greek influence, it goes well with a spinach, olive and avocado salad, and rice to mop up the gravy. It can be made in advance and reheated to allow the full flavor to develop.

2¼ lb lamb shanks, sliced
scant 1 lb eggplants
oil
2 large onions, chopped
2 large garlic cloves, crushed
3 medium tomatoes, skinned
  and chopped
good ⅓ cup flour
1½ cups hot stock
scant ½ cup white wine
3 tbsp chopped parsley
1 tsp brown sugar
1 tsp dried oregano
¾ cup natural yogurt
1 tbsp mayonnaise

The lamb shanks should be cut into 1-in slices; don't buy hefty chunks in all sorts of untidy shapes. Trim, cube and degorge (page 135) eggplants.

Fry lamb slices well on both sides in a little oil, doing it in batches, and transferring to large baking dish when browned. To skillet add a little more oil, and add onions and garlic. When lightly browned, add tomatoes, and simmer for a few minutes until soft. Sprinkle in flour and slowly stir in hot stock and wine. Stir until sauce becomes thick and chunky. Remove from heat and add eggplant cubes, parsley, sugar and oregano. Pour over lamb and mix well so that eggplants don't lie on top.

Cover and bake at 325°F for 1 hour 20 minutes, by which time lamb should be tender. Cool. Reheat, covered, at 325°F for about 30 minutes.

To finish off, mix yogurt and mayonnaise and swirl in lightly, then return to oven for 5–10 minutes.
Serves 4.

## Crumbed Lamb Chops with Herbs

**Dipped in yogurt and herbs, crumbed and then slowly baked until tender, this is a delicious way of preparing loin or thick rib lamb chops.**

2¼ lb lamb chops
¾ cup plain drinking yogurt or
    buttermilk
1 tsp dried thyme
1 tsp dried marjoram
2 tsp garlic salt
2 tsp prepared mustard
2½ cups toasted crumbs or 6
    wholewheat crackers, crushed

Trim excess fat from chops. Mix remaining ingredients, except crumbs. Coat chops with yogurt mixture, then roll in crumbs, patting on firmly. Chill for at least 2 hours to set crumbs.

To bake, preheat oven to 325°F. Brush one large or two medium shallow baking dishes with oil and heat for 5 minutes in oven. Turn chops once in hot oil, then cover and bake for 45 minutes. Uncover and bake for a further 30 minutes or until browned and tender. A potato and onion casserole goes well with this dish.
Serves 6.

## Spiced Lamb Casserole

**Choose small, meaty shanks for this satisfying casserole, and serve with rice.**

¼ cup oil
3 lb lamb shanks, sliced
1 large onion, chopped
2 garlic cloves, crushed
1 tsp turmeric
1 tsp ground cinnamon
1 tsp peeled, grated gingerroot
2 tsp ground coriander
½ tsp ground cumin
2 Granny Smith apples, peeled
    and diced
¼ cup chutney
2 tsp brown sugar
1 tsp salt
½ cup white wine
1 cup stock
⅓ cup seedless raisins

Heat oil in large, heavy skillet and add shanks. When well browned remove to baking dish. Turn heat to low, add a dash more oil if necessary and sauté onion. Add garlic and all the spices and toss for a minute, then add apples and remaining ingredients. Mix well, pour over lamb, cover and bake at 325°F for 2 hours. Adjust seasoning and thicken gravy if necessary.
Serves about 6.

### Hint

Add interest and color to plain boiled rice by forking in a handful of chopped parsley, 1 or 2 seeded, diced and lightly blanched red Bell peppers, and a knob of butter to moisten.

## Lamb Chop Casserole

**This casserole of shoulder chops in a savory sauce is so easy to prepare. The chops turn out tender, juicy and full of flavor.**

**6 x 6 oz shoulder chops**
**3 tbsp oil**
**2 large onions, chopped**
**2 garlic cloves, crushed**
**1 green Bell pepper, seeded and diced**
**¼ cup flour**
**¼ cup tomato sauce**
**1 tbsp Worcestershire sauce**
**1 tbsp light brown sugar**
**5 tsp brown vinegar**
**1 cup meat stock**
**2 bay leaves**
**salt and ground black pepper**
**1 tsp mixed dried herbs**

Preheat oven to 400°F. Arrange chops in large baking dish to fit in single layer, and put into oven for

15 minutes. While baking, make sauce by heating oil and frying onions, garlic and green pepper. When softened, remove from heat and stir in flour. When well mixed, add tomato sauce, Worcestershire sauce, sugar, vinegar, stock and bay leaves and stir to combine.

Remove chops from oven and sprinkle with salt, pepper and herbs. Pour sauce over and cover securely. Reduce temperature to 325°F and bake for about 1½ hours, or until tender.
Serves 6.

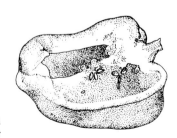

## Lamb Stew with Squash

**This unusual, spicy stew is baked, instead of simmered on the stove, and requires little attention.**

**1¾ lb loin chops (weight after trimming)**
**3 tbsp flour**
**1 tsp salt**
**2 tsp ground coriander**
**1 tsp turmeric**
**3 tbsp oil**
**2 onions, chopped**
**2 garlic cloves, crushed**
**½ cup stock or water**
**2 tsp brown vinegar**
**1¾ lb squash (weight before peeling)**
**1½ tsp ground cinnamon**
**pinch of ground cloves**
**1 tsp ground ginger**
**1 tbsp brown sugar**

Preheat oven to 325°F. Having removed excess fat from chops, slice into fairly large pieces. Mix flour with salt, coriander and turmeric and dust meat on both sides. Heat oil in large skillet and brown meat lightly over medium heat to prevent scorching. Remove to 12 x 8-in baking dish. Add a little more oil to skillet if necessary and add onions and garlic. Cover the pan and allow to sweat gently. Add to lamb, pour stock over, sprinkle with vinegar, cover and bake for 45 minutes.

Peel squash and cut into smallish dice. Mix spices with sugar and shake cubes in this mixture until coated. Add to lamb, stir to mix, then return to oven and bake, covered, for 1 hour, stirring twice and adding a little more stock or water if necessary to ensure a rich gravy. Serves 4.

# Herb-Crusted Lamb

Crusty, herby, lovely lamb.

1 x 5½ lb leg of lamb
3 garlic cloves, thinly sliced
1 small onion, grated
1 tbsp prepared mustard
1 tbsp soy sauce
1½ cups fresh wholewheat
  breadcrumbs
½ tsp dried thyme
½ tsp crushed dried rosemary
½ tsp finely grated lemon zest
salt and ground black pepper
2 tsp oil
1 onion, chopped

Wipe leg, remove outer membrane and insert garlic in small slits all over. Mix grated onion with mustard and soy sauce. Using a pastry brush, paint this mixture all over the lamb, put it on a rack in a baking dish, fat-side up, and leave for 2 hours. Mix crumbs with herbs, lemon zest and seasoning. Moisten with oil and set aside.

To roast lamb, preheat oven to 325°F, add chopped onion and 1½ cups water to roasting pan and roast for 1½ hours. By this time it should be nut-brown, so cover loosely with a tent of foil, shiny-side up. Roast for another 45–60 minutes, then remove.

Pour a little of the pan juices into crumb mixture to make a paste, then spread firmly all over top of lamb. Return to oven and roast for a further 30–60 minutes, basting occasionally. As it's a big leg, a total of 3½ hours should give you a pinkish middle with a crisp exterior. Remember to check level of juices in roasting pan occasionally, adding hot water or stock as necessary for the gravy, and using the tent of foil again towards the end if the meat is browning too rapidly.

Remove lamb to serving dish and keep warm. Pour juices into a saucepan, and either reduce or thicken.

Serve with roast potatoes or Oven-Baked Spicy Rice (page 101). Serves about 10.

## Note
**When pressed for time, the following simple method is useful and still very good. Mix 1½ cups brown breadcrumbs with ½ tsp each dried sage, thyme and marjoram, 1 small grated onion, ¼ cup chopped parsley and salt and pepper. Moisten with ¼ cup melted butter or oil. Spike lamb with garlic, but omit all the other ingredients. Roast on rack as above, then pat crumb mixture all over exposed surfaces 20 minutes before it's done and baste several times while browning.**

# Yogurt Sauce

Serve a small portion of this garlicky sauce with each serving of Herb-Crusted Lamb.

¾ cup thick natural yogurt
2 small garlic cloves, crushed
1 tbsp chopped chives
1 tsp olive oil
pinch of salt
pinch of sugar
ground black pepper

Mix ingredients, cover and stand at room temperature for 2 hours. Makes about ¾ cup.

Roast Leg of Lamb with Fresh Herbs (left) and Savory Lamb Stew (right)

## Savory Lamb Stew

**A simple, homely casserole in which the lamb is slow-baked in a rich gravy.**

4 x 6 oz blade chops
½ tsp paprika
½ tsp dried thyme
½ tsp dried oregano
½ tsp curry powder
1 tbsp flour
½ tsp salt
oil
1 large onion, chopped
2 garlic cloves, crushed
1½ cups beef stock
2 medium tomatoes, skinned
   and chopped
¼ cup chopped parsley
¼ cup seedless raisins
1 tsp brown sugar
2 tsp Worcestershire sauce

Cut chops in half to make 8 neat pieces and remove any excess fat.

Mix together the paprika, herbs, curry powder, 3 tbsp flour and ½ tsp salt and coat meat on both sides. Heat 3 tbsp oil in pan and brown chops lightly on both sides over medium heat, in 2 batches, to avoid stewing. Transfer to baking dish to fit closely. Add a little more oil to pan and fry onion and garlic. Sprinkle in 2 tsp flour, then add stock. Boil up, remove from heat, add tomatoes, and remaining ingredients. Mix well and pour over chops. At this stage you can set dish aside for a while if working ahead.

   Bake, covered, at 325°F for 1½ hours, stirring once to mix meat and sauce. Serve with baked potatoes and green vegetables. Serves 4.

## Roast Leg of Lamb with Fresh Herbs

**A traditional roast, lightly spiked with herbs, which is sure to become a family favorite.**

1 x 5½ lb leg of lamb
2 x 2-in rosemary sprigs
4 x 2-in thyme sprigs
4 x 2-in marjoram sprigs
½ cup fresh wholewheat
   breadcrumbs
3 garlic cloves, finely chopped
¼ cup chopped parsley
½ onion, grated
2 tsp salt
1 tsp ground coriander
¼ cup wholewheat flour
oil

Wipe lamb with vinegar and remove thin outer membrane. Chop rosemary needles, thyme leaves and marjoram leaves. Mix with breadcrumbs, garlic, parsley, onion and 1 tsp salt. Make deep slits all over lamb and stuff with little wads of crumb mixture.

   Mix remaining salt with coriander and flour and rub all over leg. Dribble a little oil over top, and place leg on rack over roasting pan. Add a little water to pan to prevent scorching, and roast at 325°F for 3½ hours, adding water or stock to pan when necessary, and covering loosely with foil, shiny-side up, when browned sufficiently. Stand for 10 minutes in warming drawer before carving, while you make gravy from juices in roasting pan.
Serves 8–10.

## Curried Chops

Marinated in a curry sauce, these chops may be barbecued or roasted in the oven.

6 x ¼ lb lamb loin chops
salt and ground black pepper

MARINADE
3 tbsp oil
1 large onion, chopped
2 garlic cloves, crushed
1 tbsp curry powder
1 tsp ground coriander
1 tsp turmeric
1 tsp peeled, grated gingerroot
1½ cups water
¼ cup brown vinegar
3 tbsp smooth apricot jam
2 bay leaves

Trim chops and arrange in a non-metallic dish for marinating. Heat oil and soften onion and garlic. Lower heat and add curry powder, spices and ginger and fry gently for 2 minutes. Add water, vinegar, jam and bay leaves and simmer for 5 minutes. Pour over chops, cool and refrigerate, uncovered, for 2 days, turning several times. Barbecue over coals, or roast in oven.

To roast, preheat oven to 325°F. Place chops on rack in roasting pan. Add water to pan to prevent scorching, then roast for 45 minutes. Turn, season with salt and ground black pepper and baste. Roast for a further 45 minutes, or until very tender. Serve with Oven-Baked Rice (below) and the heated marinade.
Serves 6.

## Oven-Baked Rice

about ¾ lb brown rice
good 3 cups water
1 tsp turmeric
2 cinnamon sticks
¼ cup seedless raisins
1 tsp ground coriander
2 tsp oil
½ tsp salt
chopped parsley

Put all ingredients into 9-in pie dish, cover and bake at 325°F for 1¼ hours or until liquid is absorbed. Remove cinnamon and fork in a little chopped parsley for color. Serves 6.

Marinated Roast Leg of Pork

## *Marinated Roast Leg of Pork*

1 x 6 lb leg of pork
½ cup white wine
3 tbsp soy sauce
1 tsp ground ginger
3 tbsp brown sugar
3 garlic cloves, crushed
1 tbsp oil
12 fresh sage leaves
salt and ground black pepper
prepared mustard
1 onion, chopped

Remove rind from pork and score fat. Place in dish suitable for marinating – do not use copper or aluminum. Mix wine, soy sauce, ginger, sugar, garlic and oil. Pour over pork and leave in refrigerator overnight. Turn over in the morning. Just before roasting, dry leg well and make slits all over with a sharp knife. Insert tightly rolled sage leaves, season very lightly and spread top thinly with mustard. Reserve marinade.

Place on rack in roasting pan, fat side up. Pour some water into roasting pan and add onion. Roast at 325°F for 2½ hours. Pour over half the reserved marinade and cover loosely with foil, shiny-side up, as it should be beautifully browned. Roast for another hour, then pour over remaining marinade and add water or stock to roasting pan if necessary. Continue roasting until cooked through, about 4 hours total. Uncovered roasts always take longer than pot roasts, and pork must be cooked through.

Stand in warming drawer for about 15 minutes before carving, and thicken gravy if desired, or reduce by fast boiling. Braised cabbage and baby potatoes make good accompaniments.
Serves about 12.

## *Pork with Orange*

**Seasoned with sage and mustard, simmered in wine and laced with orange, this oven-baked pot roast is succulent and delicious. The joint you buy is important as it must be a center piece leg roast, that is, cut from the middle of the leg. This is a popular cut and easily available.**

1 x 4½ lb leg of pork
1 large onion, chopped
1 tsp dry mustard
2 tsp dried sage
salt
paprika
½ cup white wine
1 cup water
3 tbsp orange marmalade
coarsely grated zest of 1 orange
2 bay leaves

Remove rind and all the fat from meat, then brown on all sides with onion in a heavy pan just smeared with oil. Place joint in baking dish and set pan aside. Mix mustard, sage and seasoning and sprinkle over meat.

Return pan with onion to low heat and add remaining ingredients. Heat, stirring to mix, then pour around pork. Cover, then bake at 350°F for 1½ hours. Turn, cover and cook until done – about 1½ hours more. Remove meat to serving platter and keep warm. Skin the gravy, then pour into saucepan and reduce over high heat, or thicken. Adjust seasoning. Serve with small boiled potatoes, stir-fried cabbage and carrots. Serves 8.

# Pineapple Pork Chops

**These chops are a boon to the busy cook. There is no frying involved, they are simply marinated for a few hours and then baked until tender. The only last-minute attention is the reduction of the slightly fruity rich brown syrup.**

**6 x ¼ lb pork loin chops (weight after trimming)**
**1 large onion, coarsely grated**
**2 garlic cloves, crushed**
**10 fresh sage leaves, finely chopped or ½ tsp dried**
**1 x 6 fl oz can unsweetened pineapple juice**
**4 tsp soy sauce**
**2 tsp honey**
**3 tbsp golden raisins**

The chops should be well trimmed before weighing. Arrange to fit closely in glass baking dish. Sprinkle onion, garlic and sage over. Mix pineapple juice, soy sauce and honey. Pour over chops, cover and leave for about 3 hours, turning twice.

Add golden raisins and bake, covered, at 325°F for about 1 hour 20 minutes or until tender. Remove chops to serving dish and keep warm. Pour juices into a small saucepan and boil over high heat until slightly reduced and a rich, caramel brown. Pour over chops. Especially good served with rice tossed with mushrooms and green onions, and vegetables or a salad. Serves 6.

# Pork Chops with Apple and Port

**These chops are baked in a piquant sauce containing fruit, honey, cinnamon, lemon and port, which reduces to a spicy syrup. The flavor is bold, and unusual, and best accompanied by stir-fried cabbage and creamy mashed potatoes.**

**6 x 3½ oz pork loin chops (weight after trimming)**
**oil**
**salt and ground black pepper**
**1 tbsp flour**
**scant 1 cup stock or water**
**⅓ cup port**
**2 Golden Delicious apples, peeled and finely chopped**
**¼ cup golden raisins**
**generous pinch of ground cinnamon**
**1 tbsp lemon juice**
**1 tsp honey**

Trim rind and excess fat off chops. Heat a little oil in a heavy skillet, and brown chops on both sides. Transfer to baking dish, to fit in a single layer, then season.

Add flour to fat in pan, and stir to absorb juices, then add stock and port and stir until smooth and thick. Remove from heat and add apples, golden raisins, cinnamon, lemon juice and honey. Spread this mixture over tops of chops and cover securely before baking at 325°F for 1¼ hours, or until chops are done.
Serves 6.

## Note
**Unless otherwise stated, Golden Delicious apples are my preference when cooking. Apart from the appeal of their creamy yellow color, they hold their shape when cooked and have a delicate flavor which enhances both sweet and savory dishes.**

## Baked Pork Chops with Soy Sauce and Honey

**Minimal preparation and no frying makes this one of the easiest ways of serving pork chops. They are simply soaked in a light marinade and then baked until tender. Good with baby potatoes tossed in parsley butter, and a green salad.**

2–2¼ lb pork loin chops
2 large garlic cloves
5 tsp soy sauce
3 tbsp honey
¼ cup dry white wine
½ tsp ground ginger
1 tbsp dried sage

Remove rind and most of the fat from chops and arrange to fit in glass dish suitable for both

marinating and baking. Crush garlic directly over chops and rub in with back of knife. Mix remaining ingredients, pour over chops and marinate for about 4 hours at room temperature, or all day in the refrigerator. Turn chops occasionally while marinating.

Remove dish 1 hour before baking and bake, covered, at 325°F for 1 hour. Remove cover, turn chops and bake uncovered for another 20 minutes or until tender and juices are slightly reduced and syrupy. Ladle a spoonful over each serving.
Serves about 6.

## Lemon Pork Chops with Mustard Sauce

**These chops, lightly flavored with lemon and sage, are crumbed and baked and served with mustard sauce made in the old-fashioned way.**

2¼ lb pork chops
1½ tsp dried sage
1⅔ cups fine, toasted breadcrumbs or 5 wholewheat
   crackers, crushed
1 tsp salt
scant 1 cup yogurt or buttermilk
¼ cup mayonnaise
5 tsp lemon juice
½ tsp finely grated lemon zest

MUSTARD SAUCE
1 cup milk
1 egg yolk
2 tsp dry mustard
4 tsp flour

2 tsp brown sugar
1 tbsp brown vinegar
pinch of salt
small knob of butter

Remove rind and most of the fat from chops. Crush sage between fingers after measuring and mix with crumbs and salt. Mix yogurt, mayonnaise, lemon juice and rind. Dip chops into yogurt mixture, then into crumbs and chill for 2–3 hours.

To bake, preheat oven to 325°F. Lightly oil base of large baking dish, heat for a few minutes, then arrange chops in single layer, turning once. Cover and bake for 1 hour, then uncover and bake for 30 minutes more.

For the sauce, put all ingredients, except butter, into the top of a double saucepan, beat well and then stir over simmering water until thick and smooth. Finally, stir in butter.
Serves about 6.

## Roast Pork with Orange and Port

Gently seasoned with herbs, spices and orange zest, the gravy flavored with orange juice and a dash of port, this is a simple but rather special way of treating a joint.

1 x 4½ lb leg of pork
1½ tsp salt
1 tsp paprika
1 tsp dry mustard
1 tsp ground ginger
1 tsp dried sage
1 tsp finely grated orange zest
1½ cups water
1 onion, chopped
1 cup fresh orange juice
scant ½ cup port

Remove rind from leg and score underlying fat. (The rind may be salted and roasted separately.) Wipe leg with vinegar. Mix salt, paprika, mustard, ginger, sage and orange zest and rub into the leg. Place on rack in large roasting pan. Pour in the water and add the onion. Roast at 350°F for 1 hour, then reduce temperature to 325°F and roast for a further 1½ hours, adding more water to the roasting pan as necessary to prevent scorching. When nicely browned, cover the top loosely with foil, shiny-side up.

Pour the orange juice and port over, and roast for another hour, basting twice. (Total cooking time about 3½ hours.) Remove to serving platter and leave in warming drawer for about 15 minutes before carving. The gravy should have reduced sufficiently, but may be thickened if desired. Serves about 8.

## Apple Pork Chops

Oven-baked chops with a light gravy.

6 x ¼ lb pork loin chops
3 tbsp flour
½ tsp turmeric
½ tsp salt
generous pinch of ground
  cinnamon
4 tsp oil
onion rings
dried apple rings, soaked†
freshly chopped sage
brown sugar
good ¾ cup apple juice

Remove rind and excess fat from chops and rub with a mixture of flour, turmeric, salt and cinnamon. Heat oil and brown chops on both sides, then arrange in a single layer in baking dish to fit without crowding.

On each chop place two large onion rings and two apple rings. Sprinkle each chop with ½ tsp freshly chopped sage and a generous pinch of brown sugar. Pour in apple juice at the side, then cover and bake just below center of oven at 350°F for about 1 hour or until cooked through.

Remove chops to warm serving dish and tip juices into a small saucepan. Reduce by rapid boiling until syrupy – this takes only a few minutes – then pour over chops and serve.
Serves 6.

† Soak apple rings in water to cover, until soft.

## Pork Casserole with Mustard, Capers and Sage

This is a simple casserole with a subtle flavor – a family favorite, with a classy touch.

6 x 6 oz pork loin chops
3 tbsp oil
salt and ground black pepper
1 onion, finely chopped
2 garlic cloves, crushed
¼ cup flour
1 cup chicken stock
¼ cup white wine
14 fresh sage leaves, finely
  chopped
1 tsp French mustard
2 tsp capers, rinsed and chopped
pinch of salt
pinch of sugar
3 tbsp heavy cream or thick sour
  cream

Cut off rind and trim chops of most of the fat. Heat oil and brown chops very lightly on both sides. Arrange in baking dish to fit closely, in single layer. Season. To pan juices add onion and garlic. When softened, add flour, and stir for a minute, then slowly stir in stock and wine. Allow to thicken, then add sage, mustard, capers, salt, sugar and cream or sour cream. Mix well and pour over chops.

Cover and bake at 325°F for 1 hour 10 minutes, or until chops are tender and gravy is thick and aromatic – the timing depends on thickness of chops, size of dish and position in oven. Good with lemon-flavored rice.
Serves 6.

Chinese-Style Spare Ribs of Pork

## *Chinese-Style Spare Ribs of Pork*

These ribs are first steamed until tender, marinated and then baked – which is not the usual way of dealing with them, but it does save hours of broiling, basting and drying out in the oven. They are neither overly sticky nor sweet, but do need to be eaten using fingers, with forks for the Chinese rice.

2¼–3 lb spare ribs, cut into one
  or two pieces
1 tbsp oil
1 onion, chopped
2 garlic cloves, crushed
¼ cup soy sauce
scant 1 cup dry white wine
3 tbsp honey
1 knob gingerroot, peeled and
  crushed

1 tbsp brown vinegar
2 tsp brown sugar

Steam ribs over simmering water for about 1½ hours or until tender. Meanwhile, make marinade by heating oil and frying onion and garlic until soft. Remove saucepan from heat and add soy sauce, wine, honey and ginger.

As soon as ribs are cool enough to handle, slice lengthwise into long strips. Arrange in a single layer in a large glass baking dish and pour marinade over while they are still hot. Leave at room temperature for about 3 hours, turning occasionally.

Before baking, sprinkle with vinegar and sugar and then bake at 350°F for 30 minutes or until browned.

Place ribs on serving platter and surround with rice. Don't forget the finger bowls.
Serves 4.

## *Chinese Rice*

2 leeks, thinly sliced
3 tbsp oil
scant 1 cup white, long-grain
  rice
2 cups heated chicken stock
5 tsp soy sauce
scant ½ cup mung bean sprouts
2 tbsp almonds, toasted and
  chopped

Soften leeks in heated oil. Add rice and toss until coated with oil. Add stock and soy sauce, cover and simmer for 25 minutes or until cooked. Fork in sprouts and almonds.
Serves 4–6.

## *Fruity Pork Chops*

1 lb 14 oz pork loin chops
2–3 garlic cloves
½ cup pure apple juice
5 tsp soy sauce
5 tsp brown sugar
½ tsp dried rosemary
thin slices of orange and apple
brown sugar
ground cinnamon
butter

Arrange chops in baking dish. Crush garlic over chops. Mix apple juice, soy sauce, sugar and rosemary and pour over. Place 1 thin slice of orange and apple on each chop. Sprinkle a little sugar and cinnamon over apple, and dot with butter. Bake, uncovered, at 325°F for 1½ hours until tender, and liquid is slightly syrupy.
Serves 4–6.

Roast Pork with Apple Juice and Sage

## Roast Pork with Apple Juice and Sage

1 x 5½ lb leg of pork
¾ cup fresh wholewheat
   breadcrumbs
12–16 fresh sage leaves, finely
   chopped
1 tsp finely grated lemon zest
3 tbsp finely chopped parsley
3 tbsp chopped chives
1 tbsp oil
salt and ground black pepper
paprika and dry mustard
1 onion, chopped
2 cups apple juice
1¾ cup water or stock
2 Granny Smith apples, peeled
   and finely diced
3 tbsp honey

Remove rind from pork (salt and
roast it separately if desired) and
make deep incisions all over top
and sides. Mix crumbs, sage, lemon
zest, parsley, chives and oil. Gather
the herby crumbs into little wads,
and push into the holes. Season leg
and place on rack in large roasting
pan. Dust top with paprika and
mustard.

   Put onion into roasting pan and
pour in 1 cup apple juice and 1 cup
water or stock. Add apples and
dribble with honey. Roast just
below center of oven at 400°F for
45 minutes. Baste well, then cover
top loosely with foil, shiny-side up.
Pour remaining apple juice and
water into pan. Reduce oven
temperature to 325°F and roast for
about 3 hours more, basting twice
and adding more liquid if
necessary. The pork should be
cooked right through, and the
gravy reduced to a rich, thick
sauce. Check seasoning. Stand pork
in a warming oven for about
15 minutes before carving. Serves
about 10.

## Pork Chops with Cheese and Crumb Topping

1–1¼ lb pork loin chops
1 onion, chopped
½ tsp salt
½ tsp ground black pepper
½ tsp dried sage
scant 1 cup chicken stock
scant 1 cup semi-sweet
   white wine
1 garlic clove, crushed
2 bay leaves
paprika

TOPPING
¼ cup fresh brown breadcrumbs
3 tbsp finely chopped parsley
¾ cup grated mozzarella cheese
¼ cup reserved pan juices
1 tsp prepared mustard

Brown trimmed chops on both
sides, together with onion. Sprinkle
with salt, pepper and sage. Add
stock, wine, garlic and bay leaves.
Bring to a boil, cover and simmer
over low heat for about 45 minutes
until tender. Mix remaining
ingredients, except paprika, and
spread over each chop. Sprinkle
with paprika. Place under
preheated broiler until melted and
lightly browned. Thicken pan
gravy, if desired. Serve separately.
Serves 4.

# Ginger-Glazed Ham

A change from ham and pineapple, this ham is brushed with a sweet apricot glaze and surrounded with spiced apricots. Serve with a tangy mustard sauce.

1 x 11 lb ham
beer
water
2 whole, peeled onions each stuck with 3 cloves
2 whole carrots
4 bay leaves
12 peppercorns
whole cloves

GLAZE
1 lb 14 oz can apricot halves
good ¼ cup soft brown sugar
1½ tsp ground ginger
3 tbsp smooth apricot jam

Soak ham overnight in cold water to cover. Next day, remove and wash well. Place in large saucepan and cover with beer and water – the beer makes it especially succulent. Add remaining ingredients, except cloves, then cover and simmer for 4–5 hours or until tender. As soon as it can be handled, remove skin and return ham to liquid to cool.

Score ham, insert cloves in squares and bake at 325°F for 45 minutes, basting with the glaze until crisp and golden brown.

For the glaze, drain syrup from apricots, measure out ½ cup and reserve the remainder. Place apricot syrup, sugar, ginger and jam in a small saucepan and melt over low heat, stirring.
Serves about 20.

# Spiced Apricots

reserved apricot syrup from glaze
4 whole cloves
1 cinnamon stick
½ tsp ground mixed spice
2 tsp white wine vinegar
reserved apricots
maraschino cherries

Make up reserved apricot syrup to 1 cup with water, if necessary. Heat syrup, spices and vinegar in a large shallow saucepan. Add apricots, hollows down, and simmer very gently for 5 minutes. Remove from heat and cool apricots in syrup.

Place a cherry in each half and arrange around ham.

# Mustard and Sour Cream Mayonnaise

Serve chilled, with cold ham.

1 cup thick mayonnaise
1 cup sour cream
3 tbsp French mustard
1 tsp lemon juice
¼ cup chopped chives
pinch each of salt and sugar

Stir all ingredients together until well blended, then refrigerate, covered, for several hours before serving. Makes about 2 cups.

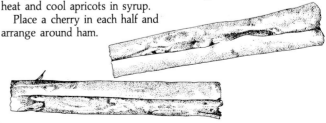

## Glazed Roast Pork

**A beautiful, mahogany-colored leg, larded with sage and marinated in soy sauce, honey and wine.**

1 x 4½ lb leg of pork
1 thick slice wholewheat bread,
  crumbled
8–12 fresh sage leaves, chopped
2 garlic cloves, crushed
2 tbsp oil
salt
paprika

MARINADE
5 tsp soy sauce
3 tbsp honey
1 tsp ground ginger
1 cup dry white wine
1 large onion, chopped
2 bay leaves

Remove rind from leg as thinly as possible, cut small incisions on all surfaces. Mix bread, sage, garlic and oil and push little wads of breadcrumb mixture into the incisions. Place pork, fat-side down, in glass dish for marinating. Mix ingredients for marinade and pour over. Arrange pork rind round sides. Refrigerate overnight, turning in the morning.

To roast, sprinkle each side of leg with salt and paprika. Place, fat-side up, on rack in roasting pan, and pour over one-third of the strained marinade. Roast at 325°F for 1 hour. Pour over another third of the marinade and roast for another hour. If browning too rapidly, cover loosely with a tent of foil, shiny-side up. Pour over remaining marinade and continue roasting until done – up to 4 hours in total. When deeply pricked, the juices should run clear. Serve hot with apple sauce, or cold with coleslaw.
Serves about 8.

## Pork Fillet in Sweet and Sour Sauce

**This dish is quite different from the batter-dipped fried pork served with a sticky, sweet and sour sauce. Instead, strips of lean fillet are slow-simmered with vegetables and pineapple in a sauce subtly flavored with sherry, sugar, soy sauce and vinegar.**

1½ lb pork fillet
oil for frying
1 large onion, chopped
1 green Bell pepper, seeded and
  diced
2 celery stalks, chopped
1 x 15 oz can pineapple rings in
  natural juice
⅔ cup water
3 tbsp light brown sugar
5 tsp soy sauce
5 tsp brown vinegar
¼ cup sherry
1 tbsp cornstarch

Remove any sinewy bits from fillet, slice into long strips, and then into thin slices across the grain. Heat 3 tbsp oil in large skillet. Fry half the pork and set aside. Repeat. Add a little more oil to pan juices if necessary and stir-fry onion, green pepper and celery. Return meat to pan. Drain pineapple and add juice and water to meat. Bring to a boil, then cover and simmer gently until pork is cooked and tender. Add pineapple rings, cut into small cubes. Stir together sugar, soy sauce, vinegar, sherry and cornstarch until smooth. Add to pan, cover and simmer about 15 minutes to blend flavors. Adjust seasoning.
Serves 4–6.

# Moussaka

My version of this popular
Greek dish.

1–1¼ lb eggplant
olive and vegetable oil for
    frying
1 large onion, chopped
2 garlic cloves, crushed
½ tsp dried oregano
1–1¼ lb ground veal
5 tsp tomato paste
scant ½ cup dry white wine
¼ cup chopped parsley
½ tsp ground cinnamon
salt and ground black pepper
1 tsp sugar
2 eggs, separated
3 tbsp butter
⅓ cup flour
⅔ cup milk
grated Cheddar cheese
1 tsp freshly grated nutmeg

Wash and trim ends off eggplants.
Slice into thin rounds and dégorge
(page 135). Pat dry with absorbent
paper towels and fry on both sides
in mixture of olive and vegetable
oil. Keep the heat fairly low and
occasionally cover the pan and the
slices will brown and soften
without absorbing quite so much
oil. Do them in batches and drain
on absorbent paper towels.
    In same pan sauté onion and
garlic. Sprinkle in oregano, then
add veal. Cook, stirring, until
browned and no longer lumpy.
Mix tomato paste, wine, parsley,
cinnamon, seasoning and sugar.
Pour over veal, stir well, cover and
simmer for 20 minutes. Beat egg
whites until foamy. Remove pan
from heat and stir in egg whites.
The meat sauce should be moist
but not sloppy. Make a thick white
sauce with butter, flour and milk.
Stir in 4 tbsp cheese and when
melted remove from heat. Add a
little cheese sauce to the beaten
egg yolks, then mix into remaining
sauce. Stir in nutmeg and season.
To assemble, cover bottom of
baking dish with half the eggplant
slices, top with meat sauce, cover
with remaining eggplant, then
pour cheese sauce over top.
Sprinkle with extra cheese, then
bake, uncovered, at 350°F for
35–40 minutes. Turn off oven and
leave for 15 minutes before
serving.
Serves 5–6.

## Veal Schnitzel with Tomato and Mozzarella

A wonderful way of serving schnitzels: first crumbed and fried, then baked in a bright tomato and vermouth sauce topped with melting mozzarella. This dish may be assembled in advance. Serve with risotto or Saffron Rice (page 114) and a crisp, garlicky salad.

6 x 2½ oz veal schnitzels
1 egg
2 tsp water
¾ cup toasted breadcrumbs, finely crushed
salt and ground black pepper
3 tbsp grated Parmesan cheese
oil for frying
1 onion, chopped
1 garlic clove, crushed
1 x 14 oz can tomatoes, chopped
½ tsp dried basil
2 bay leaves
3 tbsp chopped parsley
¼ cup dry vermouth
1 tsp sugar
1⅔ cups mozzarella cheese, sliced
generous pinch of dried oregano

Slice each schnitzel into 2 equal pieces. Beat egg with water and mix crumbs with ½ tsp salt, a little pepper and Parmesan. Brush veal with egg, then dip into crumbs, coating both sides. Chill at least 1 hour to set crumbs.

Heat 3 tbsp oil in skillet and brown veal very lightly, turning once. Do this in batches and add a little more oil when necessary. Arrange schnitzels to fit closely in a single layer in a large 12 x 9-in baking dish.

To make sauce, lightly sauté onion and garlic. Add tomatoes, plus juice, ½ tsp salt, basil, bay leaves, parsley, vermouth and sugar. Cover and simmer gently for 30 minutes. Remove bay leaves and spoon sauce over veal. Top with mozzarella and dust with oregano. If preparing in advance, set aside at this point. Bake, uncovered, at 325°F for 40 minutes, then pour in a little water or stock at the side — the finished dish should be moist and juicy — and bake for 10 minutes longer. Serves 4.

## Casserole of Veal in Mustard Cream Sauce

**Slices of veal shin with marrow bones make a singularly succulent dish. Serve with saffron rice and a bold green bean and olive salad.**

**¼ cup flour**
**½ tsp salt**
**1½ tsp dry mustard**
**1¾ lb veal shank, cut in 1-in slices**
**¼ cup oil**
**1 onion, chopped**
**4 leeks, sliced**
**2 tomatoes, skinned and chopped**
**scant ½ cup white wine**
**scant ½ cup chicken stock**
**2 bay leaves**
**1 tsp sugar**
**½ cup sour cream**
**5 tsp French mustard**

Mix flour, salt and mustard. Nick edges of veal and coat with flour mixture. Heat oil in large skillet and brown veal on both sides. Remove to baking dish in single layer. Add a little more oil to pan, if necessary, and soften onion and leeks. Add tomatoes, wine, stock, bay leaves, sugar and any left-over flour mixture. Boil up, then pour over veal. Cover and bake at 325°F for 1 hour. Turn carefully, stir gravy, and continue baking for a further 30 minutes until tender.

Mix sour cream with mustard, stir into casserole and return to oven until heated through. Adjust seasoning, and sprinkle with chopped parsley and basil, if available, before serving.
Serves 4.

## Veal Goulash with Noodles

**A richly colored, Hungarian stew using simple ingredients.**

**3 tbsp oil**
**2 tbsp butter**
**1¾ lb veal, cubed**
**2 large onions, chopped**
**2 garlic cloves, crushed**
**1 red Bell pepper, seeded and diced**
**2 tsp paprika**
**¼ cup flour**
**1¼ cups chicken stock**
**½ cup tomato paste**
**scant ½ cup white wine**
**salt and ground black pepper**
**large pinch of sugar**
**2 bay leaves**
**9 oz ribbon noodles**
**knob of butter**
**5 tsp poppy seeds**
**½ cup sour cream**
**chopped parsley**

Heat oil and butter in a very large skillet. Add meat and brown in batches to avoid stewing. Remove meat and set aside. Add a little more oil to pan if necessary and soften onions, garlic and pepper, sprinkle in paprika and flour. Keep heat low, as over-heated paprika becomes bitter. Return meat and stir in stock, tomato paste, wine, salt, pepper, sugar and bay leaves.

Stir to mix, then cover and simmer very gently, stirring occasionally, for abut 1½ hours or until meat is very tender. Remove bay leaves and if sauce needs to be thickened, tilt lid of pan and simmer over low heat.

Cook noodles in plenty of salted water. Drain, then toss with butter and poppy seeds.

Swirl sour cream into meat mixture, turn out onto large, warmed platter, sprinkle with chopped parsley and surround with the noodles.
Serves 4 generously.

## Osso Bucco

This unpretentious Milanese dish consists of veal shank in a robust gravy. It is important that each slice of veal has a thick marrow bone in the center, that the fresh garnish, or gremolada, is used, and that the dish is served with Saffron Rice (see right) or risotto.

¼ lb flour
1 tsp salt
ground black pepper
2¾ lb veal shin cut in 2-in slices
¼ cup oil
2 onions, chopped
2 garlic cloves, crushed
1⅓ cups chicken stock
⅔ cup dry white wine
1 x 14 oz can tomatoes, chopped
2 bay leaves
½ tsp sugar
½ tsp dried rosemary

GREMOLADA
3 tbsp finely chopped parsley
1 garlic clove, crushed
1 tsp finely grated lemon zest

Mix flour, salt and pepper and use to coat veal slices. Heat oil and brown lightly on both sides in large skillet or casserole. Towards end of frying period add onions and garlic and a little more oil if necessary. Continue frying for 1–2 minutes, then remove from heat and add 1 cup stock, wine, tomatoes plus the juice, bay leaves and sugar. Either bake in casserole, or transfer to large baking dish, arranging veal so that there is no chance of the marrow falling out. Cover securely and bake at 325°F for 1½–2 hours, or until tender. If dish is well covered there should be no need to turn or baste slices. Remove from oven and cool.

Add rosemary and remaining chicken stock 45 minutes before required. Cover and reheat at the same temperature. Mix the ingredients for gremolada, sprinkle over the top and serve with Saffron Rice, a green salad, and triangles of toast for the marrow.
Serves about 6.

## Saffron Rice

½ tsp saffron threads
5 tsp hot water
butter
1 tbsp oil
1 onion, finely chopped
scant 1 cup white long-grain rice
2 cups hot chicken stock
salt and ground black pepper
1–2 cinnamon sticks

Soak saffron in the hot water for at least 1 hour. Heat oil and butter, add onion and allow to soften. Add rice and toss until glistening, then slowly stir in hot stock. Add saffron plus water, seasoning and cinnamon. Bring to a boil, then cover and simmer over very low heat for about 25 minutes. Remove cinnamon sticks and serve.
Serves 4–6.

## Saddle of Venison

A saddle is surely the prime cut of venison and, if treated correctly, turns out tender and juicy.

about ½ lb pork fat
2 garlic cloves, crushed
1 tsp mixed dried herbs
small saddle of venison
3 tbsp oil
1 large onion, chopped
salt and ground black pepper
½ cup water
1 tbsp chutney
smooth apricot jam

MARINADE
1 cup red wine
¼ cup brown vinegar
½ cup water
2 lemon slices
1 carrot, sliced
8 peppercorns
1 bay leaf
1 tsp salt

Cut pork fat into cubes, reserving 2 thin strips. Roll cubes in garlic and dried herbs. Remove thin covering membrane from saddle and lard meat with pork fat. Place in glass or non-metallic dish.

Mix ingredients for marinade, pour over saddle and refrigerate for 48 hours, turning several times.

Heat oil in roasting pan with lid, and fry onion. Dry saddle, reserving marinade, and brown lightly. Season. Add water, chutney and ½ cup strained marinade. Place strips of pork fat on top, cover and roast until done, allowing about 30 minutes per 1 lb plus an extra 30 minutes. Remove, spread with a thin layer of jam and brown quickly under the broiler. Thicken gravy, adding a little more water, wine or stock if necessary. Serve with Red Wine Jelly (see below).

## Red Wine Jelly

1 cup dry red wine
1 tsp powdered gelatin
2 tsp sugar
4 blades of mace
1 tsp finely grated orange zest

Put ingredients into a saucepan, bring to a boil, stirring, and boil for at least 1 minute. Strain into small pots and leave to set.
Makes 1 cup.

## Vegetable Biriani

**Based on a dish from Northern India, this is an aromatic combination of rice, lentils, vegetables and spices.**

scant 1 cup brown rice
good ½ cup brown lentils, picked over and rinsed
1 tsp salt
1 tsp turmeric
1 tsp ground coriander
½ tsp ground cumin
1 cinnamon stick
3¼ cups water
½ lb eggplant
2 tbsp butter
3 tbsp oil
2 leeks, sliced
1 large onion, chopped
2–4 garlic cloves, crushed
½ tsp masala paste (or more to taste)
1 red Bell pepper, seeded and diced
4 juicy tomatoes, skinned and chopped
¾ lb zucchini, peeled and sliced
1½ cups green peas
pinch of salt
pinch of sugar
½ cup flaked almonds
2 tbsp butter
½ cup golden raisins

Put rice, lentils, salt, spices and water into a saucepan. Bring to a boil, cover, lower heat and leave to cook gently for about 50 minutes, by which time liquid should be absorbed. Fluff up with a fork and remove cinnamon stick.
Meanwhile dégorge eggplant (page 135), and cube. Heat butter and oil in large skillet and sauté leeks, onion, garlic and masala paste. When softened, add eggplant, red Bell pepper, tomatoes, zucchini and peas. Cook for approximately 10 minutes, stirring occasionally, until zucchini are translucent. Remove from heat and add salt and sugar. In a large, deep, buttered dish, layer one-third of the rice, half the vegetable mixture, another third of the rice, remaining vegetable mixture, then remainder of the rice. Bake, covered, at 325°F for 30 minutes. Just before end of baking time, fry almonds in butter. When lightly browned, add golden raisins, heat through and spoon over top of biriani.
Serves about 8.

Crêpes Ratatouille

## *Crêpes Ratatouille*

In this dish, pancakes are wrapped round a savory vegetable filling, covered with a white sauce, sprinkled with cheese, and then baked. This dish can be assembled successfully in advance.

BLENDER CRÊPES
**1 cup flour**
**generous pinch of salt**
**1 egg**
**1 cup milk**
**½ cup water**
**5 tsp oil**
**½ tsp dried oregano (optional)**

FILLING
**1 tbsp vegetable oil**
**1 tbsp olive oil**
**1 medium eggplant, cubed**
**1 green Bell pepper, seeded and diced**
**1 onion, chopped**

**½ lb zucchini, scrubbed and sliced**
**salt and ground black pepper**
**2 large tomatoes, skinned and chopped**
**2 garlic cloves, crushed**
**1 tsp dried basil**
**1 tsp sugar**

SAUCE
**knob of butter**
**¼ cup flour**
**2 cups milk**
**salt and pepper**
**1 tsp prepared mustard**

**grated Cheddar or Gruyère cheese**
**3 tbsp grated Parmesan cheese**

Put all ingredients for crêpes into a blender and blend well, stopping to scrape down sides once or twice. Stand for 1 hour, blend again, then make thin crêpes in a 7-in skillet. As they are done, stack on large plate with a circle of waxed paper between each one.

For the filling, put oils, eggplant, green pepper, onion, zucchini, and seasoning into a large saucepan. Cover and stew slowly, stirring occasionally, for about 35 minutes or until soft. Add tomatoes, garlic, basil and sugar. Half-cover saucepan and cook until tomatoes are pulpy. If necessary, remove lid and boil rapidly to reduce excess liquid. Cool, then divide between crêpes, roll into cigar shapes and place side by side in buttered baking dish. The filling is enough for 8–10 crêpes.

Make white sauce by melting butter, stirring in flour, then adding milk slowly, stirring constantly. When thick, add seasonings and pour over crêpes. Sprinkle generously with cheese, top with Parmesan and heat through at 325°F for about 40 minutes. Serve 1–2 crêpes per person.

## *Garbanzo Stew*

**2 tbsp butter**
**¼ cup oil**
**1 large onion, chopped**
**2 garlic cloves, crushed**
**2 carrots, diced**
**1 red Bell pepper, seeded and diced**
**¾ lb brown mushrooms, sliced**
**¾ lb tomatoes, skinned and chopped**
**5 tsp tomato paste**
**3 tbsp chopped parsley**
**½ tsp dried basil**
**½ tsp dried thyme**
**1½ lb cooked garbanzo beans**
**½ cup vegetable stock**

Heat butter and oil in large saucepan. Stir-fry onion, garlic, carrots, red Bell pepper and mushrooms. Add remaining ingredients. Season, cover and simmer for 30 minutes. Thicken sauce with beurre manié. Serves 6.

Wholewheat Pitta (page 215) with (left to right) Eggplant Salad, Tzatsiki (page 123), Hummus and Felafel

## Hummus

¾ lb cooked garbanzo beans
¼ cup lemon juice
3 garlic cloves
¼ cup tahini
¼ cup olive oil
salt
finely chopped parsley
olive oil

Drain garbanzo beans, reserving scant ½ cup of cooking liquid. Using the grinding blade of a food processor, purée garbanzo beans, lemon juice, garlic, tahini and olive oil. With motor running, pour in reserved cooking liquid or scant ½ cup water. The consistency should be that of thick mayonnaise. Add salt to taste, cover and chill. To serve, sprinkle with parsley and dribble with a little olive oil. Serves 4–6.

## Eggplant Salad

1 medium eggplant
3 tbsp vegetable oil
3 tbsp olive oil
2 leeks, thinly sliced
1 green Bell pepper, seeded and diced
1 garlic clove, crushed
½ tsp dried oregano
½ tsp dried basil
salt and ground black pepper
1 tomato, chopped
toasted pine nuts or walnuts (optional)

Dégorge eggplant (page 135) and then cube. Heat oils in skillet and add eggplant, leeks, green Bell pepper, garlic, herbs and seasoning. Cover and stew gently until soft, then spoon into bowl and add tomato. Sprinkle with nuts, if desired, cover and leave to cool. Serves 4.

## Felafel

Serve these baked felafel with creamy tzatsiki (page 123).

1–1¼ lb cooked garbanzo beans, drained
½ tsp salt
¼ cup finely chopped parsley
2 garlic cloves, crushed
1 tsp ground cumin
1 tsp ground coriander
3 tbsp wholewheat flour
1 egg, beaten
oil for baking

Place garbanzo beans in food processor and, using the grinding blade, grind to a dry mealy mixture. Put into bowl and add salt, parsley, garlic and spices. Sprinkle in flour and bind with egg, then roll into 15 small balls. Preheat oven to 350°F. Cover base of jelly roll pan with a fairly generous layer of oil and heat in oven. Roll balls in the hot oil, then bake for 20 minutes. Using a spatula, turn them carefully. Raise heat to 425°F and bake for another 15 minutes or until crisp and brown. Makes 15.

## Haricot Bean Salad

¾ lb cooked haricot beans
2 tsp lemon juice
3 tbsp olive oil
½ tsp dried oregano
1 tomato, diced
6 black olives, sliced
4 green onions, chopped
salt and freshly ground pepper
crumbled feta cheese

Toss to mix, cover and stand for at least 30 minutes.

## Note

Serve these dishes with **Wholewheat Pitta (page 215)** for a complete meal.

# Mushroom and Lentil Moussaka with Soufflé Topping

As with all moussakas, this dish takes some time to put together, but it makes a most delicious and nourishing meal served with a crisp salad and chunks of hot garlic bread.

1 lb 5 oz eggplants
oil for frying
good 1 cup brown lentils, picked over and rinsed
2 cups salted water
3 tbsp olive oil
1 large onion, chopped
1 green Bell pepper, seeded and diced
2 garlic cloves, crushed
¾ lb brown mushrooms, wiped and sliced
3 medium tomatoes, skinned and chopped

2 tsp brown sugar
½ tsp ground cinnamon
1 bay leaf
½ tsp salt
2 tbsp chopped parsley

TOPPING
3 tbsp butter
¼ cup flour
2 cups milk
2 eggs, separated
salt and pepper
½ tsp freshly grated nutmeg
1½ cups grated Cheddar cheese

Cut stem ends off eggplants, slice into ¼-in thick rings, then dégorge (page 135). Fry on both sides until lightly browned and soft. If fried on a fairly low heat in a heavy-based skillet, and half-covered every now and then, the amount of oil absorbed will be considerably reduced.

Meanwhile, boil lentils in salted water for 50 minutes or until soft, and water is absorbed. In a large skillet heat olive oil and soften onion, green pepper and garlic. Add mushrooms, and when softened add tomatoes, sugar, cinnamon, bay leaf, salt and parsley. Cover and simmer for 20 minutes, stirring occasionally. Remove bay leaf and stir in cooked lentils. The mixture should be moist and fairly thick.

Make topping by melting butter, then stirring in flour. Cook for 1 minute, remove from heat and slowly stir in milk (semi-skimmed may be used). Return to heat and cook, stirring, until thickened. Beat egg yolks, add a little hot sauce, then return yolk mixture to sauce and mix in, using balloon whisk. Season with salt, pepper and nutmeg. Stiffly beat the egg whites and fold in.

To assemble, cover base of 12 x 8in baking dish with half the eggplant slices, then spoon lentil mixture over. Cover with remaining eggplant slices, then pour topping over. Sprinkle with grated cheese and bake at 350°F for 30 minutes, then turn off oven and leave for another 15 minutes to settle.
Serves 6.

## Note
**This dish reheats well: bake initially for 30 minutes at 350°F and remove. Reheat at 325°F for 30 minutes.**

## Pot Beans

This is a hot and savory version of fasoulia, the popular Greek dish. Economical, easy to prepare, and remarkably good served on brown rice with a green salad.

1–1¼ lb haricot beans
scant ½ cup oil
2 large onions, sliced
1 tsp dried thyme
1 tsp dried oregano
4 oz can tomato paste
4 garlic cloves, crushed
2 bay leaves
1 tbsp honey
salt and ground black pepper
stock or water
1 bunch spinach, shredded
    (optional)
3 tbsp chopped parsley
soy sauce
grated Cheddar cheese
    (optional)

Soak beans overnight, then drain and rinse. Heat oil in a large saucepan and add onions. When softened, add beans and toss over medium heat for 5 minutes. Add herbs, tomato paste, garlic, bay leaves, honey and seasoning. Add enough stock or water to cover, then cover saucepan and simmer gently for 1½ hours, or until beans are soft and liquid is thick and reduced. Add spinach, if using, and parsley. Cover and simmer for another 30 minutes. To serve, add soy sauce to taste, then spoon over servings of rice and top with grated cheese.
Serves 6–8.

## Spicy Lentil Curry

A surprisingly delicious curry. Serve on rice with sambals (page 95) and a tomato and onion salad.

2 tbsp butter
3 tbsp oil
2 large onions, sliced
1 green Bell pepper, seeded and
    diced
2 garlic cloves, crushed
2 celery stalks, thinly sliced
3 carrots, coarsely grated
2 tsp curry powder
1 tsp ground cumin
1 tsp turmeric
1 tsp ground fennel
1⅔ cups brown lentils, picked
    over and rinsed
1½ pints water
1 bay leaf
2 tbsp chopped parsley
1 tsp salt
3 tbsp brown sugar

⅔ cup tomato paste
sour cream
snipped chives

Heat oil and butter and sauté onions, green pepper, garlic, celery and carrots. When softened, add spices and stir over low heat for a few minutes.

Add lentils, water, bay leaf, parsley, salt, sugar and tomato paste. Mix well and spoon into a large baking dish. Bake, covered, at 350°F for about 1 hour, or until lentils are soft, stirring once or twice. Remove from oven and streak in a few spoons of sour cream, sprinkle with chives and warm through for another 5 minutes before serving.
Serves 6.

## Casserole of Lentils and Rice with Pizza Topping

good 1 cup brown lentils, picked
over and rinsed
scant ½ cup brown rice
3 tbsp oil
1 tbsp butter
2 medium onions, finely
chopped
2 green or red Bell peppers,
seeded and diced
2 tbsp chopped parsley
½ cup fresh wholewheat
breadcrumbs
2 eggs
½ cup buttermilk
salt and ground black pepper
3–4 firm tomatoes, thinly sliced
grated mozzarella or Cheddar
cheese
grated Parmesan cheese
½ tsp dried oregano

generous pinch of dried basil
3 tbsp olive oil

Simmer lentils in 2 cups salted
water for about 50 minutes or until
soft. In another saucepan cook
brown rice in 1¼ cups salted water
for about 45 minutes. Heat oil and
butter and sauté onions and
peppers. Spoon lentils and rice into
a large bowl and add cooked
onions and peppers, parsley and
breadcrumbs. Beat eggs with
buttermilk and add together with
seasoning. Mix well, without
mashing, and spoon into a deep,
buttered 9-in pie dish.

Level top and cover with
tomatoes. Cover tomatoes with
plenty of grated mozzarella or
Cheddar, and add a sprinkling of
Parmesan. Sprinkle herbs over
cheese and dribble with oil. Bake at
350°F for about 25 minutes, until
bubbling and cheese has melted.
Serve with creamy mashed
potatoes and a salad.
Serves 6.

## Lentils and Eggplants in Barbecue Sauce

A thick, savory stew, which is
delicious served on pasta or
brown rice, topped with
crumbled feta or grated Cheddar
or Parmesan cheese. A lettuce
and avocado salad tossed with
French dressing is a good
accompaniment, with crusty
rolls an optional extra.

good 1 cup brown lentils, picked
over and rinsed
2 cups salted water
¼ cup oil
¾ lb young eggplants, cubed
1 large onion, chopped
2 garlic cloves, crushed
1 small green or red Bell pepper,
seeded and diced
bare ½ lb zucchini, scrubbed and
sliced

1 cup tomato paste
1 tbsp honey
5 tsp soy sauce
2 tbsp chopped parsley
1 cup water
1 tsp dried basil

Boil lentils gently in the water for
about 50 minutes until soft.
Meanwhile, heat oil in large skillet
and add eggplant, onion, garlic,
pepper and zucchini. Toss over low
heat for 5 minutes.

Add remaining ingredients,
cover and simmer gently for
30 minutes. Add cooked lentils
and, if necessary, another ½ cup
water, or enough to make a good
gravy. Simmer very gently for
another 15 minutes. Adjust
seasoning – it may need a pinch of
salt, or a little sugar – then leave to
stand to allow flavors to mellow.
Reheat and serve as suggested.
Serves 4.

## Lentil and Potato Pie

Brown lentils are a good source of protein, and if you like their distinctive, rather earthy flavor, you'll enjoy this pie, in which they're baked between layers of sliced potatoes and onions, and topped with cheese. This simple dish is one of our favorite vegetarian meals, accompanied by buttered cabbage.

¾ lb brown lentils, picked over and rinsed
1 lb 14 oz potatoes, thinly sliced
2 large onions, thinly sliced
salt and ground black pepper
1½ pints hot stock or 3 tbsp Marmite in 1½ pints hot water
grated Cheddar cheese
butter
paprika

Cover lentils with water and leave to soak for about 2 hours. Grease a deep 9-in pie dish and cover the base with half the potatoes and onions. Season lightly. Top with drained lentils, evenly spread. Cover with remaining onions and potatoes, and season lightly again. Pour over hot stock, cover with greased foil, shiny-side up, or with a lid, and bake at 350°F for 1 hour.

Remove cover and sprinkle thickly with cheese, dot with butter, and dust with paprika. Bake, uncovered, for a further 20 minutes, by which time potatoes and lentils should be soft, liquid absorbed, and cheese melted and bubbling.
Serves 6–8.

## Spiced Garbanzo Beans

A fragrant stew to serve on brown rice with bowls of coconut and chopped nuts, and a green salad.

¼ cup oil
2 onions, chopped
2–3 garlic cloves, crushed
½ tsp ground cumin
½ tsp turmeric
½ tsp ground cinnamon
½ tsp ground ginger
1 tsp ground coriander
2 celery stalks, chopped
1 green Bell pepper, seeded and diced
1–1¼ lb cooked garbanzo beans, drained
3 tbsp chopped parsley
1 x 14 oz can tomatoes, chopped, plus juice
2 bay leaves
1 cup water or vegetable stock
1 tsp salt or 2 tsp vegetable salt
1 tsp sugar

Heat oil in a large saucepan. Add onions, garlic, spices, celery and pepper. Cover and cook over very low heat until onions are soft. Add remaining ingredients, bring to a boil, then cover and simmer on low heat for about 30 minutes, stirring occasionally. Add a little water if necessary for a good gravy. Check seasoning and serve as suggested. Serves 4–6.

### Note
Garbanzo beans have been popular for centuries. Round, and cream-colored, they are fairly bland in flavor and slightly nutty in texture, and require a long soaking and cooking period before being used in spreads, salads and stews.

# Haricot Bean Salad

This happy combination of French and Greek flavors is an economical, substantial salad to serve with wholewheat bread.

1–1¼ lb haricot beans
2 bouquets garnis
2 bay leaves
1 tsp salt
3–4 leeks, thinly sliced
1 green or red Bell pepper, seeded and chopped
1 large celery stalk, sliced
2 tbsp chopped parsley
large pinch of sugar
tomato, black olives and feta cheese

DRESSING
scant ½ cup vegetable oil
¼ olive oil
1 garlic clove, crushed
5 tsp lemon juice
½ tsp salt
1 tsp dried oregano

TZATSIKI
½ cucumber
1 cup plain drinking yogurt
½ cup sour cream
2 tsp honey
1 garlic clove, crushed
salt and ground black pepper
8–10 mint leaves, finely chopped

Soak beans overnight. Next day drain, rinse, cover with fresh water, add bouquets garnis and bay leaves and boil until soft, adding salt towards the end of the cooking period.

Make dressing by mixing all ingredients, and leave to stand while beans are cooking.

Make tzatsiki several hours in advance and chill thoroughly. Peel and grate cucumber coarsely and squeeze very dry between pieces of absorbent paper towels. Mix with remaining ingredients, cover and chill.

Drain cooked beans and spoon into large bowl. Toss while hot with dressing, using a fork and taking care not to mash them. Add leeks, pepper, celery, parsley and sugar. Cover and stand for at least 2 hours, or chill overnight. To serve, adjust seasoning in bean salad, then spoon onto large serving platter. Surround with chunks of tomato and top with black olives. Sprinkle generously with crumbled feta, and serve tzatsiki separately.
Serves 8.

## Greek Vegetable Casserole with Beans and Feta

A delicious medley of Mediterranean-style vegetables. Served in a large earthenware casserole, topped with crumbled feta and black olives, it's beautiful to look at and good to eat. Serve on brown rice, with a lettuce and avocado salad tossed in garlicky French dressing.

3 tbsp vegetable oil
3 tbsp olive oil
1 large onion, chopped
2 leeks, sliced
1 green Bell pepper, seeded and diced
2 garlic cloves, crushed
1 medium eggplant, rinsed and cubed
good 1 lb zucchini, peeled and sliced
4 large, juicy tomatoes, skinned and chopped
2 cups cooked soya or haricot beans
1 tsp salt
ground black pepper
1 tsp dried oregano
1 tsp dried basil
1 tsp sugar
1 cup stock or 1 beef bouillon cube in 1 cup water
black olives
2 cups coarsely crumbled feta cheese

Heat oils in large skillet and sauté onion, leeks, pepper and garlic. When softened, add eggplant, zucchini and tomatoes. Cover and sweat for 5 minutes over low heat. Add drained beans, salt, pepper, herbs, sugar and stock. Stir to mix, then turn into a large baking dish. Bake, covered, at 300°F for 1 hour 15 minutes, stirring once or twice and adding a little more liquid if necessary.

About 10 minutes before serving, add a handful of sliced black olives and then sprinkle with feta. Return to oven just to heat through.
Serves 4–6.

# *Cannelloni*

An Italian dish, traditionally made with rectangles or tubes of pasta rolled around a filling, covered with a tomato sauce and cheese, and baked. Instead of pasta, I have used crêpes, stuffed with low-fat soft cheese, smothered in a mushroom or tomato sauce and melting mozzarella. A good choice for an informal meal because the crêpes, filling and sauce can all be made in advance. Good with a lettuce, avocado and herb salad, and a hot garlic loaf.

BLENDER CRÊPES
**1 cup flour**
**generous pinch of salt**
**1 egg**
**1 cup milk**
**½ cup water**
**5 tsp oil**

FILLING
**3 cups low-fat soft cheese**
**2 egg yolks**
**3 tbsp grated Parmesan cheese**
**1 garlic clove, crushed**
**1 tsp dried oregano**
**generous pinch of salt**
**ground black pepper**
**2 green onions, chopped**

MUSHROOM SAUCE
**3 tbsp oil**
**1 tsp butter**
**bare ¾ lb brown mushrooms, wiped and sliced**
**1 large onion, chopped**
**1 garlic clove, crushed**
**1 fresh rosemary sprig**
**¼ cup flour**
**1 cup stock**
**1 cup milk**
**salt and ground black pepper**
**lemon juice**

TOMATO SAUCE
**3 tbsp oil**
**1 large onion, chopped**
**1 garlic clove, crushed**
**1 tsp dried basil**
**3 medium ripe, juicy tomatoes, skinned and chopped**
**2 bay leaves**
**generous pinch of salt**
**1 tsp honey or 2 tsp brown sugar**
**2 tbsp chopped parsley**
**¼ cup white wine**

**mozzarella cheese for topping**

To make crêpes, put all ingredients into blender and blend until smooth, stopping to scrape down sides with a spatula. Cover and stand for 1 hour, then blend briefly before making thin crêpes, stacking them between sheets of waxed paper as they're done.

Mix the filling ingredients together until smooth, using a wooden spoon. If working ahead, chill filling until required.

To make mushroom sauce, heat oil and butter and sauté mush-rooms, onion, garlic and rosemary. When just beginning to soften and shrink, remove rosemary and add flour, then slowly stir in stock and milk. When thickened, remove from heat, season, and add a dash of lemon juice.

To make tomato sauce, heat oil and sauté onion, garlic and basil. Add tomatoes and remaining ingredients. Cover and simmer for approximately 30 minutes, stirring occasionally, until sauce is thick and syrupy. Remove bay leaves.

To assemble, divide cheese filling between crêpes, roll into cigar shapes, and place side by side in greased baking dish. Pour mushroom or tomato sauce over and top with sliced mozzarella. Bake at 350°F for about 25–30 minutes, until bubbling.
Makes 8 small portions.

## Vegetable Stir-Fry

¼ cup oil
**2–4 garlic cloves, crushed**
**about ¾ lb brown mushrooms,**
**wiped and sliced**
**3–4 leeks, sliced**
**3 large celery stalks, sliced**
**salt and ground black pepper**
**½ cauliflower**
**½ cucumber, peeled and diced**
**4 young carrots, cut in julienne**
**1⅓ cups chopped pecan nuts**

SAUCE
¼ cup sherry or port
**1 cup vegetable stock**
**5 tsp soy sauce**
**1 tsp peeled, grated gingerroot**
**4 tsp cornstarch**

Heat 3 tbsp oil in large skillet or
wok and add garlic, mushrooms,
leeks and celery. Stir-fry for about
5 minutes, then remove to baking
dish, plus any pan juices. Season
lightly.

Break cauliflower into flowerets.
Add another 3 tbsp oil to pan and
add cucumber, cauliflower and
carrots. Reduce heat and stir-fry,
half covered, until tender but crisp.
The mixture will reduce somewhat
and could take up to 15 minutes
with regular tossing. Add to
vegetables in baking dish.

Beat together ingredients for
sauce and stir into vegetable
mixture. Finally add pecan nuts,
tossing until ingredients are
thoroughly combined. Bake,
covered, at 350°F for 20–30
minutes until deliciously aromatic.
Serves 4–6.

## Eggplant Stuffed with Rice and Walnuts

**These crunchy, stuffed
eggplants may be assembled in
advance. Serve with a simple
green salad and a hot French
loaf.**

**4 x ¼ lb or 2 x ½ lb eggplants**
**3 tbsp olive oil**
**4–6 green onions, chopped**
**2 garlic cloves, crushed**
**scant 1 cup walnuts, coarsely
chopped**
**1 celery stalk, chopped**
**2 medium tomatoes, skinned
and chopped**
**salt and pepper**
**pinch of sugar**
**generous pinch of dried oregano**
**1 cup cooked brown rice**
**1 tbsp mayonnaise**
**grated mozzarella cheese**
**paprika**
**stock or water**

Wash and trim eggplants, then boil
in unsalted water for about
10 minutes until beginning to
soften. Halve lengthwise and when
cool remove pulp, leaving cases
about ¾ in thick. Cube flesh. Heat
oil and sauté green onions, garlic,
walnuts and celery. When
softened, add tomatoes,
seasonings, oregano and eggplant
cubes. Cover and simmer for 5–10
minutes until tomatoes are pulpy.
Stir in rice and mayonnaise.

Mound this mixture into
reserved cases, arranged close
together in baking dish, and top
generously with grated cheese.
Sprinkle with paprika, and carefully
pour about 1 in stock into dish.
Bake, uncovered, at 325°F for 45
minutes.
Serves 4.

# Brown Rice with Lentils, Mushrooms and Almonds

**Served with a creamy green salad, this vegetarian main dish is a real delight.**

good 1 cup brown lentils, picked
  over and rinsed
1 bay leaf
knob of butter
1 tsp ground cumin
pinch of salt
1 cup brown rice
knob of butter
pinch of salt
1 tsp mixed dried herbs
2 tbsp butter
3 tbsp oil
2 onions, sliced
1 red Bell pepper, seeded and
  sliced
¾–1 lb brown mushrooms,
  wiped and sliced
2 celery stalks, chopped
2 tbsp chopped parsley
3 cups mung bean sprouts
¼ cup soy sauce
scant ½ cup almonds, halved
  and toasted

Put lentils into saucepan with 2 cups water, bay leaf, butter, cumin and salt. Bring to boil, then cover and simmer gently for about 50 minutes until water is absorbed and lentils are soft. At the same time, cook the rice in another saucepan with 3⅓ cups water, butter, salt and herbs and simmer, covered, over low heat for about 45 minutes. Toss lentils and rice together and spoon into large, buttered baking dish, discarding bay leaf. Cover and keep warm in low oven, or set aside to reheat gently at dinnertime.

To prepare the vegetables, heat butter and oil in a large skillet and add onions and red Bell pepper. When soft and browning, increase heat and add mushrooms, celery and parsley. Stir-fry for 5 minutes and then add sprouts and soy sauce. Reduce heat and cook for a further 2 minutes, tossing with a wooden spoon. Pour mixture over warmed rice and lentils, and scatter with almonds.
Serves 8–10.

## Note
**The soy sauce should season the dish sufficiently, so don't be tempted to add salt before tasting.**

## Green Beans with Mushrooms and Sour Cream

3 tbsp oil
1 large onion, finely chopped
1 tsp chopped fresh rosemary
   needles
1 garlic clove, crushed
¾–1 lb green beans, trimmed
   and sliced
½ cup stock or water
salt and ground black pepper
good ¼ lb brown mushrooms,
   wiped and sliced
3 tbsp sherry
⅓ cup sour cream

Heat oil and sauté onion, rosemary, garlic and beans. Toss for a few minutes until coated with oil, then add stock or water and seasoning. Half-cover and simmer until tender, stirring occasionally. After about 15 minutes the liquid should have been absorbed.

Add mushrooms and sherry. Cook for a further 2–3 minutes, stirring, then spoon into serving dish. Swirl in the sour cream and place in low oven just to heat through.
Serves 4–6.

Savory Zucchini

Broccoli with Lemon Cream Sauce

## Savory Zucchini

3 tbsp olive oil
1 onion or 2 leeks, sliced
2 garlic cloves, crushed
½ lb tomatoes, skinned and
    chopped
¾–1 lb zucchini, peeled
    and sliced
½ green Bell pepper, seeded and
    sliced
2 tbsp chopped parsley
½ cup dry white wine
1½ tsp dried basil
½ tsp salt
pinch of sugar

Heat oil and lightly sauté onion (or leeks) and garlic. Add tomatoes, zucchini, green Bell pepper and remaining ingredients. Stir to mix, then cover and simmer slowly for about 20 minutes, stirring occasionally. Serve hot, or else cool, cover, chill and serve as a salad. Serves 4–6.

## Braised Fennel and Carrots

Bulb fennel is the perfect partner for fish, and the carrots add color.

1 large bulb fennel
½ lb carrots
¾ cup chicken stock
2 tsp lemon juice
salt and ground black pepper
2 tbsp butter
pinch of sugar
snipped chives

Wash and trim fennel bulb and cut into long, thin strips; cut carrots into thin matchsticks. Melt butter, add vegetables and stir until coated. Add remaining ingredients. Cover and cook very gently for about 30 minutes until tender. The liquid should all be absorbed. Serve sprinkled with snipped chives. Serves 4–6.

## Broccoli with Lemon Cream Sauce

1–1¼ lb broccoli
paprika

SAUCE
½ cup sour cream
¼ cup mayonnaise
1 tbsp fresh lemon juice
1 tsp French mustard
very generous pinch of finely
    grated lemon zest

Trim and slice broccoli lengthwise. Poach in a little water until tender. To retain the bright color, do not overcook. Chop coarsely, place in serving dish and keep warm.

Combine ingredients for sauce in a small saucepan, and heat gently while stirring. Do not allow to boil. When hot, pour over broccoli, dust with paprika and serve at once.
Serves 6.

## Glazed Pearl Onions

1–1¼ lb pearl onions
1 tsp salt
¼ cup brown sugar
¼ cup water
2 big knobs of butter
pinch of nutmeg

Pour boiling water over onions. Stand 10 minutes, then drain, nick off tops and bottoms, and slip off the skins. Cover with cold water, bring to a boil, add salt and cook for 3 minutes. Drain. You can do all this in advance.

To finish off, melt remaining ingredients in a large skillet. Add onions. Cover and cook over medium heat, for 10–15 minutes, shaking pan occasionally until liquid has evaporated and onions are evenly browned.
Serves 6.

## Brussels Sprouts with Mustard Sauce

The sweet and sour mustard sauce which coats these sprouts makes this dish particularly suitable for serving with pork or ham.

1–1¼ lb young Brussels sprouts

EASY MUSTARD SAUCE
1 cup milk
1 egg yolk
2 tsp dry mustard
4 tsp flour
2 tsp brown sugar
1 tbsp brown vinegar
generous pinch of salt
small knob of butter

Trim sprouts and boil in a little salted water until just tender.

The sauce may be made ahead and gently reheated when required.

Put all the ingredients, except butter, into a small saucepan. Whisk to mix, then bring to a boil, stirring. Allow to bubble for a few minutes to thicken and cook flour, then remove from heat and stir in butter.

To serve, spoon hot sprouts into serving dish, pour hot sauce over, and toss gently until mixed.
Serves 6.

### Hint
For sprouts with a difference, remove outer leaves from ¾ –1 lb sprouts, cut a cross in the stem ends of each, and rinse. Put ⅔ cup chicken stock, a pinch of ground mace and 1 tbsp runny honey into saucepan. Add sprouts and boil until just tender. Season with salt and pepper, add 2 tsp lemon juice and 1 tbsp butter, and serve.
Serves 4.

## Stir-Fried Chinese Cabbage

This is definitely the aristocrat of the cabbage family. Leafy, tender and mild in flavor, Chinese cabbage should never be overcooked, and braising or stir-frying are the best cooking methods. It is also very good in a salad.

3 tbsp oil
4 green onions, chopped
2 celery stalks, thinly sliced
1 green Bell pepper, seeded and diced
small knob of gingerroot, peeled and grated
½ head of Chinese cabbage, shredded
2½ cups lentil sprouts
5 tsp soy sauce
large pinch of sugar
toasted flaked almonds

Heat oil in large skillet or wok and add green onions, celery, green pepper and ginger. When vegetables have softened, add cabbage. Toss in sprouts. Mix well, cover and steam over low heat until cabbage is just wilted, but still a good color. Stir in soy sauce and sugar and serve at once with a scattering of almonds.
Serves 4–5.

### Hint
There are several different varieties of soy sauce, and some are saltier than others. When using soy sauce in cooking, do not add salt, as the soy sauce usually seasons the dish sufficiently – if necessary, adjust at the end of the cooking period.

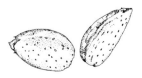

## Oven-Baked Carrots

The following two recipes are convenient ways of preparing carrots because they can be baked at the same time as any meat dish or casserole requiring a low oven temperature.

### Carrots in sherry

scant ¾ lb young carrots
¼ cup sherry
1 tbsp honey
¼ cup finely chopped parsley
½ tsp salt
2 tbsp butter

Peel and slice carrots lengthwise into thin strips and arrange in a pie dish, more or less in a single layer. Pour in sherry and honey, sprinkle with parsley and salt and dot with butter. Cover and bake at 325°F for about 1 hour 10 minutes.
Serves 4.

## Orange Carrots

1–1¼ lb carrots
½ cup fresh orange juice
3 tbsp honey
¼ cup finely chopped parsley
½ tsp finely grated orange zest
½ tsp salt
butter

Scrape and slice carrots lengthwise into thin strips. Arrange in a large pie dish, and pour orange juice and honey over. Sprinkle with parsley, orange zest and salt and dot with butter. Cover and bake at 325°F for about 1 hour or until just cooked.
Serves 5–6.

## Braised Belgian Endive

Called chicory in Europe, this delicate vegetable has long whitish leaves and very pale green tips, and should not be confused with curly endive. Cooked very simply, as follows, it is especially good with fish or chicken.

¾–1 lb Belgian endive
3 tbsp oil
1 tbsp butter
2 leeks, thinly sliced
2 tsp lemon juice
½ cup chicken stock
½ tsp salt
2 garlic cloves, crushed
2 tbsp chopped parsley
½ tsp sugar
grated Cheddar cheese
  (optional)

Remove any discolored outer leaves from endive, and cut off a thin slice from the corky base. Wash carefully. Heat oil and butter in wide, shallow pan. Cover bottom with a layer of leeks. Halve heads of endive lengthwise if large and arrange on top of leeks in a single layer. Sprinkle with lemon juice and add stock, salt, garlic, parsley and sugar. Cover securely and simmer gently for 30 minutes or until soft. Sprinkle with cheese, if desired, and melt under the broiler before serving.
Serves 6.

# Orange Sweet Potato Casserole

Sweet potatoes are now found in many supermarkets as well as in Indian or oriental stores. The simplest way of preparing them is to bake them in their skins and serve them with butter. The following recipe, with orange as the predominant flavor, is particularly suitable for serving with ham, pork or turkey.

1¾ lb sweet potatoes
cold water
salt
good ¾ cup fresh orange juice
3 tbsp honey
½ tsp finely grated orange zest
¼ cup sherry
2 tsp brown sugar
½ tsp ground cinnamon
butter

Scrub potatoes, cover with cold water, add salt and parboil for about 20 minutes – they should be half-cooked. Peel, slice into medium-thick fingers and arrange in a single layer to cover the base of a buttered 9-in pie dish. Mix orange juice, honey, rind and sherry. Bring to a boil and pour over potatoes. Sprinkle with sugar and cinnamon, dot with slivers of butter and bake, uncovered, at 350°F for 45 minutes to 1 hour, until soft and lightly browned. Serves 6.

# Baked Fried Potatoes

Chips the easy way, with no splattering, deep-frying or fuss.

potatoes, peeled, washed and
    dried
oil
salt

Cut potatoes into long, thin slices. Cover bottom of baking sheet with a generous layer of oil. Place in 325°F oven to heat, then arrange chips in single layer, tossing to coat evenly. Bake on bottom shelf until lightly browned and cooked through. Drain on absorbent paper towels, sprinkle with salt, and serve.

## Spiced Red Cabbage

Good with duck, venison and pork. Red cabbage tastes even better if prepared in advance and reheated.

2¼ lb red cabbage, finely
   shredded
2 onions, chopped
¼ cup oil
2 large cooking apples, peeled
   and cubed
2 tsp salt
ground black pepper
½ cup water
½ cup red wine
1 tsp ground mixed spice
good ½ cup seedless raisins
3 tbsp brown sugar
knob of butter

Soak cabbage in salted water to cover for 1 hour, then drain and rinse. In a large saucepan, lightly fry onions in oil, then add cabbage and cover and simmer for 10 minutes. Add apples and remaining ingredients, except butter. Cover and simmer gently for 1 hour, adding a dash more water or wine if necessary. Cool and reheat gently when required, adding butter just before serving.
Serves 8.

### Hint
Add interest to green cabbage as follows: bring a little salted water to a boil and add 1–1¼ lb shredded cabbage, 4 thinly sliced leeks and 2 crushed garlic cloves. Boil for a few minutes until tender-crisp. Drain and spoon into top of large double saucepan. Mix ⅔ cup sour cream, 1 tsp paprika, ½ tsp Worcestershire sauce and 2 tsp French mustard. Stir into cabbage, cover and cook over simmering water for 20 minutes.
Serves 8.

## Cauliflower Puff

This cauliflower dish can be prepared well in advance and requires only last-minute attention in whipping up the egg whites for the topping.

1 medium head cauliflower
lemon juice
3 tbsp butter
¼ cup flour
1⅔ cups milk
salt and pepper
1 tsp prepared mustard
⅓ cup grated Cheddar cheese
2 egg whites, stiffly beaten
grated Parmesan cheese
paprika

Break cauliflower into flowerets, removing any really thick stalks. Sprinkle with lemon juice and poach in lightly salted water until soft. Do not overcook. Drain well, then place in buttered pie dish – the flowerets should just cover the base.

Melt butter and stir in flour. Stir for 1 minute, then remove saucepan from heat and slowly add milk. Return to heat, stir until thick, then remove and add salt, pepper, mustard and Cheddar cheese. Stir to melt, then cool.

When ready to serve, fold stiffly beaten egg whites into cheese sauce and spoon evenly over cauliflower. Sprinkle with Parmesan and paprika and bake at 400°F for 12 minutes until puffy and golden brown.
Serves 6.

## Greek-Style Squash

A simple medley of vegetables that is particularly good with roast lamb.

1 x 1¾ lb winter squash
3 tbsp oil
2 onions, chopped
2 tomatoes, skinned and
 chopped
2 garlic cloves, crushed
½ tsp ground cinnamon
½ tsp dried oregano
2 tbsp chopped parsley
½ cup chicken stock
2 tsp honey
salt and ground black pepper

Peel squash. Cut flesh into long strips, discard seeds and pith and cut into small dice – you should have about 1¼ lb.

 Heat oil in large saucepan and soften onions. Add tomatoes, garlic, cinnamon, oregano, parsley and squash. Toss to mix, then add stock – the amount depends on the juiciness of the tomatoes. Add honey and seasoning. Cover and simmer until squash is tender, stirring occasionally.
Serves 5–6.

### Note

*Origanum vulgare* **is closely related to marjoram, but is more pungent in flavor, especially when dried. It is used extensively in Greek and Italian cooking, and is without equal for flavoring lamb and tomato dishes, pizzas and pasta. The name is derived from the Greek words for mountain, and joy, because of the way in which the herb proliferates on the hillsides of certain Greek islands.**

## Stuffed Squash

**Pattypans are rather quaint examples of the huge squash family. Serve them whole, or add interest by scooping out the insides, then filling them with a simple stuffing before popping the lids back on.**

6 x 2–2½ oz pattypan squash
¼ cup grated Cheddar cheese
2 green onions, chopped
2 tsp finely chopped parsley
generous pinch of ground mace
salt and ground black pepper
knob of butter

Wash and boil squash in a little salted water for about 12–15 minutes until just tender, but not too soft. Cool, slice off pointed tops and carefully scoop out most of the pulp. Chop, then mix with cheese, green onions and remaining ingredients. Fill shells and replace caps. Arrange in small baking dish brushed with oil, and heat through at 325°F for about 15 minutes.
Serves 6.

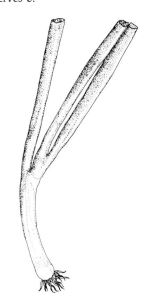

# Ratatouille with Olives

2 medium eggplants, diced
2 large zucchini, or 6 small ones,
  peeled and sliced
¼ cup olive oil
1 large onion, sliced
3 tomatoes, skinned and
  chopped
1 large red Bell pepper, seeded
  and diced
1 garlic clove, crushed
½ tsp dried basil
salt and ground black pepper
pinch of sugar
⅓ cup black olives, pitted and
  sliced

Dégorge (see box) eggplant and
zucchini. Heat the olive oil in a
large, heavy saucepan and fry
onion until soft but not browned.
Turn heat to very low and toss in
the eggplant, zucchini, tomatoes,
red bell pepper, garlic, basil and salt
and pepper.

  Simmer very gently, half-
covered, for about 45 minutes,
stirring occasionally. Vegetables
should be soft, but not mushy, with
very little liquid. Add sugar and
olives, and adjust seasoning. Stir to
mix and serve with broiled steak or
a roast. Cool if serving as a first
course. I like to top the cold
ratatouille with a little sour cream
and snipped chives, although this is
taking a great liberty with a
traditional Provençal dish.
Serves 4–6.

**TO DÉGORGE EGGPLANT,
ZUCCHINI AND CUCUMBERS**
Remove stem and calyx and
slice or dice vegetable. Score
the surface of the flesh,
sprinkle with salt and leave
on a tilted plate or in a
colander for about 30
minutes, so that the liquid
can run off. Rinse off excess
salt and dry thoroughly with
absorbent paper towels
before proceeding with the
recipe.

**TO SKIN TOMATOES**
Pour boiling water over,
stand for 5 minutes, then
rinse under cold water. Skins
should slip off easily. Nick
out stem end before using.

## Ground Beef and Pasta Casserole

First cousin to lasagne, but without mozzarella or ricotta cheese or the traditional Bolognese sauce. Although I prefer this ratio of noodles to ground beef, as the result is never stodgy, 11 oz noodles may be used if you wish to make the dish go further.

9 oz medium ribbon noodles

CHEESE SAUCE
3 tbsp butter
6 tbsp flour
1½ pints milk
1 tsp dry mustard
scant 1 cup grated Cheddar
  cheese
salt and pepper

MEAT SAUCE
3 tbsp oil
1 large onion, chopped
1 large celery stalk, sliced
2 garlic cloves, crushed
1–1¼ lb lean ground beef
1 x 14 fl oz can tomato soup
1 tsp dried oregano
½ tsp dried basil
2 tbsp chopped parsley
grated Parmesan cheese

Boil noodles in plenty of salted water. Drain and toss with a little oil to keep the strands separate.

Make the cheese sauce by melting the butter and stirring in the flour. Remove from heat and gradually stir in the milk, preferably heated. Return to heat and stir until thick, then beat in mustard, cheese and seasoning.

For the meat sauce, heat oil and soften onion, celery and garlic. Add meat and toss until no longer red. Add tomato soup, herbs, parsley and 1 cup of the cheese sauce. Mix well and season.

Grease a 12 x 8-in baking dish. Cover the base with half the noodles. Spoon over half the meat mixture, top with the remaining noodles, then with the remaining meat mixture. Pour the remaining cheese sauce over to cover completely. Sprinkle over a little grated Parmesan cheese. Bake, uncovered, at 325°F for 50 minutes. Serves 8–10.

# Mediterranean Vegetable Sauce for Pasta

Regard this as a basic recipe, as other vegetables, such as mushrooms or zucchini, may be added or substituted. The following is a good, simple version, which cooks into a delicious, thick stew. Ladle it over pasta and top each serving with sour cream mixed with chives, then sprinkle with crumbled feta.

3 tbsp vegetable oil
3 tbsp olive oil
4 large leeks, thinly sliced
3 garlic cloves, crushed
1 green Bell pepper, seeded and diced
2 celery stalks, sliced
2 medium eggplants, rinsed and diced
3 medium tomatoes, skinned and chopped
5 tsp tomato paste
1 tsp dried basil
2 tbsp chopped parsley
salt and ground black pepper
1 tsp sugar
½ cup stock or water
sliced black olives (optional)

Heat oils in a very large, heavy skillet. Add leeks and garlic. Reduce heat to low and simmer, covered, until soft. Add green pepper, celery, eggplant, tomatoes, tomato paste, basil, parsley, seasoning, sugar and stock. Cover and simmer for about 45 minutes, stirring occasionally and adding more liquid as required for the gravy – up to 1 cup. The mixture should not be dry or too watery – bear in mind that it should be thick enough to coat the pasta. Adjust seasoning and, if desired, add a few sliced black olives just before serving.
Serves 4.

# Noodles with Spinach, Mushrooms and Cheese

1–1¼ lb frozen spinach, thawed
9 oz medium ribbon noodles
3 tbsp oil
¾ lb brown mushrooms, wiped and sliced
1 onion, chopped
1 tsp chopped fresh rosemary needles
5 tsp soy sauce
1½ cups low-fat soft cheese
4 large green onions, chopped
2 eggs
1 cup buttermilk
salt and ground black pepper
2 tomatoes, thinly sliced
2 garlic cloves, crushed
dried oregano
mozzarella cheese
¼ cup grated Parmesan cheese

Drain spinach in a colander, pressing out all moisture with a wooden spoon. Boil noodles, drain and toss with a little oil.

Heat the oil and sauté mushrooms, onion and rosemary. When onions are browned, remove from heat and add soy sauce.

In a large bowl mix the spinach, cheese and green onions (add some of the green tops). Beat eggs with buttermilk, salt and pepper and add. Stir in the mushroom mixture and noodles. Spoon into a greased 11 x 9-in baking dish. Cover top with tomatoes and sprinkle over garlic and oregano. Top with a thick layer of thinly sliced mozzarella, and finally sprinkle with Parmesan. Bake at 325°F for 45 minutes then turn off oven and leave for about 10 minutes to settle before serving. This dish does not reheat successfully.
Serves 6.

## Ground Beef, Mushroom and Pasta Casserole

A comforting, informal supper dish, using a modest amount of pasta to ensure that it remains succulent and moist. Team with a crisp salad and a hot garlic loaf.

good ¾ lb small egg noodles
3 tbsp butter
½ cup flour
1½ pints milk
salt and pepper
3 tbsp oil
2 onions, chopped
2 garlic cloves, crushed
1 green Bell pepper, seeded and diced
scant ¾ lb mushrooms, wiped and sliced
1–1¼ lb ground beef
1 tsp dried oregano
2 x 14 fl oz can mushroom soup

3 tbsp soy sauce
grated mozzarella and Parmesan cheese

Boil noodles in plenty of salted water, drain, then toss with a little oil and set aside.

Make a thick white sauce with butter, flour and milk. Season, cover and set aside.

Heat oil in a large skillet and add onions, garlic, green pepper and mushrooms. When softened, add ground beef and oregano. Toss until meat turns brown, then spoon contents of pan into a large bowl. Stir in soup, 1 cup of the white sauce, soy sauce, a little salt and pepper, and the noodles.

Spoon into a large, lightly oiled baking dish. Cover and bake at 325°F for 30 minutes. Remove from oven and pour over the remaining 2 cups white sauce. Sprinkle generously with grated cheeses and return to oven for about 25 minutes until hot and bubbling.
Serves 8.

## Pasta with Mushroom Sauce

I find this recipe a real life-saver – all you need are a few basic ingredients and 20 minutes in hand to produce a delicious meal for 4–6 people. Protein is added by tossing the spaghetti with some chopped nuts, and topping each serving with Parmesan, Cheddar or, for a change, feta cheese.

about ¾ lb spaghetti, fettucine, tagliatelle or noodles
2 tbsp butter
3 tbsp oil
4 leeks, thinly sliced
2 celery stalks, chopped
1 green Bell pepper, seeded and diced
1–1¼ lb brown mushrooms, wiped and sliced
1 fresh rosemary sprig, chopped

2 garlic cloves, crushed
¼ cup flour
1½ cups hot stock
¼ cup soy sauce
¼ cup sherry
¼ cup sour cream

While pasta is cooking in plenty of boiling salted water, heat butter and oil in a large saucepan and add leeks, celery and green pepper. When beginning to soften, add mushrooms, rosemary and garlic. Toss over medium heat until smelling really good, then sprinkle in the flour and stir to mix. Slowly add stock, soy sauce and sherry. Stir well and then allow to thicken slowly, half-covered. Just before serving, swirl in the sour cream and spoon onto hot drained pasta.
Serves 4–6.

## Spinach Pesto

Pesto is surely one of the greatest of Italian sauces. It is very rich and highly flavored, so a little goes a long way – 3 tbsp on top of a serving of pasta is sufficient. A departure from the traditional recipe is the use of Cheddar cheese instead of Parmesan. If you prefer the latter, use less. I have also used walnuts instead of pine nuts. A processor is essential for this recipe.

2 bunches of young spinach
   leaves
⅔ cup walnuts
4 garlic cloves
6 sprigs fresh basil leaves
1 cup grated Cheddar cheese
salt and ground black pepper
1 cup vegetable oil
¼ cup olive oil

Trim and wash spinach – you'll need 1–1¼ lb leaves, weighed after preparation. Cook in the water adhering to the leaves until soft. Drain well, pressing out moisture with a wooden spoon. Using the metal blade, process the walnuts, garlic and basil until finely chopped. Add the cooked spinach, cheese and seasoning. Process again, and then add the olive and vegetable oils in a slow steady stream. You should end up with a thick, creamy green mixture. Spoon into storage jars, run a thin film of oil over the top and refrigerate. It will keep for several days.

Before serving, stir well and stand at room temperature for 30 minutes. Make sure that the pasta and the plates are very hot because the sauce is not heated.

### Note
My interpretation of traditional Pesto can be found on page 31.

## Easy Pizza with Wholewheat Crust

There are surely more varieties of pizza than there are roads in Rome – not only with regard to the topping, but also the base. Traditionally, it's a yeast dough which I, personally, find very often dry. The following is a quick alternative.

CRUST
1 cup wholewheat flour
1 cup all-purpose flour
½ tsp salt
1 tsp baking powder
5 tbsp oil
scant ½ cup skimmed milk
2 tsp lemon juice

TOPPING
scant ½ cup tomato sauce
2 tsp Worcestershire sauce
½ tsp each dried oregano and
    thyme
2 tomatoes, sliced
1 onion, coarsely grated
2 garlic cloves, crushed
grated Cheddar and Parmesan
    cheese
anchovies, black olives, cooked
    mushrooms (optional)
olive oil
½ tsp garlic salt

To make the crust, mix flours, salt and baking powder. Add oil, milk and lemon juice. Quickly mix to a ball – use an electric beater if possible – and press evenly onto the base of a lightly oiled 13 x 8-in jelly roll tin, or a pizza pan.

Mix tomato sauce, Worcestershire sauce and herbs and spread over the dough, right to the edges. Cover with tomatoes, onion and garlic. Sprinkle thickly with Cheddar cheese and dust with Parmesan. If using, soak anchovies in milk. Top pizza with anchovies, olives and mushrooms, if desired. Dribble the top with a little olive oil, sprinkle with garlic salt and bake at 400°F for about 30 minutes, until bubbly and cooked. Cut into fingers and serve very hot. Serves about 8.

### Hint
Traditionally, soft, white Italian mozzarella should be used instead of Cheddar cheese. It is the perfect pizza cheese, melting to a golden-brown blanket. Use sliced rather than grated.

## Stuffed Bell Peppers

These peppers make a lovely light lunch or, served in smaller portions, an appetizer.

3 very large or 6 medium green
   Bell peppers
1 tbsp oil
1 tbsp butter
1 onion, chopped
2 garlic cloves, crushed
good ⅓ cup long-grain rice
½ tsp each ground turmeric,
   cumin and fennel seed
1 tsp ground coriander
2 tomatoes, skinned and
   chopped
1 cup chicken stock
1 bay leaf
salt and ground black pepper
pinch of sugar
1 x 7 oz can shrimps, drained
   and rinsed
3 tbsp shredded coconut
sour cream and paprika

Halve large bell peppers or slice tops off medium ones. Remove seeds and white ribs and drop into a large saucepan of boiling water, pressing down gently to submerge. Boil for 5 minutes, then drain.

Heat oil and butter and soften onion and garlic. Add rice and spices and toss over low heat for 1 minute. Add tomatoes, stock, bay leaf, salt, pepper and sugar. Cover and simmer gently for about 25 minutes until rice is cooked. Remove bay leaf and add shrimps and coconut, tossing with a fork until mixed.

Arrange peppers, hollows up, close together in shallow baking dish. Spoon in rice mixture, pour 1 cup water round, then cover and bake at 325°F for 30–40 minutes, until soft. Top each pepper with 2 tsp sour cream, dust with paprika and return to oven, uncovered, for 10 minutes.
Serves 3 or 6.

## Stir-Fry with Mushrooms and Sprouts

oil for frying
4 leeks, thinly sliced
1 small onion, chopped
2 celery stalks, sliced
2 medium carrots, cut in julienne
2 garlic cloves, crushed
about ¾ lb mushrooms, wiped
   and sliced
3 cups shredded cabbage
½ cucumber, peeled and cubed
scant 1 cup lentil sprouts
¼ cup soy sauce
good ¾ cup chicken stock
4 tsp cornstarch
pinch of sugar
toasted almonds

In a large skillet or wok heat ¼ cup oil and stir-fry leeks, onion, celery, carrots and garlic. After about 5

minutes on medium heat, transfer to a large, warmed dish and place in preheated 325°F oven.

To pan add a little more oil and add mushrooms, cabbage and cucumber. Sauté until softened, stirring, then add the sprouts, soy sauce and stock mixed with cornstarch and sugar. Cover and simmer for a few minutes, then mix into the other vegetables in the oven dish. Return to oven for about 10 minutes, then serve on rice and top with plenty of toasted almonds. It should not be necessary to add salt.
Serves 4–6.

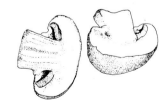

## Vegetable Paella

¼ cup vegetable oil
¼ cup olive oil
2 large leeks, sliced
1 onion, chopped
3 garlic cloves, crushed
1 green Bell pepper, seeded and
  diced
1⅓ cups brown rice
¾ lb mushrooms, wiped and
  sliced
good ½ lb eggplant, diced †
1 tsp each dried oregano, basil
  and turmeric
3 medium tomatoes, skinned
  and chopped
3 cups chopped green beans or
  3 cups peas
2 tbsp chopped parsley
salt and ground black pepper
pinch of sugar
1 cup chicken or vegetable stock
½ cup white wine
2–2½ cups diced feta or grated
  Cheddar cheese

Using a large saucepan or wok,
heat oils and add leeks, onion,
garlic and pepper. When softened,
add rice and toss until coated with
oil. Reduce heat and add
mushrooms, eggplant, herbs and
turmeric. Toss for a minute or two,
then add tomatoes, the beans or
peas, parsley, seasoning, sugar,
stock and wine.

  Mix well, then turn into a large
baking dish. Cover and bake at
350°F for 35 minutes. Stir lightly
with a fork, then continue baking
for another 20–25 minutes until
vegetables are cooked and the
liquid absorbed. The mixture
should be moist but not at all
watery. Turn off oven heat and
cover top with diced feta or grated
Cheddar, and return to oven for
5–10 minutes to heat through.
Serves 6.

† Large eggplants need to be
dégorged before use. See page
135 for instructions.

## Lentil Salad

**This is a favorite summer salad.
Surround with wedges of hard-
boiled eggs, and serve with
cheese and wholewheat bread
for a nourishing, complete meal.**

2 cups brown lentils, rinsed
  and picked over
1½ pints water
½ tsp salt
2 bay leaves
½ tsp turmeric
scant ½ cup French dressing
  (page 47)
3–4 green onions, chopped
2 large carrots, grated
2–3 celery stalks, chopped
¼ cup chopped parsley
1¾ cups mung bean sprouts (or
  sprouts of choice)
5 tsp soy sauce

Put lentils into saucepan with
water, salt, bay leaves and turmeric.

Bring to a boil, then cover and
simmer gently until soft and liquid
has been absorbed Tip into a large
bowl and discard bay leaves. Fork
in the dressing, taking care not to
mash the lentils. Add green onions,
carrots, celery, parsley, sprouts and
soy sauce. Toss lightly to mix, and
then set aside, covered, for about
2 hours – or chill for longer. Serve
as suggested – or brighten up the
lentils by dribbling over a little
plain yogurt and topping with
chopped mint, or substitute sour
cream and sprinkle with nuts.
Serves 6.

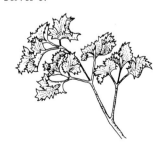

# Spinach Pancakes

or Crêpes Florentine. This dish can be prepared in advance and baked when required. The pancake batter and the cheese sauce are both made in a blender.

CRÊPES
**1 cup flour
generous pinch of salt
1 egg and 1 egg yolk
1 cup milk
½ cup water
5 tsp oil**

FILLING
**1–1¼ lb frozen spinach, thawed
generous pinch of salt
generous pinch of freshly grated
    nutmeg**

SAUCE
**2⅓ cups milk
¼ cup flour
1 cup grated Gruyère cheese
½ tsp each dry mustard and salt
3 tbsp butter, softened
grated Parmesan cheese
paprika**

Put ingredients for crêpes into blender, blend well and stand for at least 30 minutes. The consistency should be creamy and medium-thick, and the batter will be enough for 10 crêpes, 7–8-in in diameter. Stack, after cooking, with sheets of waxed paper between each crêpe.

For the filling, cook spinach, drain very well in colander and press out all moisture. Season with salt and nutmeg.

For sauce, put ½ cup milk, flour, Gruyère cheese, mustard, salt and butter into blender, blend well and then pour into saucepan and cook over low heat, stirring, until thick and cheese has melted. Stir ½ cup of this sauce into the spinach purée. Fill each crêpe with a large spoonful of the purée and roll into cigar shapes. Place side by side, close together in a shallow, buttered baking dish. Thin the remaining cheese sauce with remaining milk and pour over crêpes. Sprinkle generously with Parmesan (or Cheddar or Gruyère if preferred) and dust with paprika. Bake at 350°F for 30 minutes. Serves 10 as a first or 5 as a main course.

## Italian Quiche

Baked in a 12-in pizza pan, this is a huge and hearty quiche with a wholewheat crust and a ratatouille-style filling.

PROCESSOR PASTRY
**1 cup wholewheat flour**
**½ cup all-purpose flour**
**½ tsp salt**
**½ cup butter, diced**
**2 tsp lemon juice**
**scant ¼ cup cold water**

FILLING
**¼ cup oil**
**2 leeks, chopped**
**1 small onion, chopped**
**1 green Bell pepper, seeded and diced**
**2 garlic cloves, crushed**
**good ½ lb zucchini, peeled and diced**
**good ½ lb eggplant, diced**
**½ tsp salt**
**ground black pepper**
**¼ cup chopped parsley**
**½ tsp dried oregano**
**generous pinch of dried basil**
**¾ cup cream cheese**
**1½ cups milk**
**3 eggs**
**1 large tomato, thinly sliced**
**scant 1 cup grated Cheddar cheese**
**3 tbsp grated Parmesan cheese**

To make the pastry, use the metal blade to mix the flours, salt and butter until finely blended. With the motor running, add lemon juice and water. Stop as soon as it forms a ball, turn out onto floured board and roll out, using a floured rolling pin. Using fingers, press into pizza pan, flute edges, prick well and chill.

For the filling, heat oil in a large pan and sauté leeks, onion, pepper and garlic. When translucent, add zucchini and eggplant, then season with salt and pepper. Cover and cook over low heat, stirring occasionally until soft. Spoon into a bowl. Add parsley and dried herbs. Cool.

Bake chilled crust at 400°F for 12 minutes. Brush about 1 tbsp flour over base. Spoon in vegetable filling. Beat cream cheese, milk, eggs and large pinch of salt. Arrange tomato over vegetables, pour custard over, sprinkle with cheeses and bake at 350°F for 30–35 minutes. Turn off oven and leave for 20 minutes. Serve with a salad. Serves 8.

## Asparagus and Green Onion Quiche

CRUST
1½ cups flour
generous pinch of salt
generous pinch of baking
 powder
scant ½ cup oil
¼ cup iced water
squeeze of lemon juice
2 tsp cornstarch

FILLING
1 x 1 lb can asparagus spears,
 well drained
6 green onions, chopped
1½ cups low-fat soft cheese
½ tsp dried tarragon
½ tsp salt
ground black pepper
3 eggs
½ cup milk
½ cup light cream

3 tbsp chopped parsley
paprika and grated Gruyère

To make the crust, sift flour, salt
and baking powder. Add oil, water
and lemon juice. Mix lightly with a
fork, shape into a ball and roll out
thinly between two sheets of
waxed paper. Line a deep, 9-in
fluted tart pan, prick well and bake
at 400°F for 15 minutes. Remove
and dust base with cornstarch.
Cool.

 If asparagus stems are thick, slice
in half lengthwise and arrange on
base of crust, together with green
onions. Beat cheese with tarragon,
salt and pepper. Beat in eggs, one at a
time, followed by the milk, cream
and parsley. Pour carefully onto
crust, dust with paprika and sprinkle
with Gruyère. Reduce oven
temperature to 350°F and heat a
cookie sheet in it for a few minutes.
Place tart pan on the hot tray and
bake for 45 minutes or until set.
Serves 6–8.

## Stuffed Baked Potatoes

4 large baking potatoes
2 tbsp butter, melted
about ⅔ cup milk, heated
1 cup grated Cheddar cheese
salt and ground black pepper
½ tsp prepared mustard
3 tbsp chopped parsley
paprika

Scrub potatoes, rub skins with oil
and bake at 400°F for about 1 hour
until soft. Either slice in half
lengthwise and serve half per
person, or slice off just the tops.
Scoop flesh into a bowl, leaving a
firm shell. Mash with the melted
butter and milk, then add
remaining ingredients, except
paprika. Pile into shells, brush
lightly with milk and dust with
paprika. Reheat at 350°F.
Serves 4–8.

## Tuna-Stuffed Potatoes

4 large baking potatoes
1 x 7 oz can tuna in brine,
 drained and shredded
2 tsp capers, rinsed and chopped
1 tsp lemon juice
¼ cup mayonnaise
salt and ground black pepper
scant ⅓ cup milk, heated
grated Cheddar cheese
butter

Pre-heat oven to 400°F. Prepare
potatoes and bake as in previous
recipe. Reduce oven temperature to
350°F. Scoop out flesh into a bowl,
leaving shells intact. Mash potato
and add remaining ingredients
except cheese and butter. Pile into
shells and top with cheese and a
knob of butter. Return to oven
until cheese has melted.
Serves 4–8.

## Phyllo Packages

1 lb frozen phyllo pastry, thawed in refrigerator for 24 hours

CHICKEN, CHEESE AND SPINACH FILLING
4 chicken breasts (about 1–1¼ lb with bone)
salted water
1 onion, chopped
few parsley sprigs
1 bay leaf
1 whole carrot
2 tbsp butter
1–1¼ lb frozen spinach, thawed
2 leeks, finely chopped
1½ cups low-fat soft cheese
¼ cup grated Parmesan
1 tsp chopped fresh rosemary needles
salt and ground black pepper

EGG AND LEMON SAUCE
2 tbsp butter

¼ cup flour
2 cups hot, seasoned chicken stock
2 egg yolks
5 tsp lemon juice
generous pinch of finely grated lemon zest
pinch of sugar

Poach breasts in plenty of salted water together with onion, parsley, bay leaf and carrot. When done, remove skin and bone and chop into small dice. Strain and reserve stock for sauce. Melt butter and add spinach and leeks. Cook over low heat until all moisture has evaporated. Combine chicken, spinach, low-fat and Parmesan cheeses, rosemary and seasoning and work into a smooth mixture.

Remove 3 sheets of phyllo — they should measure about 17 x 15 in. Brush top sheet with oil, garlic oil or melted butter. Place a mound of filling in the center and then draw up the corners to form a

package, twisting the top to seal. Brush outside of package with oil or butter and sprinkle lightly with water. Make 7 more packages in the same way, place on 2 large, oiled cookie sheets and bake at 400°F for 20 minutes until golden brown.

While they are baking, make the sauce. Melt butter, stir in flour. When straw-colored, remove from stove and slowly add stock. Return to heat and stir until thickened. Beat egg yolks with lemon juice and zest, stir in a little of the hot sauce, then return to heat and stir until cooked and creamy. Adjust seasoning and add pinch sugar. Serve with chicken packages, rice, and a salad.
Makes 8 packages.

### Note
**Tissue-thin, feathery phyllo pastry requires special treatment. Refer to page 220 for full instructions.**

## Sprout, Feta and Almond Filling

**As a delicious alternative, try this vegetarian mixture when making phyllo packages.**

3 cups mung bean sprouts
½ lb feta cheese, rinsed and diced
2 tbsp chopped toasted almonds
2 egg yolks
5 tsp soy sauce
2 celery stalks, finely chopped
6 green onions, chopped
4 small zucchini, peeled and coarsely grated
pinch of sugar

Combine ingredients and make and bake 6 packages as in previous recipe. Serve with a creamy cabbage salad.
Makes 6 packages.

Mushroom Roulade

## *Mushroom Roulade*

A soufflé-type roll with a filling – this is a sophisticated first or light main course which really is not all that difficult to make. Perhaps the most difficult part is achieving a really smooth panada, but it is possible to cheat a little and start it off in a blender.

ROULADE
**4 tbsp butter, softened**
**½ cup all-purpose flour**
**2 cups milk**
**½ tsp salt**
**1 tsp dry mustard**
**1 tsp sugar**
**4 eggs, separated**

FILLING
**3 tbsp oil**
**about ¾ lb button mushrooms, wiped and chopped**
**1–2 garlic cloves, crushed**
**1 tsp chopped fresh rosemary**
**1½ cups low-fat soft cheese**
**4–6 green onions, chopped**
**1 tbsp finely chopped parsley**
**salt and ground black pepper**
**pinch of sugar**

TOPPING
**1 cup sour cream**
**chopped chives**

Put butter, flour and milk into blender, and blend until well mixed. Pour into a heavy-based saucepan and bring to a boil, using a balloon whisk to bring mixture to a very thick and smooth consistency. Allow 1–2 minutes for flour to cook. Remove and add salt, mustard and sugar and beat well.

Beat egg yolks, mix in a little of the hot sauce, then stir into rest of sauce. Beat well, then fold in the stiffly beaten egg whites. Be gentle but thorough. Oil a 13 x 8-in jelly roll pan, line with waxed paper, allowing an overhang at the ends,

brush with oil again and dust with flour, shaking off excess. Pour in soufflé mixture, spreading evenly, and bake just below center of oven at 325°F for 1 hour, or until risen, firm and golden brown. Loosen edges with a knife, invert onto a large sheet of waxed paper, remove backing paper and roll up. Cool.

To make the filling, heat oil and briskly fry mushrooms, garlic and rosemary until all liquid has evaporated – mixture must be dry. Tip into a bowl and leave until cold, then add remaining ingredients, combining thoroughly. Unroll roulade, spread with filling, and re-roll. When required, reheat in low oven, and serve in thick slices with the sour cream and chive topping.
Serves 8 generously.

## *Smoked Salmon Roulade*

A delicious alternative.

**1½ cups cream cheese**
**¼ lb smoked salmon, chopped**
**generous pinch of finely grated lemon rind**
**2 green onions, chopped**
**ground black pepper**
**3 tbsp sour cream**
**pinch of sugar**

TOPPING
**1 cup sour cream**
**chopped chives**

Following instructions in the previous recipe, make the roulade.

Combine ingredients, spread over baked roll, roll up and serve at room temperature with the sour cream and chive topping.
Serves 8 generously.

## Spinach and Brown Mushroom Quiche

*A substantial, large, cheesy quiche, which reheats well.*

PASTRY
scant 1 cup all-purpose flour
scant 1 cup wholewheat flour
pinch of salt
¼ lb butter
good ¼ cup iced water
squeeze of lemon juice
1 egg, separated

FILLING
1–1¼ lb frozen spinach, thawed
generous pinch of salt
½ tsp dried dill
3 tbsp oil
2 tbsp butter
about ¾ lb brown mushrooms,
   wiped and roughly chopped
2 leeks, sliced
1 small onion, chopped

1 fresh rosemary sprig
salt and ground black pepper
1 cup milk
2 eggs plus reserved yolk
½ cup sour cream
1 tsp French mustard
1 cup grated Gruyère or
   Cheddar cheese
½ tsp dried oregano

To make pastry, mix flours and salt. Rub in butter until crumbly, then bind with water and lemon juice. Form into a ball and chill for about 30 minutes, then roll out and line a deep 11-in diameter quiche pan. Prick well and bake at 400°F, just below center of oven for 20 minutes. Brush with lightly beaten egg white (reserve yolk for filling) and return to oven for 5 minutes.

For filling, drain spinach well, pressing out all moisture, then season with salt and dill. Heat oil and butter and sauté mushrooms, leeks, onion and rosemary. When semi-cooked, remove rosemary

and season the mixture lightly. Beat milk with eggs and egg yolk, sour cream, mustard, salt and pepper. Spread drained spinach over crust and spoon mushroom mixture over. Pour egg mixture over, sprinkle with cheese and oregano and bake at 325°F for 45 minutes or until set. Serves 8.

## Variation

SPINACH AND CHEESE QUICHE
9–10 oz frozen spinach, thawed
   and well drained
1½ cups low-fat soft cheese
½ tsp salt
generous pinch of freshly grated
   nutmeg
2 eggs, beaten
½ cup sour cream
1 small onion, grated
¼ cup chopped parsley
1 tbsp grated Parmesan cheese

Combine spinach, low fat cheese, salt and nutmeg. Add eggs, sour cream, onion and parsley. Pour into crust and sprinkle with Parmesan. Bake at 350°F for 30 minutes. Serve warm, rather than hot. Serves 8.

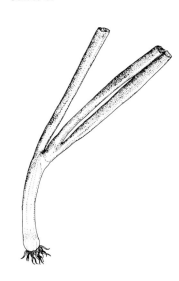

# Chilled White Mushroom and Cheese Tart

For a light lunch, an unusual appetizer, or as part of a cold buffet, this quiche is a winner. I have used a bland crumb crust which does not interfere with the delicate filling, and a garnish of sliced avocado dusted with milled black pepper ensures that no-one mistakes it for cheesecake – which it closely resembles in appearance. Use a deep 8-in pie dish, make it several hours in advance, and keep refrigerated.

CRUST
2 cups crushed savory crackers
scant ½ cup butter, melted

FILLING
3 tbsp oil
6 green onions, chopped
about ¾ lb white button
    mushrooms, wiped and sliced
1 garlic clove, crushed
2 fresh rosemary sprigs
salt and ground black pepper
1½ cups low-fat soft cheese
2 eggs, separated
4 tsp powdered gelatin
good ¾ cup chicken stock
½ cup whipping cream, whipped
few drops of Worcestershire
    sauce
pinch of sugar

Mix ingredients for crust and press onto base of greased pie dish. Chill.

Heat oil in large skillet and add green onions, mushrooms, garlic and rosemary. Toss over high heat for 3 minutes until starting to shrink and soften. Remove and set aside, and season when cold, so that juices are not extracted.

Beat cheese and yolks together until smooth. Soften gelatin in the stock, dissolve over low heat and gradually beat into cheese mixture. Add mushroom mixture to cheese mixture, discarding rosemary. Chill until starting to thicken – this takes a while. Beat egg whites with a pinch of salt and fold in together with cream, Worcestershire sauce and sugar. Pour onto crust and chill until set. Garnish just before serving.
Serves 8.

## Oranges with Sabayon Grand Marnier

Just the thing with which to round off a heavy dinner. Those who want fresh fruit can simply have a serving of orange slices; others can smother them with the sybaritic sabayon. This is often made with sherry, sometimes with rum, but Grand Marnier is good here because it complements the oranges. Brandy or whisky, however, would also be suitable.

oranges
granulated sugar

SABAYON
**6 egg yolks**
**½ cup granulated sugar**
**2 tsp cornstarch**
**⅓ cup Grand Marnier**
**good ¾ cup whipping cream,
    whipped**

Peel and thinly slice as many oranges as you'll need. Remove pith and pips. Layer on flat glass dish, sprinkle with just a little granulated sugar and pour over any juice that escaped on the cutting board. Cover and chill all day to allow the juices to "draw." Don't be tempted to make a sugar syrup — the beauty of this dessert lies in the fresh, raw orange, with the rich, sweet sauce. However, if desired, the slices may be sprinkled with very finely shredded zest cooked until soft in a light syrup.

To make the sabayon, put egg yolks, sugar and cornstarch in top of double saucepan and beat, using a balloon whisk, over gently simmering water. When very thick and light add Grand Marnier. Now stir over the simmering water with a wooden spoon until the custard is thick. It must thicken, or it will separate on standing, but it must not cook, or it will curdle. Pour into a bowl, cover once cooled, and chill thoroughly.

Just before serving, fold in cream gently but thoroughly, then pour into a large and pretty container, like a colored glass goblet. The sabayon should not be poured, but ladled over each serving.
Quantities can easily be halved.
Makes about 2½ cups of sauce.

Pavlova with Fruit and Cream

## Pavlova with Fruit and Cream

Pavlova is an Australian specialty, also claimed by New Zealand. Crisp outside, soft underneath, topped with fruit and cream. Traditionally it should be made in a pie dish, but I prefer a free-standing circle.

MERINGUE
3 egg whites
pinch of salt
scant 1 cup granulated sugar
2 tsp cider vinegar
2 tsp cornstarch

FILLING
1 x 1 lb 14 oz can peach slices
pulp of 6 fresh passion fruit
2 firm bananas, sliced and tossed in lemon juice
1 cup whipping cream
1 tbsp confectioners' sugar
few drops of vanilla extract

For the meringue beat egg whites with a pinch of salt until foamy, using an electric beater. Gradually beat in the granulated sugar, a spoonful at a time. Beat until stiff. Using a metal spoon, fold in the vinegar and cornstarch lightly but thoroughly. Spoon meringue onto cookie sheet brushed with oil and dusted with cornstarch – make a circle with a fairly thick base and a raised edge. Bake at 275°F for 1 hour. Do not open the oven door at all during the baking period. After an hour, turn off the heat and leave until absolutely cold, preferably overnight. Remove carefully, peeling off the foil slowly, and put on serving plate.

The filling can be prepared ahead and piled in just before serving. Drain peaches well, add passion fruit and bananas, cover and set aside. Whip cream with confectioners' sugar and vanilla extract and chill. To serve, fold fruit into cream and fill shell. Serves 8.

## Chocolate-Swirled Rum Crèmes

A tot of rum and circles of melted chocolate make this rich, custard-based dessert both decorative and delicious.

2 tsp powdered gelatin
¼ cup cold water
1½ cups milk
1 vanilla pod
2 eggs, separated
3 tbsp granulated sugar
pinch of salt
1 tsp cornstarch
3 tbsp dark rum
½ cup whipping cream, whipped

TOPPING
3 tbsp milk chocolate
5 tsp water

Soften gelatin in cold water. Scald milk with vanilla. Mix yolks with sugar, salt and cornstarch. Pour on a little hot milk, stir to mix, then return to saucepan and heat, stirring, until mixture coats the back of a wooden spoon. Remove from heat and stir in gelatin. Pour into a bowl and add rum. Cool and then chill briefly, or stir over ice until beginning to thicken. Beat egg whites until stiff but not dry and fold in together with cream. Pour into one large glass bowl, or 6–8 small bowls or glasses, and chill for 15 minutes.

Place chocolate and water in saucepan over hot water. Stir until very smooth and runny. Drop a large teaspoonful onto the top of each half-set crème and swirl in lightly (not deeply) in concentric circles, using the point of a skewer. Return to fridge and set firm. Serves 6–8.

## Coffee Vacherin with Cream and Fruit

**Crisp, coffee-flavored meringue rounds, sandwiched with whipped cream and pears or lychees – a sinfully sweet and irresistible dessert. The meringue rounds may be made days in advance and stored in an airtight container. Add the cream filling 4 hours before serving, and refrigerate. This softens the meringue slightly and makes for easier cutting.**

2 egg whites
¾ cup granulated sugar
2 tsp instant coffee powder
2 tsp water

FILLING
1 cup whipping cream
4 tsp confectioners' sugar
1 tsp instant coffee powder

1 tsp Tia Maria
1 x 14 oz can pears or lychees

Beat egg whites until stiff. Gradually add half the sugar, beating well, then beat in coffee powder dissolved in the water. Beat until very stiff then fold in the remaining granulated sugar, using a metal spoon. Lightly oil a large baking sheet, dust with cornstarch, and shake off the excess. Spoon on meringue to form two 8-in circles. Bake at 225°F for 1 hour 30 minutes, then turn off oven and leave until cold. Lift off sheet, and store, or fill.

Whip cream with confectioners' sugar. Dissolve coffee in liqueur, add to cream, and whip until stiff. Drain fruit thoroughly, dry well using absorbent paper towels, and then chop into small pieces. Fold into cream. Sandwich meringue rounds with half the cream and pile the remainder on top. Chill. Serves 8.

## Variation

ALMOND MERINGUE
Try this as an alternative to the Coffee Vacherin: Beat 4 egg whites until foamy. Gradually add scant ½ cup sugar, while beating. When very stiff, fold in another scant ½ cup sugar, using a metal spoon. Lastly fold in ⅔ cup ground almonds, then proceed as above.

## Sabayon Malibu

**Serve with fruit salad – include a can of mangoes for a tropical touch.**

4 egg yolks
⅓ cup granulated sugar
1 tsp cornstarch
5 tbsp Malibu
⅔ cup whipping cream, whipped

Using a balloon whisk, beat egg yolks, sugar and cornstarch in a small saucepan over gently simmering water. When thickened, stir in Malibu and continue stirring, using a wooden spoon, until mixture thickens again. Do not overheat, but the yolks must be cooked. Remove from heat, pour into a small bowl, cool, cover and chill. Fold in cream just before serving.
Makes about 1½ cups.

# Chocolate Liqueur Mousse

**As this mousse is very rich, serve small quantities in individual glasses.**

**about ¼ lb bittersweet chocolate**
**3 eggs, separated**
**5 tsp Crème de Cacao**
**1 tsp instant coffee powder**
**1 cup whipping cream, whipped**

Break up chocolate and melt in top of small double saucepan, having first smeared inside of container with a little melted butter. Don't stir more than is necessary to soften it completely.

Using an electric beater, beat egg yolks, liqueur and coffee powder. Add melted chocolate and beat well. Beat egg whites with a pinch of salt until stiff but not dry and using a metal spoon, fold in together with whipped cream. Keep folding until thoroughly combined, then pour into 6 glasses and chill for at least 4 hours. Serve plain, or decorate with chocolate curls, made by drawing a vegetable peeler down the long side of a warm slab of chocolate.
Serves 6.

## Variation
IRISH COFFEE CHOCOLATE MOUSSE
Substitute 3 tbsp Irish whiskey for the Crème de Cacao and add a few drops of vanilla with the cream.

# Chocolate Mousse Pie

**This is a simple, honest-to-goodness chocolate pie, which takes on a sophisticated flavor if decorated with rum-flavored whipped cream.**

CRUST
**2 tsp cocoa powder**
**scant ½ cup butter, melted**
**2 cups cookie crumbs**

FILLING
**1 cup milk**
**1½ oz bittersweet chocolate**
**1 tbsp cocoa powder**
**2 eggs, separated**
**⅓ cup granulated sugar**
**2 tsp powdered gelatin**
**¼ cup cold water**
**few drops of vanilla extract**
**½ cup whipping cream, whipped**

Dissolve cocoa powder in butter and mix with crumbs. Press into the base of a greased 8-in pie dish. Chill while making filling.

Scald milk, chocolate (broken into pieces) and cocoa powder, stirring to melt chocolate. Beat yolks with sugar, stir in a little hot milk mixture, then return to saucepan and cook over low heat, stirring, until thickened. Do not boil. Remove from heat. Soften gelatin in cold water then stir into custard. When dissolved, add vanilla and pour into bowl to cool. Chill until beginning to thicken. Stiffly beat egg whites with a pinch of salt, then fold in together with whipped cream. Pour into crust and chill until set.
Serves 6.

## Hint
**For the finest vanilla flavor, sink a vanilla pod into a jar of sugar or granulated sugar and keep on hand to use in desserts and cakes, instead of using sugar plus vanilla extract.**

Chocolate Pots

## Chocolate Pots

7 oz bittersweet chocolate,
  broken in pieces
¼ cup water
6 eggs, separated
1 tsp finely grated orange zest
¼ cup Curaçao

In the top of a double saucepan
melt chocolate in water. When
melted, turn heat to very low and
beat in egg yolks, one at a time,
using a wooden spoon. Stir well
after each addition and when thick
and smooth, remove from heat. Stir
in orange zest and Curaçao.

Leave to cool slightly. Beat egg
whites with a pinch of salt until stiff,
but not dry. Fold into chocolate
mixture until well blended, then
pour into 8 little pots. Set in
refrigerator for at least 4 hours.
Serve plain, or with a swirl of cream
and a little grated chocolate.
Serves 8.

## Chocolate Pudding

¼ lb bittersweet chocolate,
  broken in pieces
1 tsp instant coffee powder
2 tsp water
1 tbsp butter
2 tsp powdered gelatin,
  softened in 5 tsp cold water
few drops of vanilla extract
1 x 14 oz can evaporated milk,
  chilled and whipped
2 tsp lemon juice
¼ cup confectioners' sugar

Slowly melt chocolate, coffee,
water and butter in top of double
saucepan. When smooth remove
from heat and stir in gelatin until
dissolved. Add vanilla, allow to
cool slightly. Whip lemon juice and
confectioners' sugar into
evaporated milk until very stiff.
Beat in chocolate mixture slowly
then refrigerate.
Serves 8–10.

## Fraises Brûlée

or Burnt Strawberries – a
delicious combination of berries
and orange liqueur, topped with
cream and crusted with sugar.
Assembled in minutes, chilled
for 4 hours and then flashed
under the broiler just before
serving, it's a joy for the busy
cook. A 7-in heatproof pie dish
is essential.

2 cups ripe strawberries
¼ cup Curaçao
good ¾ cup whipping cream
½ tsp finely grated orange zest
¼ cup light brown sugar

Wash, hull and halve strawberries
and arrange to cover the base of
the pie dish. Sprinkle with Curaçao.
Whip cream with orange zest until
stiff, then spread over the fruit.
Sprinkle the sugar evenly over the
top. Leave in coldest part of
refrigerator for 4 hours.

Preheat broiler for several
minutes and place dish under heat
for about 1 minute. As soon as
sugar melts and darkens, remove
and serve.
Serves 4–5.

### Variation
GRAPE BRULÉE
Fill a 7-in heatproof dish with a
mixture of 1 sweet melon, cut into
small dice, 1½ cups halved and de-
pipped grapes, one piece finely
chopped preserved ginger and
scant ½ cup chopped hazelnuts.
Dribble with 3 tbsp ginger syrup.
Stiffly whip 1 cup cream with ½ tsp
ground cinnamon and pour over
fruit. Put in coldest part of
refrigerator for 6 hours. To serve,
sprinkle 3 tbsp light brown sugar
evenly over cream and place under
preheated broiler to melt sugar.
Serve at once.

Fruit Salad Special with Coffee Cream Topping

## Fruit Salad Special with Coffee Cream Topping

A simple but elegant fruit salad. The ingredients are rather special, so is the topping, and the color combination is superb. The effect will be lost if served in one big bowl so use 6 little glass dishes instead.

2 large bananas
1 large, firm avocado
24 strawberries
3 tbsp lemon juice
3 tbsp granulated sugar
toasted flaked almonds

CREAM TOPPING
1 cup whipping cream
5 tsp confectioners' sugar
2 tsp Kahlúa
1 tsp instant coffee powder

Slice bananas thinly, cut avocado into small dice and slice strawberries. Divide the fruit between the dishes, and to each dish add 1 tsp lemon juice and 1 tsp granulated sugar. Toss gently, then cover and chill.

Whip ingredients for cream topping together until soft peaks form. Do not over-beat. Cover and chill. Just before serving, pour a blanket of the coffee cream over each fruit salad, and sprinkle with the almonds.
Serves 6.

## Kiwi Fruit and Strawberries with Curaçao

A bright, refreshing dessert to serve at the end of a good dinner. For best effect, layer the red and green fruit in a large glass bowl, or in champagne glasses. Serve garnished with a sprig of mint, dribbled with a spoonful of sour cream, or topped with a small scoop of vanilla ice cream.

3 kiwi fruit
12–24 strawberries

SYRUP
½ cup water
¼ cup granulated sugar
1 tsp finely grated orange zest
¼ cup Curaçao

First make the syrup. Put water, sugar and zest into a small saucepan and boil rapidly for 2–3 minutes. Remove and add Curaçao.

Peel kiwi fruit and wash and hull strawberries. Slice both fruits into very thin rounds. Layer into bowl or glasses and strain 5 tsp of the syrup over each serving. Cover and chill for several hours.
Serves 6.

### Note
One is inclined to regard New Zealand as the home of kiwi fruit, but in fact it was originally imported from China, and known as the Chinese Gooseberry. Egg-shaped, with emerald green flesh, the flavor is a subtle combination of strawberry, orange, watermelon and banana and is wonderfully versatile, combining well with meat, fish and poultry. It is great for highlighting desserts and can also be made into jam.

Orange Liqueur Ice Cream

## Orange Liqueur Ice Cream

Serve fresh and pure; with chocolate sauce; or with Mandarin Orange Sauce Flambé.

4 eggs, separated
⅓ cup granulated sugar
1 tsp very finely grated orange zest
5 tbsp orange-flavored liqueur
1 cup heavy cream
few drops of vanilla extract

Using an electric beater, beat egg yolks, sugar, orange zest and liqueur at high speed for several minutes. Beat egg whites stiffly with a pinch of salt. When egg yolk mixture is thick and custardy, fold in whipped cream and egg whites. Finally add vanilla. Fold gently until well combined, then freeze quickly. Serves 6–8.

## Mandarin Orange Sauce Flambé

1 x 11 oz can mandarin oranges, drained
good ¾ cup fresh orange juice
¼ cup mixed candied peel
5 tsp honey
¼ cup seedless raisins
¼ cup chopped walnuts
5 tsp brandy

Mix all ingredients, except brandy, in a small bowl, cover and refrigerate up to 48 hours. To serve, heat thoroughly in small saucepan. Flame with the warmed brandy and serve at once. Makes about 1⅓ cups.

### Hint
Use pale, clear honey in baked desserts – the darker the honey, the stronger the flavor.

## Rich Coffee Ice Cream

This recipe was inspired by an ice cream I ate from a cone on a street corner near the Arab Market in Israel. It was quite superb and the color of mud and I would gladly have traded all my shekels for the recipe.

¼ cup instant coffee powder
scant ½ cup hot water
scant ½ cup granulated sugar
3 eggs, separated
1 cup heavy cream †
few drops of vanilla extract

In a large, deep mixing bowl dissolve the coffee powder in the hot water. Cool slightly, then add granulated sugar and egg yolks. Using an electric beater, beat very well at high speed for several minutes until the mixture becomes somewhat paler – or muddy – and slightly thickened. Beat the egg

whites with a pinch of salt until stiff. Whip cream and vanilla. Fold cream and egg whites into coffee mixture. Be gentle but very thorough – never beat it. Freeze quickly, in individual freezer ramekins, or in a 3½ pint container.

If using individual ramekins, decorate each with whipped cream and grated chocolate or chopped toasted nuts. If using a mold, line it first with plastic wrap, then unmold ice cream when firm. Garnish and then return to freezer until required. Alternatively, it may be dribbled with chocolate sauce. Serves about 8.

† For this and all ice creams, it is particularly important to use a good, thick, heavy cream.

Cold Christmas Pudding

# Ice Cream Christmas Pudding

**1 cup water**
**⅓ cup seedless raisins**
**3 tbsp mixed candied peel**
**12 cherries, chopped**
**3 tbsp chopped preserved ginger**
**½ tsp ground nutmeg**
**1 tsp ground cinnamon**
**½ cup nuts, chopped**
**3 cups very fine shortcake cookie crumbs**
**5 tsp brandy**
**5 tsp rum**
**4½ pints vanilla ice cream**
**¾–1 cup heavy cream confectioners' sugar rum**

Put water, raisins, candied peel, cherries, ginger and spices into a saucepan. Bring to a boil, then cover and simmer for 10 minutes.

Drain if necessary, then add nuts, cookie crumbs, brandy and rum. Mix well and cool.

Line a bombe mold with 3½ pints of the ice cream. Use the back of a spoon dipped in water and work quickly. Spoon the fruit mixture into the hollow in the middle. Cover with the remaining ice cream and freeze for 24 hours.

Unmold onto a freezer-proof serving plate – run base of mold under running tap, loosen round the top with a blunt knife or spatula, and ease out.

Whip cream stiffly with a little confectioners' sugar, and a large nip of rum. Cover entire surface of the bombe with the cream, either smoothly, flicked up with a spatula, or prettily piped. Return to freezer until required. Remove, decorate with holly and stand for about 5 minutes before serving. Serves about 12.

# Cold Christmas Pudding

**This is a superb alternative to hot plum pudding.**

**1½ cups mixed dried fruit**
**1 cup water**
**⅔ cup pitted dates, chopped**
**1 cup walnuts, chopped**
**⅓ cup maraschino cherries, chopped**
**1 packet lemon jello**
**1 cup hot water**
**½ cup white port**
**½ packet shortcake cookies**
**1 tsp ground mixed spice**

Boil mixed dried fruit in 1 cup water for 5 minutes. Drain and add dates, nuts and cherries. Dissolve jello in 1 cup hot water. Add port. To fruit mixture add finely crushed cookies and mixed spice. Finally add jello. Stir well, pour into rinsed mold in the traditional dome shape, and chill. Unmold and decorate with holly. Serve with whipped cream flavored with brandy or rum. Serves 8–10.

## Chocolate Liqueur Ice Cream

An extravagant and creamy ice cream, which is made in minutes. The simple sauce contains a modest amount of chocolate, no cream and no extra sugar, as the ice cream is sweet and rich.

¼ cup Crème de Cacao
2 tsp instant coffee powder
few drops of vanilla extract
1 cup heavy cream
4 egg whites
generous pinch of salt
¾ cup canned evaporated milk, chilled overnight
1 tsp lemon juice
1 x 14 fl oz can condensed milk

To make the ice cream, pour the liqueur into a cup. Add coffee powder and vanilla, and stir well to dissolve the coffee. Whip cream until fairly stiff. Beat egg whites with salt until stiff. Whip evaporated milk until very stiff, adding lemon juice while whipping. Pour condensed milk into a large bowl. Stir in the liqueur mixture – do not beat. When thoroughly combined, scoop the evaporated milk, egg whites and cream on the top. Using a spatula, fold up and over until smoothly mixed. Pour into a large container and freeze as quickly as possible. Makes about 3½ pints.

## Chocolate Sauce

1½ oz each bittersweet and milk chocolate or 3½ oz bittersweet chocolate
1⅔ cups evaporated milk
4 tsp cocoa powder
knob of butter
few drops of vanilla extract

Break up chocolate and put into small saucepan with evaporated milk, cocoa powder and butter. Heat, stirring to melt chocolate and then simmer for a few minutes, still stirring, until thickish and dark. Remove and stir in vanilla. If left to stand, put a piece of waxed paper on top to prevent a skin from forming. Reheat over hot water when required.
Makes about 1½ cups.

Irish Coffee Ice Cream

## Custard Ice Cream

I almost didn't include this recipe in the book, because it defies all the rules that go into the making of a good, smooth, creamy ice cream. It sets so hard you can cut it with a knife, it's a cheesy yellow in color, and really not the slightest bit elegant, but everybody loves it. There are two important points to remember: it should be frozen quickly to ensure a smooth texture, and it must be allowed to soften before serving. It is superb served with fresh fruit salad.

1½ pints milk
3 eggs
3 tbsp granulated sugar
1 x 14 oz can condensed milk
few drops of vanilla extract

Scald milk. Beat eggs and sugar,

and add a little of the hot milk. Stir to mix, then add to rest of milk and cook slowly, stirring, until it coats the back of a wooden spoon. Remove from heat and stir in condensed milk and vanilla. Pour into a 4½-pint container, cool and freeze.
Serves 8–10.

## Irish Coffee Ice Cream

1 x 6 fl oz can evaporated milk, chilled overnight
few drops of lemon juice
⅔ cup sifted confectioners' sugar
1 tbsp instant coffee powder
4 tsp Irish whiskey
1 cup heavy cream
3 egg whites, stiffly whisked

Chill bowl and beaters before whisking evaporated milk and lemon juice until stiff. Gradually beat in confectioners' sugar. Dissolve coffee powder in whiskey and beat into milk mixture. When very stiff, fold in whipped cream and egg whites gently but thoroughly. Pour into container and freeze quickly, folding over once or twice before it freezes firm, to prevent any chance of separating.

Serve plain, or on a pool of light, hot Chocolate Sauce (page 158).
Serves about 8.

## Strawberry Ice Cream

1½ cups ripe strawberries
⅓ cup granulated sugar
1 tbsp light honey
1 cup heavy cream
few drops of vanilla extract
1 x 6 fl oz can evaporated milk, chilled for 12 hours
1 tsp lemon juice
3 egg whites
pinch of salt

Wash, hull and slice strawberries into small pieces. Sprinkle with sugar and honey. Cover and leave to stand for 1 hour, then purée until smooth. Pour into a large bowl. Whip cream with vanilla and fold in. Whip evaporated milk with lemon juice until stiff and fold in. Beat egg whites with salt until stiff and fold in. Pour into 4½ pint container and freeze quickly.

# Irish Coffee Pie

As the name implies, this is a mixture of whiskey, coffee and cream. Combined with a rich egg custard and set in a nutty crust, it makes a lovely dessert.

CRUST
½ tsp instant coffee powder
scant ½ cup butter, melted
2 cups sugar cookie crumbs
scant ½ cup walnuts or pecan nuts, coarsely chopped

FILLING
1½ cups milk
3 eggs, separated
3 tbsp granulated sugar
pinch of salt
2 tsp powdered gelatin
¼ cup whiskey
2 tsp instant coffee powder
few drops of vanilla extract
½ cup whipping cream, whipped
whipped cream and chocolate scrolls to decorate

To make the crust, dissolve coffee powder in melted butter and then combine with remaining ingredients. Press onto base of greased 8-in pie dish, and chill.

Scald milk. Beat yolks with sugar and pinch of salt. Pour on scalded milk and then return to saucepan and stir until it thickens, without boiling. Remove from heat. Soften gelatin in the whisky and stir into custard. Add coffee powder, and when dissolved, add vanilla and set aside until cold and beginning to thicken – this can be hurried by standing the bowl in iced water. Beat egg whites until stiff but not dry, then fold in together with whipped cream.

Pour into crust and chill until set. Decorate with whipped cream and chocolate scrolls.
Serves 8.

# Lemon Soufflé

A delicately flavored, creamy textured, custard-based soufflé made with everyday ingredients. It may be set either in a straight-sided dish tied with a paper collar, or more simply in little bowls, in which case reduce the amount of gelatin by ½ tsp.

6 egg yolks
¾ cup granulated sugar
2 cups milk
finely grated zest of 2 large lemons
1 tbsp powdered gelatin
scant ½ cup fresh lemon juice
½ cup whipping cream
few drops of vanilla extract
7–8 egg whites
whipped cream and finely grated lemon zest to decorate

Using an electric beater and a deep bowl, beat yolks with granulated sugar until pale and thick. Add milk and lemon zest. Beat to mix, then turn into top of double saucepan and cook as for custard over simmering water, until mixture coats the back of a wooden spoon. Soften gelatin in the lemon juice. Pour cooked custard into a large bowl, add gelatin, stir until dissolved, then leave to cool, stirring occasionally – or hurry it up by placing the bowl in a dish of iced water and stirring until cold and beginning to thicken.

Whip cream with vanilla and fold in. Stiffly beat egg whites with a pinch of salt and fold in. Pour into prepared dish, or little dishes (or glasses) and set in refrigerator. Before serving, decorate with a lattice of whipped cream and a sprinkling of finely grated lemon zest.
Serves 10–12.

# Loganberry Yogurt Pie

A useful, basic recipe, which can be varied by using differently flavored fruit juices and yogurt – pineapple makes a delicious alternative, as does strawberry. These desserts are pleasingly large, and very easy to make. Be sure to use the thick, eating yogurt, not the fluid, drinking kind.

CRUST
**3 cups sugar cookie crumbs**
**scant ½ cup butter, melted**

FILLING
**1 tbsp powdered gelatin**
**1 x 14 oz can loganberries in natural juice**
**2 cups raspberry yogurt**
**good ¾ cup whipping cream**
**¼ cup confectioners' sugar**
**2 egg whites**
**pinch of salt**
**whipped cream to decorate**

Make crust by mixing crumbs and butter, press onto base of greased 9-in pie dish and chill.

Drain juice from canned fruit and make up to 1 cup with water. Reserve loganberries. Soften gelatin in juice, then dissolve over low heat, taking care not to let the juice boil. Pour yogurt into a large bowl. Slowly add fruit juice with dissolved gelatin, stirring all the time. Whip together cream and confectioners' sugar and beat egg whites stiffly with the pinch of salt. Fold these into the fruity mixture, pour into crust and chill until set. Before serving, decorate with whipped cream and reserved loganberries.
Serves 10.

## Variations
PINEAPPLE YOGURT PIE
Use a gingersnap crust and substitute pineapple juice and yogurt for the loganberry.

APRICOT YOGURT PIE
Use apricot yogurt and juice and increase the amount of confectioners' sugar to ⅓ cup.

# Chiffon Pie Grand Marnier

**A crunchy nut crust holds a creamy orange filling spiked with liqueur.**

CRUST
**2 cups cookie crumbs**
**5 tbsp butter, melted**
**2 tsp runny honey**
**scant ½ cup walnuts, chopped**
**½ tsp finely grated orange zest**

FILLING
**3 eggs, separated**
**1 tsp cornstarch**
**⅓ cup granulated sugar**
**½ tsp finely grated orange zest**
**½ cup fresh orange juice**
**2 tsp powdered gelatin**
**5 tsp cold water**
**¼ cup Grand Marnier**
**½ cup whipping cream, whipped**

Mix ingredients for crust and press onto base of greased pie dish, 8–9 in in diameter and 1¼ in deep (to take the filling) and chill.

Beat egg yolks, cornstarch, granulated sugar, orange zest and juice. Soak gelatin in cold water. Cook yolk mixture in small saucepan or double saucepan, stirring constantly until it thickens like custard. Remove from heat and add Grand Marnier. Add softened gelatin and stir until dissolved, then set aside to cool and thicken. If you're in a hurry, stir it over ice, or chill it — but very briefly — because it must not start to set.

Beat egg whites with a pinch of salt and fold in together with the cream. Pour into chilled crust and set in refrigerator. Serve plain, or garnish with cream and nuts. Serves 8–10.

Orange Syllabub

## *Apple Chiffon Pie*

A delicious and simple pudding, for which Golden Delicious apples are essential.

CRUST
**1¾ cups gingersnap cookie crumbs**
**¾ cups shortcake cookie crumbs**
**scant 1 cup butter, melted**

FILLING
**1¾ lb Golden Delicious apples, peeled and sliced**
**1 cinnamon stick**
**knob of butter**
**⅔ cup water**
**¼ cup honey or 5 tsp each honey and sugar**
**1 tbsp powdered gelatin**
**few drops of vanilla extract**
**½ cup whipping cream, whipped**
**ground cinnamon**

To make crust, mix crumbs and butter and press into greased 8-in pie plate and chill.

Put apples, cinnamon, butter, scant 1 cup water and honey into saucepan. Cover and simmer gently for about 10 minutes or until soft. Remove from heat. Soak gelatin in ¼ cup water, add to hot apple mixture and stir until dissolved.

Cool for 10 minutes, then remove cinnamon stick and spoon into blender (plus all the juices) and add vanilla. Blend until smooth, then pour into a bowl to cool. Fold in cream. Pour into crust, sprinkle generously with cinnamon and chill for 8–12 hours before serving. Serves 8–10.

## *Orange Syllabub*

Syllabub is a dessert you can make before you've even put on your apron. Normally it is made with brandy, wine or sherry, but in the following recipe I have given it a fresh new flavor.

**5 tsp orange-flavored liqueur**
**¼ cup fresh orange juice**
**3 tbsp granulated sugar**
**generous pinch of very finely grated orange zest**
**1 cup whipping cream, whipped**

Mix liqueur, juice, sugar and zest in a deep container. Stir to dissolve the sugar, then cover and chill for 2–3 hours. Pour the cream into the same container and whip everything together until stiff, then spoon into 4–6 wine glasses and chill for another 2 hours at least. Serve with unfilled cigar cookies. Serves 4–6.

## *Lemon Cheese Cream*

This dessert tastes like cheesecake and looks like ice cream, but leaves them both standing when it comes to speed of preparation.

**1½ cups low-fat soft cheese**
**¼ cup granulated sugar**
**½ tsp very finely grated lemon zest**
**½ tsp powdered gelatin**
**¼ cup lemon juice**
**⅔ cup whipping cream**
**4 egg whites, stiffly beaten**

Whip together cheese, sugar and lemon zest until smooth. Soften gelatin in lemon juice and dissolve over hot water. Beat slowly into cheese mixture. Fold in whipped cream and then egg whites. Pour into 8 wine glasses and chill for a few hours. Garnish with cream and a maraschino cherry. Serves 8.

Whisky Oranges

# Whisky Oranges

**4 medium to large navel oranges
scant ½ cup granulated sugar
1 cup water
shredded zest of 1 orange
5 tsp whisky**

Peel oranges, removing all pith, and slice into very thin rings. Place in shallow pie dish, adding the juices from the cutting board.

Put sugar, water and shredded zest into a small saucepan. The zest should be free of any white pith and cut into very thin julienne. Bring to a boil, stirring, then cover and simmer gently for 30 minutes. Remove and cool for 10 minutes. Add whisky. Pour warm syrup over oranges and scatter the cooked zest evenly over the top. Cover and chill for 2–3 days. Serve plain, or with ice cream or cream. Serves 4–6.

# Tipsy Peaches

**scant ½ cup granulated sugar
1½ cups water
2 cinnamon sticks
2 tsp lemon juice
4 large fresh peaches
orange- or coconut-flavored
   liqueur**

Slowly bring sugar, water, cinnamon and lemon juice to a boil in a large skillet and simmer for 5 minutes. Plunge peaches first into boiling water and then into cold water and slip off skins. Halve and remove pits. Place, hollow-side down, in the boiling syrup, then cover and poach until tender. Cool in syrup, then slice and divide between 6 smallish dessert dishes. Into each dish pour 3 tbsp of the poaching liquid and 1 tbsp liqueur. Cover and chill for several hours, preferably overnight.
Serves 6.

# Pears in White Wine

**10 firm pears
2 cups semi-sweet white wine
1 cup water
¼ cup orange marmalade
⅓ cup granulated sugar
coarsely grated zest of 1 orange
¼ cup honey
sour cream or fresh cream to
   serve**

Peel pears smoothly, leaving stalks on. Bring the remaining ingredients, except the cream, to a boil in a deepish saucepan in which the pears will all fit, preferably on their sides. Add pears to boiling syrup, cover and poach gently for about 20 minutes until soft, turning occasionally and carefully. Remove pears to serving dish, standing upright, then reduce syrup in saucepan to 2 cups by fast boiling.

Strain syrup over pears, cool, cover with a tent of foil and chill thoroughly. Serve with some of the syrup poured over each pear and a bowl of thick, sour cream, or lightly whipped fresh cream. Serves 10.

### Variation
PEARS IN FRUIT JUICE AND PORT
Peel, core and halve 1¾ lb firm pears. Arrange in large skillet. Mix 1 cup grape juice with ¼ cup runny honey. Pour over pears. Add 1 cinnamon stick and 2 whole cloves. Cover and simmer until soft, basting occasionally. Remove pears to serving dish, rounded sides up. Pour juices into small saucepan. Remove spices, stir in ¼ cup port mixed with 2 tsp cornstarch and bring to a boil. Pour over pears, basting as they cool. Cover, chill thoroughly, and serve with thick cream.

Strawberry Cream

## Pears in Whisky Cream Sauce

Fresh pears are poached in a light sugar syrup, which is then blended with cream, laced with whisky and thickened by adding a whole puréed pear. This refreshing dessert tastes just as good as it looks.

scant ½ cup sugar
2 cups water
2 cinnamon sticks
4 whole cloves
4 large slightly under-ripe firm pears
1 cup cream
¼ cup whisky
toasted flaked almonds

Put sugar, water, cinnamon and cloves into large saucepan and bring to a boil, stirring to dissolve sugar. Peel, halve and core pears

and place, rounded side up, in syrup. Cover and poach until soft. Remove pears to serving dish (choose one with sides, to hold the sauce) and reserve two pear halves. Strain poaching liquid, return to saucepan and then reduce by boiling rapidly, uncovered, for about 10 minutes, until it measures 1 cup and becomes syrupy. Slowly stir in cream. Remove from heat and add whisky. Chop reserved pears and add. Cool slightly and then purée in blender until smooth.

Pour slowly over pears and leave to cool, then chill for a few hours. Scatter with almonds just before serving.
Serves 6.

## Strawberry Cream

The simplest way of serving strawberries and cream short of putting the one in a bowl and the other in a jug.

3¼ cups strawberries
¾ cup granulated sugar
4 tsp powdered gelatin
¼ cup water
2 egg whites
⅔ cup whipping cream, whipped
whipped cream and strawberries to decorate

Hull, wash and slice strawberries, sprinkle with granulated sugar and stand for about 30 minutes to draw the juices. Purée in blender until smooth, then pour into a bowl. Soften gelatin in water, dissolve over low heat, then stir into strawberry purée. Set aside until beginning to thicken. Stiffly beat egg whites with a pinch of salt and

fold in together with cream. Pour into a mold and chill until set. Unmold and decorate with extra whipped cream and strawberries. Serves 8–12.

### Note
You may prefer to set the mixture in individual molds, or, instead of unmolding, you could tie a band of waxed paper round the rim of a straight-sided dish to form a collar, for the "risen soufflé" look.

Pear Tart Praline

## *Pear Tart Praline*

There are three steps to this dessert: the pears, the praline and the pastry. The pears are poached with wine and cinnamon; the cream layer flavored with almonds and caramelized sugar, and the short pastry spiked with spices. The only requirements then, are a little patience, and an 8-in tart ring.

PRALINE
**scant ½ cup granulated sugar**
**½ cup whole, unblanched almonds**

PASTRY
**⅓ cup butter, softened**
**3 tbsp confectioners' sugar**
**1 egg yolk**
**1 cup all-purpose flour**
**1 tsp ground cinnamon**
**generous pinch of nutmeg**
**pinch of salt**

FILLING
**1–1¼ lb firm pears**
**½ cup semi-sweet white wine**
**1 cinnamon stick**
**1 tbsp lemon juice**
**scant 1 cup water**
**¼ cup sugar**
**1 cup whipping cream**

Make praline by heating sugar and almonds slowly in a small, heavy saucepan. Allow the sugar to melt and caramelize with the almonds, while stirring slowly. When melted and brown, pour onto buttered cake pan or small cookie sheet and leave until cold. Remove (it should lift off in one piece) and grind until fine, or crush in a strong plastic bag with a rolling pin. Set aside.

To make the pastry, cream butter and confectioners' sugar. Beat in egg yolk. Sift dry ingredients and add. Mix well, form into a ball, wrap in waxed paper and chill for about 1 hour until firm. Put the tart ring on a

cookie sheet and press the pastry into it. Do not let it get warm – if it does, put into freezer for 5 minutes before baking. Prick sides and bottom well, and bake at 400°F for 15 minutes. Don't worry if it should puff up a bit, it will subside when cooled. When cold, remove ring and carefully transfer pastry shell to flat serving dish.

Poach the pears while the pastry is chilling. Peel, halve and core pears. Put wine, cinnamon, lemon juice, water and sugar into saucepan. Bring to a boil, then add pears. Poach gently until soft, then cool in liquid.

To assemble, whip cream until stiff. Fold in about 3 oz of the praline and spoon into pie crust. Arrange drained pears on top – 8 halves should just fit. Sprinkle thickly with more praline.
Serves 6 generously.

## *Athol Brose*

This potent little number from the Highlands of Scotland combines oats and honey and whisky in amazing proportions, and the result is about as heady as a neat drink.

**¼ cup porridge oats**
**¼ cup thin honey**
**¼ cup Scotch whisky**
**1 cup whipping cream, stiffly whipped**

Spread porridge oats on cookie sheet and toast lightly under broiler, then rub until fine between your palms. Stir honey and whisky into cream, then fold in 4 tsp oats. Spoon into small glasses, sprinkle with remaining oats and chill.
Serves 4.

## Old-Fashioned Trifle

To my mind, one should never trifle with trifle. It's a simple dessert, basically just cake, sherry and custard, with a flurry of trimmings. A good trifle needs neither the addition of jelly nor canned fruit to turn it into one of the most satisfying endings to a special meal.

7-in sponge cake layer
strawberry jam
about ½ cup sherry
finely chopped candied fruit
a handful of chopped nuts
a little preserved ginger
  (optional)
whipped cream, cherries and
  angelica to decorate

CUSTARD
3 cups milk
3 eggs
1 egg yolk
5 tsp cornstarch
3 tbsp granulated sugar
pinch of salt
few drops of vanilla extract
small knob of butter

Cut sponge cake in half, horizontally, and spread liberally with jam. Break it up and use to cover the bottom of the bowl. Sprinkle with sherry and strew with candied fruit, nuts and ginger if using. Allow to stand while you make the custard.

Scald milk. Beat eggs, egg yolk, cornstarch, sugar and salt. Pour on the hot milk, stirring, then return to saucepan and cook over low heat until it coats the back of a wooden spoon. Remove from heat and add vanilla and butter. Cool slightly, then pour over cake, cutting in gently. When cold, cover and chill. Before serving, decorate boldly and brightly on a thick layer of whipped cream.
Serves about 8.

## Rum and Ricotta Creams

A most useful dessert for the hostess-in-a-hurry; quick to prepare, with a memorable flavor. Ricotta is a low-fat, Italian cheese with a very light texture. Nevertheless, this is a rich mixture, so it should be set in smallish glasses. Make these creams at least 6 hours ahead of serving, but preferably a day in advance.

1–1¼ lb ricotta cheese
½ cup granulated sugar
2 eggs, separated
2 tsp instant coffee powder
¼ cup dark rum
few drops of vanilla extract
good ¾ cup whipping cream,
  whipped

Beat ricotta, sugar and yolks until very light. Dissolve coffee in rum, then stir into cheese mixture. Add vanilla. Beat egg whites with a pinch of salt until stiff and fold in gently together with cream until thoroughly blended. Spoon into 10 glasses and chill.

Serve plain, or topped with whipped cream and a chocolate scroll.
Serves 10.

Fruit Salad with Nuts, Yogurt and Honey

## Fruit Salad with Nuts, Yogurt and Honey

It's all in the title: a nutritious, fairly low-calorie dessert, always enjoyed by health enthusiasts and those on a diet. The addition of avocado in a fruit salad is possibly a bit surprising, but it really does add a special touch. This fruit salad is most effective if served in a shallow glass dish rather than a deep bowl.

2 small Golden Delicious apples
2 ripe pears
2 bananas
½ pineapple
1 large avocado
5 tsp fresh lemon juice
scant ½ cup nuts of choice, chopped and toasted

1 cup plain drinking yogurt
5 tsp runny honey
generous pinch of finely grated orange zest
chopped nuts and/or grated orange zest to decorate

Peel and cube apples and pears. Slice bananas thinly, cube pineapple and dice avocado. Put into bowl and toss with lemon juice. Mix in nuts. Beat yogurt, honey and orange zest. Pour over fruit, allowing it to dribble down. Cover and chill for 2–4 hours. For decoration, sprinkle with a few more nuts and/or a little grated orange zest.
Serves about 6.

## White Chocolate Mousse

Chocolate mousses are amongst the riches of desserts, and this one is no exception, except that it does contain only 2 eggs, no extra yolks, and sour cream instead of fresh. Nevertheless, the result is still melt-in-the-mouth and the flavor elusive, with a trace of toffee liqueur.

scant ¼ lb white chocolate, broken up
3 tbsp milk
small knob of butter
5 tsp Old English Toffee or Bailey's Irish Cream liqueur
few drops of vanilla extract
2 eggs, separated
¼ cup granulated sugar
2 tsp powdered gelatin
¼ cup water
good ¾ cup sour cream
pinch of salt

Put chocolate in top of small double saucepan with milk and butter. Melt over simmering water and when smooth, remove from heat and stir in liqueur and vanilla. Set aside.

Beat egg yolks with sugar until pale and thick. Soak gelatin in water and dissolve over low heat, then stir into yolk mixture. Beat to blend, then add the slightly cooled chocolate mixture and beat again. Stir in sour cream. Beat the egg whites with the pinch of salt, until stiff, then fold in.

Pour into small bowls or glasses, cover, and chill for about 6 hours to allow flavors to blend. Serve plain or whip a little cream with a dash of the liqueur and pipe a small swirl on the top of each. Serve icy cold.
Serves 6.

## Peaches in Red Wine

**This is the sort of dessert that deserves to be photographed: large, fresh peaches smothered in a thick, slightly spicy red wine sauce. Make it at the height of summer when peaches are really ripe and juicy, and buy the biggest you can find.**

**1¾ lb large fresh peaches**
**1½ cups good red wine**
**⅓ cup granulated sugar**
**3 tbsp honey**
**1 large cinnamon stick**
**4 small whole cloves**
**2 tsp cornstarch**

Plunge peaches into boiling water and remove skin. Halve, remove stones, and arrange in a heavy skillet to fit quite snugly. Heat wine, sugar and honey in a small saucepan. Stir to dissolve sugar, then pour over peaches. Add cinnamon and cloves. Bring to a boil, then cover and poach gently for about 20 minutes, basting each peach several times. When soft, remove peaches with slotted spoon to serving dish – a large pie dish would be just right. Arrange hollow-sides down and cool. Remove spices from syrup and leave to cool.

Dissolve cornstarch with a little of the cooled wine syrup, stir into the rest in the pan, and then boil up again until thickish. Spoon syrup over each peach, coating several times. When cold, cover and chill up to 12 hours. Serve with a bowl of thick cream.
Serves 6–8.

## Toffee Liqueur Creams

**This is a truly dreamy dessert: liqueur-flavored custard set in pretty glasses, topped with liqueur-flavored cream.**

**2 eggs, separated**
**¼ cup granulated sugar**
**1½ cups milk**
**1 vanilla pod**
**2 tsp powdered gelatin**
**scant ⅓ cup Old English Toffee or Bailey's Irish Cream liqueur**
**scant ½ cup whipping cream**

Beat yolks with sugar. Scald milk with vanilla. Pour onto beaten eggs, then return to saucepan and cook as for custard. Remove from heat. Soften gelatin in ¼ cup liqueur, then beat into custard until dissolved. Pour into a bowl and allow to cool. Beat egg whites with a pinch of salt until stiff. When custard begins to thicken, fold in egg whites gently, but thoroughly, until combined. Pour into 6 glasses, leaving room for the cream, and set in refrigerator.

Whip cream with remaining liqueur until as stiff as it will go, then pour in an even layer over top of set puddings. Return to refrigerator until required. This dessert may be prepared up to a day in advance.
Serves 6.

## Sherry Bavarian Crème

This is a delicious but pale-colored dessert, so serve it prettily in a big glass bowl, decorated like a trifle, or in individual glasses topped with chocolate curls.

5 tsp powdered gelatin
scant ½ cup cold water
4 egg yolks
⅓ cup granulated sugar
pinch of salt
2 cups milk
⅔ cup sweet or medium cream sherry
7–8 egg whites
1 cup whipping cream, whipped

Soften gelatin in cold water. Beat egg yolks with sugar and salt. Scald milk. Pour hot milk onto egg mixture, stirring to dissolve the sugar, then pour back into saucepan. Add softened gelatin and then stir over low heat until it thickens like custard – do not boil. Remove from heat and stir in sherry, then pour into a bowl and leave until cold and beginning to thicken, stirring occasionally. Or chill briefly. Beat egg whites stiffly with a pinch of salt and fold in together with cream. Pour into bowl, or glasses, and set in refrigerator.
Serves 10–12.

### Variation

IRISH COFFEE BAVARIAN CRÈME
A delicious variation may be made by substituting the following ingredients: 2 tsp gelatin; ¼ cup cold water; 2 eggs, separated; pinch of salt; 3 tbsp sugar; ⅔ cup milk; 2 tsp instant coffee powder; 2 tsp Irish whiskey; good ¾ cup cream.
Serves 6.

## Stuffed Oranges

A fresh and fruity dessert.

8 medium, sweet oranges
1 x 11 oz can mandarins, drained
1 piece preserved ginger, finely chopped
¼ cup orange-flavoured liqueur whipped cream and walnuts to decorate

As this fruit salad is served in the orange shells, choose round, unblemished ones. Cut off the tops and with a grapefruit knife scoop out the insides. Be careful not to puncture the skins. Remove seeds and membranes and chop the flesh, catching the juices. Spoon into a bowl and add mandarins, ginger and liqueur. Cover and chill for a few hours. Leave shells upside down to drain.

To serve, fill shells with fruit. If desired, flavor the whipped cream with a little finely grated orange zest or liqueur to taste, or leave plain. Pipe generously on top of each orange to cover completely, top with a walnut, and serve.
Serves 8.

### Variation

ORANGE SOUFFLÉ
Use to fill the orange shells: 2 cups fresh orange juice; 1 tbsp gelatin; 4 eggs, separated; 2 tsp finely grated orange zest, 3 tbsp granulated sugar; 1 cup cream, whipped.

Soak gelatin in scant ½ cup of the juice. Heat remaining juice with zest. Beat yolks and sugar, pour in strained hot juice, then return to heat and cook as for custard. Remove, stir in gelatin, pour into bowl and cool. Fold in egg whites, stiffly beaten with a pinch of salt, and the cream. Set in refrigerator.
Serves 8.

## Cheese Creams with Mango Purée

Rich yet refreshing, and a beautiful color: citrus-flavored creams scooped onto a smooth sauce with a hint of liqueur. An elegant dessert which is surprisingly easy to prepare; serve icy cold on your prettiest plates.

½ tsp powdered gelatin
3 tbsp cold water
1½ cups cream cheese
3 tbsp granulated sugar
few drops of vanilla extract
1 egg, separated
generous pinch of finely grated lemon zest or ½ tsp finely grated orange zest
scant ½ cup whipping cream, whipped
1 x 14 oz can mango slices in syrup
¼ cup Malibu
fresh mint sprigs to garnish

Soften gelatin in water and dissolve over low heat. Beat cream cheese, sugar, vanilla, egg yolk and zest until smooth. Slowly beat in the dissolved gelatin. Beat egg white with a small pinch of salt and fold in together with cream. Chill. Drain mango slices and place in blender with ¼ cup of the syrup. Add liqueur and blend until smooth. Pour into a jug and chill.

To serve, dribble a small pool of the sauce onto each plate. Place 1–2 scoops of the softly set cheese mixture on top – use an ice cream scoop or 2 dessert spoons to shape. Decorate with sprigs of mint. Serves 6.

## Variation
When sweet melons are in season, substitute the following sauce for the mango purée:

SWEET MELON AND RUM SAUCE
Using a blender, purée enough ripe sweet melon to give you 1½ cups purée. Stir in 1½–2 tsp dark rum. If desired, add a little granulated sugar, but if sweet melon is juicy and ripe, this should not be necessary. Pour into a jug and chill before using as a base for the cheese creams.

# Strawberry Cheesecake

This recipe, using a mere handful of strawberries, makes a really big cheesecake. Topped with fresh berries and whipped cream, it makes a bright and beautiful ending to a meal.

CRUST
2 cups shortcake cookie crumbs
⅓ cup ground almonds
   (optional)
2 tsp confectioners' sugar
5 tbsp butter, melted

FILLING
1½ cups strawberries, washed
   and hulled
¼ cup milk
⅓ cup sugar
1½ cups low-fat soft cheese
2 eggs, separated
few drops of vanilla extract
1 tbsp powdered gelatin
¼ cup cold water
pinch of salt
½ cup whipping cream, whipped

To make the crust, mix ingredients and press onto base of greased 9-in pie dish and chill.

Slice strawberries and purée in blender with milk and 3 tbsp granulated sugar. Beat together cheese, 5 tbsp granulated sugar, egg yolks and vanilla. Soften gelatin in water and dissolve over low heat. Beat into cheese mixture together with the purée. Beat egg whites stiffly with a pinch of salt and fold in together with cream. Pour into chilled crust and return to refrigerator until set. Garnish as suggested before serving.
Serves about 10.

## Hint
Soft margarine is best for greasing dishes for chilled desserts as it does not set as hard as butter.

# Vanilla Cheesecake

**A simple cheesecake, unfailingly popular, and possibly the one I make most most often.**

CRUST
3½ oz shortcake cookies
scant ⅓–½ cup butter, melted

FILLING
1½ cups low-fat soft cheese (or cream cheese)
⅓ cup granulated sugar
2 eggs, separated
2 tsp powdered gelatin
¼ cup cold water
few drops of vanilla extract
pinch of salt
½ cup whipping cream, whipped

Crush cookies. Instead of using a processor, which can reduce them to a fine dust, I prefer putting the cookies into a plastic bag and rolling until crumbly with a rolling pin. Toss with melted butter and press onto the base of a greased 8-in pie dish. Chill while making filling.

Using an electric beater, beat the cheese, sugar and egg yolks until smooth. Soften gelatin in cold water and dissolve over low heat. Slowly beat into cheese mixture – if you dribble it directly onto the beaters it won't form little strings. Add vanilla. Beat egg whites stiffly with the pinch of salt and fold in. Finally fold in the cream.

Pour onto pastry shell and set in refrigerator. Serve plain or decorated with a lattice of whipped cream.
Serves 8.

# Fruity Cheesecake

**Laced with sherry and rich with fruit and nuts, this cheesecake is rather like a cold and creamy Christmas pudding.**

CRUST
2 cups sugar cookie crumbs
scant ½ cup butter, melted

FILLING
¾ cup mixed dried fruit
6 maraschino cherries, chopped
¼ cup chopped walnuts
3 tbsp finely chopped preserved ginger
3 tbsp honey
¼ cup sweet sherry
2 tsp powdered gelatin
3 tbsp water
¼ cup light brown sugar
1½ cups low-fat soft cheese
⅔ cup sour cream
2 egg whites
pinch of salt
ground cinnamon

Mix crumbs and butter and press onto the base of greased 8-in pie dish. Chill.

To make the filling, put dried fruit, cherries, walnuts, ginger, honey and sherry into the top of a double saucepan, cover and steam gently over simmering water for 10 minutes. Remove and pour into a bowl. Soak gelatin in the water. Add to hot fruit mixture and stir until dissolved. Stir in brown sugar. When dissolved, stir in cheese and sour cream. When thoroughly combined, leave to cool, but do not allow it to set. Beat egg whites with the pinch of salt until stiff and fold in. Pour into chilled crust, sprinkle with cinnamon and set in refrigerator.
Serves 8–10.

## Chocolate Rum and Raisin Cheesecake

CRUST
**2 cups sugar cookie crumbs**
**5 tbsp butter, melted**
**½ tsp ground cinnamon**

FILLING
**3 tbsp seedless raisins**
**3 tbsp dark rum**
**2 eggs, separated**
**⅓ cup granulated sugar**
**1½ cups low-fat soft cheese**
**3 squares plain chocolate**
**1 tsp instant coffee powder**
**scant ⅓ cup water**
**2 tsp powdered gelatin**
**½ cup whipping cream, whipped**
**few drops of vanilla extract**
**chocolate curls to decorate**

First soak raisins in rum for at least 4 hours.

Mix ingredients for crust and press onto the base of a greased 8-in pie dish. Chill.

Beat egg yolks, sugar and cheese until smooth. Break up chocolate and put into small container with coffee and 3 tbsp water. Melt over low heat, mix until smooth, then cool slightly before beating slowly into cheese mixture. Soak gelatin for a few minutes in ¼ cup water, then dissolve over low heat. Slowly add to cheese mixture, beating all the time. Reserve a little whipped cream for garnishing and fold remainder into the chocolate mixture. Beat egg whites with a pinch of salt, and fold in. Finally fold in vanilla and raisins, plus any rum not absorbed, gently but thoroughly. Pour into crust and chill well. Decorate with a few rosettes of whipped cream topped with chocolate curls.
Serves 8.

## Cheesecake with Strawberry topping

CRUST
**5 oz shortcake cookies, crushed**
**scant ½ cup butter, melted**

FILLING
**1½ cups low-fat soft cheese**
**1 x 14 oz can condensed milk**
**¼ cup lemon juice**
**1 cup sour cream**
**1 tbsp powdered gelatin**
**3 tbsp water**

TOPPING
**14 oz can strawberries in syrup**
**1 tbsp custard powder**

For the crust, mix crumbs and butter and press into a greased 9-in pie dish. Chill.

Mix cheese and condensed milk. Slowly stir in lemon juice, then add sour cream. Soften gelatin in water and dissolve over low heat. Add slowly to cheese mixture, stirring well, then pour into crust and chill until set.

Drain can of strawberries, reserving syrup. Mix a little of the syrup with the custard powder, and pour the remainder into a small saucepan. Add custard powder mixture and boil up until thickened. Remove from heat, add strawberries and beat with a wooden spoon until pulpy. Allow to cool completely before spooning over the set filling. Return to refrigerator until firm enough to slice.
Serves 8.

Orange Liqueur Cheesecake (left) and Baked Orange Cheesecake (right)

# Orange Liqueur Cheesecake

**This cheesecake contains only one egg and no fresh cream so is slightly lower in calories than most.**

CRUST
**2 cups sugar cookie crumbs**
**½ tsp finely grated orange zest**
**5 tbsp butter, melted**

FILLING
**2 tsp powdered gelatin**
**¼ cup cold water**
**1½ cups low-fat soft cheese**
**⅓ cup granulated sugar**
**½ tsp finely grated orange**
**1 egg, separated**
**5 tsp orange-flavored liqueur**
**good ¾ cup sour cream**
**pinch of salt**

Mix ingredients for crust and press onto base of greased 8-in pie dish. Chill.

Soak gelatin in cold water. Beat cheese with sugar and orange zest and egg yolk until smooth. Dissolve gelatin over low heat and then beat into cheese mixture in a slow stream. Stir in liqueur and sour cream. Stiffly beat egg white with a pinch of salt, then fold in. Pour into crust and chill for a full day if possible. Decorate with a gentle sprinkling of orange zest and a little whipped cream or canned, well-drained mandarin segments.
Serves 8

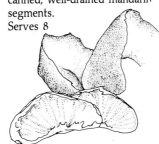

# Baked Orange Cheesecake

CRUST
**2 cups sugar cookie crumbs**
**scant ⅓ cup butter, melted**
**1 tsp honey**
**scant ½ cup pecan nuts, chopped (optional)**

FILLING
**1½ cups low-fat soft cheese**
**2 eggs, separated**
**⅓ cup granulated sugar**
**few drops of vanilla extract**
**2 tsp cornstarch**
**½ cup light cream**
**½ tsp finely grated orange zest**

TOPPING
**good ¾ cup sour cream**
**few drops of vanilla extract**
**2 tsp light brown sugar**
**½ tsp finely grated orange zest**
**ground cinnamon**

Mix ingredients for crust. Press onto base of greased 8-in pie dish with fairly high sides. Bake at 325°F for 10 minutes, then cool.

For the filling, beat together all the ingredients, except the egg whites, until smooth. Beat egg whites, fold in, then pour onto crust. Place dish on cookie sheet and bake for 40 minutes or until just set.

Mix ingredients for topping, except cinnamon, pour evenly over cheesecake and dust lightly with cinnamon. Bake for another 10 minutes, turn off heat then open oven door and leave until cold. Serves 8.

## Note
**The filling can also be baked in ramekins and served as little soufflés. Spoon cheese mixture into 8–10 greased ramekins. Sprinkle with cinnamon, arrange on cookie sheet and bake for about 40 minutes or until well risen and firm.**

## Brandy Tart with Ginger and Pecans

**Closely related to the traditional old favorite, but with a delicious new flavor.**

1½ cups pitted dates, chopped
1 tsp baking soda
1 cup boiling water
2 knobs preserved ginger, finely chopped
3 tbsp butter
¾ cup granulated sugar
1 egg, beaten
1½ cups flour
½ tsp baking powder
generous pinch of salt
½ cup pecan nuts, chopped
few drops of vanilla extract

SYRUP
⅔ cup light brown sugar
1 cup water
pinch of salt
small knob of butter
½ cup brandy

Put dates and baking soda into a bowl. Pour boiling water over. Add ginger. Cool completely, stirring now and then. Cream together the butter and granulated sugar. Add egg and beat until very light. Sift dry ingredients and stir into creamed mixture alternately with cooled date mixture, beginning and ending with flour. Add nuts and vanilla. Bake at 325°F in a buttered 9-in pie dish just below center of oven for 1 hour, until risen and dark brown.

Meanwhile, boil brown sugar and water for 5 minutes. Add remaining syrup ingredients, stir well, then pour slowly over the hot pie. Serve at room temperature with whipped cream.
Serves 8–10.

# Raisin Pecan Pie

This is a spicy, rich pie full of raisins and nuts and laced with brandy. Serve warm or at room temperature with whipped cream.

CRUMB CRUST
**2 cups crushed graham cracker crumbs**
**½ tsp ground cinnamon**
**⅓ cup butter, melted**

FILLING
**½ tsp ground nutmeg**
**½ tsp ground cinnamon**
**⅔ cup seedless raisins**
**¾ cup pecan nuts, chopped**
**⅓ cup soft brown sugar**
**¼ cup honey**
**2 tsp cornstarch**
**1 x 14 oz can evaporated milk**
**2 eggs**
**¼ cup brandy**
**pinch of salt**

Mix ingredients for crust and press onto base of greased 8-in pie dish.

To make the filling, toss together nutmeg, cinnamon, raisins and nuts and set aside. Beat remaining ingredients together until well mixed. Add to raisin mixture and combine thoroughly. Pour evenly into crust and sprinkle lightly with a little extra ground cinnamon. Bake at 325°F for 30 minutes or until set.
Serves 8.

# Baked Bananas

**Fried bananas flamed with rum are a delicious old favorite, but do involve some last-minute attention. Done this way, however, you can assemble them before dinner and bake them during the main course – they'll come out soft, sweet and flavored with rum. Serve with vanilla ice cream.**

**4 large, ripe but firm bananas**
**scant ⅓ cup fresh orange juice**
**¼ cup light rum**
**2 tsp pale honey**
**4 tsp brown sugar**
**a little ground cinnamon**
**few knobs of butter**

Peel bananas, halve lengthwise and then halve again, so that each banana is cut into four. Put into shallow baking dish in single layer, close together.

Pour over orange juice and rum, dribble with honey, and sprinkle with sugar and cinnamon. Dot with butter, cover and bake at 325°F for 30–40 minutes.
Serves 4–6.

## Variation
BAKED APPLES FLAMBÉ
Peel, core and slice 4 large Golden Delicious apples into eighths. Pack tightly into buttered 8-in pie dish. Sprinkle with 5 tsp lemon juice and ¼ cup each golden raisins and halved, toasted almonds. Dribble with ¼ cup honey and sprinkle with 1 tbsp brown sugar and ½ tsp each ground cinnamon and ginger. Dot with slivers of butter and bake, covered, at 350°F for about 45 minutes. Remove cover, flame with 5 tsp brandy and serve hot with ice cream or cream.

Orange Crème Caramel

# Caramel Crème Caramel

**A light caramel in both color and flavor, this is a velvet-textured, ever popular dessert.**

¾ cup granulated sugar
5 tsp water
1 x 14 oz can condensed milk, caramelized (see Hint)
3 cups hot water
6 eggs
pinch of salt
few drops of vanilla extract

In a heavy saucepan, over low heat, melt sugar with 5 tsp water. Do not keep stirring, simply shake the pan now and then until sugar has dissolved and the mixture turns a deep caramel color. Being careful not to splash, pour into ovenproof soufflé dish, turning quickly to coat bottom and sides. (Individual ramekins may also be used, in which case reduce baking time by about 25 minutes.)

Empty condensed milk into a bowl and add hot water, beating until well mixed. Beat eggs with salt. Slowly pour on the milk mixture. Add vanilla, then strain into caramel-coated dish. Place in baking dish with hot water coming halfway up the sides, and bake at 325°F for about 1 hour until just set. Cool, then chill thoroughly before unmolding. Run a knife round the edges and invert onto platter.
Serves about 8.

# Orange Crème Caramel

**Another version of crème caramel, beautifully smooth and delicate, with a different flavor.**

1¼ lb granulated sugar
7 cups milk
grated zest of ½ large orange
8 eggs
¼ cup orange-flavored liqueur
pinch of salt

Melt 1⅓ cups sugar in a large, heavy skillet over low heat. Spread it out evenly and stir now and then as it starts to dissolve. As soon as it is smooth and golden-brown in color, remove from heat and carefully pour onto the base of 2–3 small soufflé dishes, or 12–16 ramekins, turning to coat sides evenly.

Scald milk with the orange zest.

Beat remaining ingredients together. Pour hot milk onto egg mixture, then strain into molds. Stand in pan of hot water to come halfway up the sides, and see that the dishes aren't touching. Bake at 300°F for about 45 minutes for ramekins, 1½ hours for larger dishes. When done, they'll still be a bit wobbly, but will firm up on standing. Cool, then chill very well. Unmold by running a knife round the edges, and inverting onto serving plates.
Serves 12–16.

## Hint
**To caramelize condensed milk, place a thick wad of newspaper in the bottom of a saucepan of hot water. Bring to a boil and stand can of condensed milk on the paper. Simmer for 3 hours, adding more water if necessary, and keeping can away from hot base and sides of saucepan.**

## Cheese Blintzes

Thin little pancakes, filled with low-fat soft cheese (in this case lightly flavored with orange and orange liqueur), folded up, and traditionally fried in butter. However, as this involves standing over the stove while everyone waits for their dessert, I prefer to make them in advance, chill them and then heat them through just before serving. Choose a light main course, as blintzes are rich and filling.

BLENDER CRÊPES
**2 eggs**
**pinch of salt**
**1 cup flour, sifted**
**½ cup water**
**½ cup milk**
**3 tbsp granulated sugar**
**2 tsp brandy**
**2 tsp oil**

FILLING
**¼ cup seedless raisins**
**1½ cups low-fat soft cheese**
**½ tsp finely grated orange zest**
**¼ cup confectioners' sugar**
**1 tbsp orange-flavored liqueur**
**1 egg yolk**

**melted butter or sour cream**
**3 tbsp soft brown sugar**
**generous pinch of ground**
  **cinnamon**

Put ingredients for crêpes into blender. Blend well. Scrape down sides with a rubber spatula and blend again. Cover and stand for about 1 hour. Blend again briefly before using to make thin pancakes in small skillet lightly brushed with oil.

Plump raisins in boiling water, drain and mix with cheese, zest, sugar, orange liqueur and egg yolk. Put a heaped spoonful onto the center of each crêpe. Flap sides over to middle and bottom ends up, to make a neat parcel. Arrange close together, in lightly buttered ovenproof dish (and it must be suitable for taking directly from refrigerator as the crêpes are not brought to room temperature.)

Just before baking, pour over either a little melted butter or sour cream, sprinkle with sugar and cinnamon and heat through at 350°F for 15 minutes. If using melted butter, serve a jug of sour cream separately. Serves 6–8.

# Soufflé Grand Marnier

One of the few desserts in this book that can't be completed in advance, but a hot soufflé, served at its height, never fails to impress. The size of the dish is important to ensure a slightly creamy middle with a high, light-brown "hat."

3 tbsp butter
1¾ cups flour
1¼ cups milk
¼ cup granulated sugar
pinch of salt
3 egg yolks
¼ cup Grand Marnier
½ tsp finely grated orange zest
4 egg whites

Melt butter, stir in flour, cook for a minute, then remove from heat and slowly add milk. Return to heat and cook, stirring with a balloon whisk, until very thick. Stir in sugar and salt until dissolved. Beat egg yolks, add a little of the hot sauce, mix well, then add the yolks to the sauce together with the Grand Marnier and orange zest.

When mixed, spoon into a large bowl. Beat egg whites until stiff. Stir a quarter into egg sauce, then fold the remainder in gently but thoroughly. Grease a 3-in soufflé dish with butter and sprinkle with granulated sugar. Pour mixture into prepared dish and bake at 350°F for about 30 minutes. Serve immediately.
Serves 5–6.

# Spicy Peach and Nut Crumble

Another winter's dessert, first cousin to apple crumble.

1 x 1 lb 14 oz can peach slices in syrup
1 Granny Smith apple, peeled and cubed (optional)
1 tsp ground cinnamon

TOPPING
1¼ cups self-rising flour
pinch of salt
¼ cup brown sugar
½ cup chopped walnuts
1 egg
generous pinch of ground cinnamon
½ tsp ground nutmeg
5 tbsp butter, melted

Lightly butter a deep 8-in pie dish. Spoon in the peach slices plus the syrup. Add the apple if using – it adds a nice tart touch – and sprinkle with cinnamon.

To make the topping, mix the flour, salt, sugar and nuts. Drop the unbeaten egg into the middle and, using a fork, mix until very well combined and crumbly. Sprinkle evenly over fruit. Sprinkle spices over topping and finally dribble the melted butter over.

Bake at 350°F for 50 minutes or until crisp and bubbling. Best served warm rather than very hot, with thick cream.
Serves 5–6.

## Variation
WHITE CURRANT CRUMBLE
Make as for peach crumble, but for the filling substitute same quantity of white currants, undrained, and add 2 Golden Delicious apples, peeled and chopped. Reduce cinnamon to ½ tsp. Omit nuts in the topping.

## Grape Tart with Almond Pastry

A basic recipe, which is wide open to variations. The tart case, made with plenty of butter and ground almonds, is short and crisp, and may be made some days in advance, ready to be filled with any cream and fruit combination. I have used green and black grapes because they look so attractive – but any fruit may be used, and the filling spiked with complementary flavors: strawberries and Kirsch for example, or bananas and rum. The pastry is enough for two 8-in pies, the filling for one.

ALMOND PASTRY
**2¼ cups all-purpose flour**
**⅓ cup confectioners' sugar**
**generous pinch of salt**
**scant ½ cup ground almonds**

**¾ cup + 2 tbsp soft butter**
**1 egg yolk**
**2 drops of almond extract**

FILLING
**⅔ cup whipping cream**
**3 tbsp confectioners' sugar**
**5 tsp Amaretto**
**1½ tsp powdered gelatin**
**5 tsp water**
**½ cup sour cream**
**1 egg white**
**pinch of salt**

TOPPING
**1 bunch green grapes**
**1 bunch black grapes**
**smooth apricot jam**
**toasted almonds**

Make pastry by sifting flour, confectioners' sugar and salt. Add ground almonds. Using an electric beater, work in the butter, egg yolk and extract. When very finely crumbled, form into a ball with your hands. Do not add any liquid.

Press thinly into two ungreased 8-in loose-bottomed tart pans with fluted sides. Prick very well all over and bake at 350°F for 15 minutes. The pastry should not brown, but be a pale color. Cool completely before removing the rings. The cases may now be stored in an airtight container, to be filled a few hours before dinner.

Whip cream, confectioners' sugar and liqueur. Soften gelatin in water and dissolve over low heat. Stir into sour cream, and pour into a bowl. Beat egg white with the pinch of salt and fold in together with whipped cream mixture. Now taste it – you may want it sweeter or sharper or more potent. Sprinkle base of pastry case lightly with granulated sugar to keep it crisp. Pour in filling and set in refrigerator.

Halve and seed grapes, but do not peel. Arrange rounded sides up, over cream filling in concentric circles, to cover completely. Melt a little smooth apricot jam with a little water. Using a pastry brush, brush glaze lightly over grapes until shiny. Tuck in a few toasted almonds. Return to refrigerator until required.
Serves about 8.

Strawberry Tart

# Strawberry Tart

This tart looks every bit as professional as those on display in a patisserie: feather-light pastry holding a creamy confection which is topped with bright, glazed strawberries.

PASTRY
scant ½ cup butter, softened
¼ cup confectioners' sugar
1 egg yolk
few drops of vanilla extract
1¼ cups all-purpose flour
pinch of salt

FILLING
1½–2 cups strawberries
3 tbsp sugar
good ½ cup cream cheese
¾ cup heavy cream
¼ cup confectioners' sugar
½ tsp finely grated orange zest
5 tsp Grand Marnier or few drops of vanilla extract

3 tbsp strawberry jam
1 tsp water
whipped cream and almond flakes to decorate

If possible, use an electric beater to make the pastry. Cream butter and confectioners' sugar and beat in egg yolk and vanilla. Sift flour with salt and add. Dough will be soft. Form into a ball, wrap in waxed paper and chill for about 1 hour. Press thinly into 9-in loose-bottomed pie ring. Prick bottom and sides well and bake at 400°F for 10–12 minutes or until pale gold in color – on no account must it brown. When cold, remove ring carefully and put tart crust onto serving plate.

Hull and wash strawberries and sprinkle with sugar. Leave to drain in a colander for about 15 minutes. Beat cream cheese, cream, confectioners' sugar, orange zest and liqueur or vanilla until thick. Spoon evenly into pastry shell. Halve the strawberries and arrange

on top of filling to cover completely.

Heat jam and water and pour into a small strainer. Glaze by holding strainer over berries and pushing liquid through, using back of spoon. Chill tart. It will hold well for about 4 hours without going soggy. Before serving, decorate with whipped cream piped in a lattice pattern. Fill the squares with toasted almond flakes.
Serves about 6.

# Lychee Cobbler

1 x 1¼ lb can peeled and pitted lychees, drained
¼ cup all-purpose flour
2 tsp ground ginger
generous pinch of salt
3 tbsp smooth peach jam
½ cup butter, melted
1 tsp baking soda

Chop lychees coarsely and cover bottom of lightly greased 8-in pie dish. Pour over 1 cup of the syrup. Sift together flour, ginger and salt. Add jam, then pour in melted butter and baking soda dissolved in 3 tbsp hot water. Using a knife, mix until combined and then drop in large spoonfuls over lychees – do not try to cover them, the mixture will spread as it bakes. Bake on middle shelf of oven at 350°F for 30 minutes.
Serve 5–6.

# Apple and Pear Tart with Sour Cream Topping

Baked in a fluted tart pan, this pastry case holds a fruity filling covered with a butterscotch-colored, creamy topping. This is really quite a simple tart using basic ingredients, but for sheer eye appeal it's hard to beat.

PASTRY
1½ cups all-purpose flour
½ tsp baking powder
½ tsp salt
¼ cup granulated sugar
½ tsp ground mixed spice
scant ½ cup butter
iced water

FILLING
**1 x 13 oz can unsweetened apples**

3 tbsp honey
¼ cup seedless raisins
1 x 14 oz can pear pieces
½ tsp ground cinnamon

TOPPING
1 egg yolk
⅔–¾ cup sour cream
3 tbsp light brown sugar
½ tsp ground cinnamon

Make pastry by sifting together the flour, baking powder, salt, granulated sugar and mixed spice. Cut in butter until crumbly and slowly add enough iced water to bind. Mix quickly into a ball, wrap in waxed paper then chill about 1 hour. Roll out thinly on a floured board, and line a loose-bottomed 9-in fluted pan. Sprinkle base lightly with a little flour.

Chop apples into small pieces and mix with honey and raisins. Drain and chop pear pieces and add to apple mixture, then stir in the cinnamon. Spoon evenly into shell

and bake at 400°F on middle shelf for 20 minutes.

Beat together ingredients for topping. Pour over fruit filling (be prepared for it to puff up a bit). Lower heat to 325°F and return tart to oven for 30 minutes. Remove and allow it to stand for about 10 minutes before lifting off the tart ring. Serve warm or at room temperature.
Serves 8–10.

## Hint

**For a more wholesome crust, brown flour may be substituted for half the flour. You will need about ¼ cup iced water to bind this mixture, slightly less if using only white flour and about ⅓ cup if using only brown flour.**

## Baba au Rhum

Usually babas are baked in small dariole molds, and savarins in rings, but personally I like the look of a ring, with the cream piled up in the middle. Deep muffin pans can be used if preferred.

5 tsp warm water
½ tsp sugar
2 tsp dried yeast
4 eggs
1½ cups all-purpose flour (sifted before measuring)
⅓ cup granulated sugar
½ cup butter, melted
whipped cream and/or strawberries to serve

SYRUP
2 cups water
¾ cup sugar
5 tbsp rum

Put water into a cup – it should not be hot, but warmer than lukewarm. Sprinkle in the sugar and dried yeast and leave for 15 minutes. Don't stir, just give it a shake now and then, and it will melt and start to bubble. Stir to a smooth cream just before using. Beat 3 eggs well. Warm flour in a very low oven, then stir into egg mixture, using a wooden spoon. Stir in the bubbly yeast. Beat well, still using a wooden spoon. The mixture will be tacky, like soft chewing gum. Cover and allow to rise in a warm place for about 25 minutes. When spongy and bubbly on the surface, add the remaining egg, beaten, the sugar and the melted butter. Beat again until well mixed – it will still be soft and tacky – then scoop into an oiled and floured 9-in ring mold. Cover, stand on a cookie sheet, and return to a warm place for about 1 hour 20 minutes, until risen and spongy. Bake at 425°F for 10 minutes, then reduce heat to 400°F

and bake for 5 minutes more.

Meanwhile make syrup by boiling water and sugar rapidly for 5 minutes. Remove from stove and stir in rum.

Remove baba from oven, turn over, cover with 2 tea towels and leave for 5 minutes before loosening spring. Loosen edges with a knife and ease out gently onto a rack with a plate underneath. Prick all over with a skewer, then spoon syrup over slowly until it has all been absorbed, re-using any drips left on the plate. Cool, then fill center with whipped cream, either plain or mixed with fresh strawberries. Serves 8–10.

# Dutch Milk Pie

I have taken several liberties with this recipe. I have not, as in the traditional version, made a flaky pastry the night before, hung it up in a cloth and rolled it out at dawn. Nor have I flavored it with tangerine peel. I have further broken with tradition by folding in the egg whites at the end, because I prefer the resulting lighter texture.

PASTRY
½ cup butter, softened
¼ cup granulated sugar
1 egg
2¼ cups all-purpose flour
pinch of salt

FILLING
2½ cups milk
1 cinnamon stick
¼ cup all-purpose flour
scant ⅓ cup sugar
pinch of salt
2 tbsp butter
3 eggs, separated
few drops of vanilla extract
3 drops of almond extract
  (optional)
ground cinnamon and sugar

To make the pastry, beat together butter and sugar. Beat in egg. Sift in the flour and salt, form into a ball and chill while making the filling.

Using a heavy-based saucepan, scald 2 cups milk and cinnamon stick. Mix flour, sugar and salt to a paste with the remaining milk, then return to saucepan and cook until thick, stirring, and keeping heat low to prevent scorching. When thick and smooth, remove and add butter. Cool. Remove cinnamon stick and then beat in yolks, one at a time, using a wooden spoon. Add vanilla and almond extract. Beat whites and fold in.

Press chilled dough evenly into 9-in pie dish – not too shallow as the filling puffs up. Cover base with a circle of waxed paper and weight with dried beans. Bake at 350°F for 10 minutes. Remove paper and beans and bake for further 5 minutes. Pour in filling and bake just below center of oven for 20–25 minutes until set. Sprinkle generously with cinnamon and sugar.
Serves 8–10.

## Pear Tart with Yogurt

This tart has a very special appeal for those who are into health foods.

NO-ROLL CRUST
½ cup wholewheat flour
½ cup white flour
½ tsp salt
2 tsp granulated sugar
scant ½ cup butter
1 tsp lemon juice
¼–⅓ cup cold water

FILLING
about 1¾ lb nearly-ripe eating
  pears
2 egg yolks
1 cup plain drinking yogurt
3 tbsp honey
2 tsp cornstarch
1 tbsp light brown sugar
¼ cup seedless raisins
1 tsp ground cinnamon
2 tsp brown sugar
3 tbsp honey
whipped cream to serve

To make the crust, use a flour sifter to sift both flours, salt and sugar into a bowl. Return husks to bowl, and rub in butter. Add lemon juice and cold water, just enough to be able to form a ball, using a knife and then your finger tips. Working quickly, press dough evenly into a loose-bottomed 9-in fluted tart pan. Chill while making the filling.

Peel, core and slice enough pears to give you 1 lb 5 oz, weighed after preparation. Beat egg yolks with yogurt, honey and cornstarch. Remove tart shell from refrigerator and sprinkle the 1 tbsp light brown sugar over the bottom (this helps to prevent the crust from becoming soggy). Cover with the thinly sliced pears.

Sprinkle with raisins, cinnamon and sugar and dribble with the honey. Pour the yogurt mixture over. Put tart pan on a baking sheet and bake at 400°F just below the center of the oven for 45 minutes. Remove and stand at room temperature until cool. Remove ring and serve with whipped cream.
Serves about 8.

## Apple Crumble

High on the list of old-fashioned favorites, this apple crumble never fails to please. The apple juice ensures that it turns out juicy, and the nuts and spices add a tasty crunch.

1 x 1¾ lb can pie apples
6 cups apple juice (or water)
3 tbsp white sugar
3 tbsp runny honey
¼ cup golden raisins
2–3 whole cloves (optional)
whipped cream to serve

TOPPING
1 cup all-purpose flour
1 tsp baking powder
scant ⅓ cup brown sugar
2 tsp ground cinnamon
½ tsp ground nutmeg
½ cup chopped walnuts
scant ½ cup butter

Spread apples in buttered 9-in pie dish. Pour apple juice (or water) over. Sprinkle with sugar. Dribble with honey, add the golden raisins and tuck in the cloves if you like it spicy.

For the crumble, mix flour, baking powder, sugar, spices and walnuts. Rub in butter. Sprinkle evenly over apples, then bake at 350°F for 45 minutes. Serve warm rather than bubbling, with a bowl of whipped cream.
Serves 6–8.

NOTE
As an alternative to serving whipped cream with sweet desserts, try the following: stir 1⅓ cups thick yogurt until smooth. Whip scant ½ cup whipping cream, and fold in. Cover and chill.

## Apple Pie with Cinnamon Pastry

PASTRY
2¼ cups all-purpose flour
3 tbsp cornstarch
⅔ cup confectioners' sugar
2 tsp ground cinnamon
2 tsp baking powder
pinch of salt
¾ cup butter, softened
1 egg, beaten
¼ cup chopped nuts
few drops of vanilla extract

FILLING
1¾ lb can unsweetened pie
    apples
¼ cup granulated sugar
¼ cup brown sugar
½ cup golden raisins
ground cinnamon
thick cream to serve

To make pastry, sift together flour,

cornstarch, sugar, cinnamon, baking powder and salt. Rub in butter until crumbly, then add egg, nuts and vanilla. Mix well, knead and form into a ball. Wrap in waxed paper and leave in freezer for a few hours until hard. Grate two-thirds of the pastry coarsely onto the bottom of an ungreased deep 9-in pie dish or loose-bottomed cake pan. Cover bottom completely, distributing dough evenly, but don't press down-use a fork to spread it around.

Chop apples and mix with sugars and golden raisins. Spoon on top of pastry, top with a sprinkling of cinnamon, then grate remaining dough evenly over the top. Bake at 325°F for 1 hour. Serve hot or at room temperature, dusted with confectioners' sugar, and with a bowl of thick cream. If baked in a cake pan, remove sides when quite cold.
Serves 8.

## Upside-Down Apple Pie

Tarte des Demoiselles Tatin is a famous French dessert named after two ladies from Orléans. Traditionally, thinly sliced apples are arranged in carefully patterned circles in a pan lined with caramel, and then covered with a rich, sweet pastry. Tarte Tatin is always served upside down once baked. This is my simplified version of this excellent but tricky dessert.

PASTRY
**1 cup all-purpose flour**
**generous pinch of salt**
**1 tbsp granulated sugar**
**generous pinch of ground**
   **cinnamon**
**4 tbsp cold butter**
**scant ¼ cup iced water**

FILLING
**⅓ cup light brown sugar**
**1 tsp ground cinnamon**
**scant ½ cup chopped walnuts**
   **(optional)**
**¼ cup golden raisins**
**1–1¼ lb Granny Smith apples**

To make pastry, sift dry ingredients, rub in butter and slowly add enough water to bind. This may all be done using a hand-held electric beater. Form into a ball, wrap and chill briefly while preparing the pan and making the filling. It is essential to use a round 8-in cake pan that is deep enough to take the filling and the crust.

Lightly oil the base and cover with a circle of waxed paper to fit. Butter the paper and the sides of the pan. Sprinkle with the sugar, pressing down firmly with the back of a spoon to make an even layer. Over this sprinkle the cinnamon, nuts and golden raisins. Top with peeled and thinly sliced apples –

the slicing blade of a processor is perfect for the job. Press down firmly.

Roll out pastry on a floured board to a circle about 1½ in larger than the diameter of the pan, then place it directly onto the apples. Turn overlapping pastry inwards and press firmly against the inner edge of the pan. The pastry must rest on the apples. Bake at 350°F for 45 minutes. Stand at room temperature until cool. Unmold by running a knife round the edges, then put a large round plate on top and turn the tart upside down. Remove paper. The top should be toffee-colored and juicy. Serve with whipped cream flavored with brandy or rum.
Serves 6.

## Baked Stuffed Apples

**6 medium Granny Smith apples**
**⅓ cup dates, chopped**
**⅓ cup golden raisins**
**¼ cup chopped walnuts**
**1 large piece of preserved**
   **ginger, chopped**
**1 tbsp honey**
**butter**
**1 cup unsweetened apple juice**
**¼ cup brown sugar**
**3 whole cloves**
**1 cinnamon stick**
**1 tbsp honey**

Make large cavities in the apples. Remove a strip of peel around the middle of each. Mix dates, golden raisins, walnuts, ginger and honey. Stuff apples and arrange in pie plate. Top each with a knob of butter. Heat remaining ingredients, pour around apples and bake at 350°F for about 1 hour or until soft, basting often. Serve at room temperature. Serves 6.

Fruit Flambé

# *Peach Küchen*

**The dish you use for this dessert is quite important – it can be square or round, but must be a bit larger than the average 8-in pie dish, with sides at least 1¼ in high.**

CRUST
**1¾ cups flour
½ tsp baking powder
generous pinch of salt
3 tbsp granulated sugar
½ cup butter, softened
1 tbsp light brown sugar**

FILLING
**1 x 1 lb 14 oz can peach slices
3 tbsp light brown sugar
1 tsp ground cinnamon**

TOPPING
**1 egg yolk
1 cup sour cream
few drops of vanilla extract
1 tsp cornstarch**

To make the crust, sift flour, baking powder and salt. Add granulated sugar. Using an electric beater if possible, work in the butter. Beat until mixture is like fine cornmeal, and press into ungreased dish. No liquid must be added. Use the back of a spoon and press firmly to form a thin shell on the base and sides, but not on the rim. Sprinkle base with the light brown sugar.

Drain peaches very well and arrange on crust: Sprinkle with sugar and cinnamon. Bake at 400°F for 15 minutes.

Beat ingredients for topping together and pour evenly over peaches. Sprinkle with a little extra brown sugar and cinnamon, and return to oven to bake for another 15 minutes. Remove, and while still hot, neaten the edges of the crust. Serve warm or at room temperature, with or without cream.

Serves about 8.

# *Fruit Flambé*

**A flexible dessert, using canned fruit, that can be prepared in advance. A good (and economical) combination is peaches and pears. The following is slightly more exotic.**

**1 x 1 lb 14 oz can peach slices, drained
1 x 14 oz can fruit cocktail, drained
1 x 14 oz can lychees, drained, pitted and sliced
¼ cup light brown sugar
1 knob preserved ginger, chopped
½ tsp finely grated lemon zest
few slivers of butter
¼ cup brandy
½–1 cup heavy cream**

Mix fruits together. Sprinkle base of a large 9-in pie dish with the sugar. Spoon in the fruit. Add the ginger, sprinkle with lemon zest and dot with butter. Cover and leave at room temperature until required.

Bake, covered, at 325°F for 40 minutes. Remove and uncover. Have ready the warmed brandy in a small long-handled saucepan. Flame, then pour over the hot fruit. Swirl in the cream, and serve at once.
Serves 6.

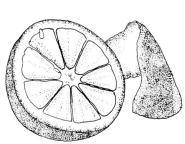

Jam Roly Poly

## Jam Roly Poly

2¼ cups all-purpose flour
2 tsp baking powder
generous pinch of salt
2 tbsp butter
1 egg
scant ½ cup milk or water
smooth apricot jam
chopped nuts

SYRUP
1 lb sugar
1 tbsp butter
1 tsp ground cinnamon
4¼ cups boiling water

Sift flour, baking powder and salt.
Rub in butter. Beat egg and milk (or
water) and add to flour mixture.
Mix to a soft, easy-to-handle
dough. Roll out about 1¼ in thick
into a 12 x 9-in rectangle on a
floured board. Spread liberally with
jam and scatter with nuts. Roll up
from the long side like a jelly roll,

pinching edges together. With a
sharp knife cut into 1-in thick slices
and place in a single layer in a 14 x
10-in buttered baking dish, leaving
plenty of room for spreading.
    To make the syrup, put sugar,
butter and cinnamon into a bowl.
Add the boiling water, mix well,
then pour over rolled up dough in
baking dish. Bake at 350°F for 35–
40 minutes, or until golden brown
and well risen. Serve hot with
cream or custard.
Serves 10.

### Variation
APPLE ROLY POLY
Substitute the following filling for
the apricot jam and nuts: peel and
grate 2 large Golden Delicious
apples and mix with 3 tbsp golden
raisins, 2 tbsp chopped nuts and
3 tbsp honey.

## Orange Liqueur Crêpes

CRÊPES
2 eggs
3 tbsp granulated sugar
pinch of salt
½ cup milk
1 tsp oil
1 cup all-purpose flour, sifted
½ cup lukewarm water
½ cup soda water

SAUCE
3 tbsp butter
1¼ cup fresh orange juice
½ tsp finely grated orange zest
2 tsp honey
¼ cup orange-flavored liqueur
sugar
½ tsp ground cinnamon
1 tsp brown sugar
3 tbsp warmed brandy

Make crêpes by beating eggs with

sugar. Add salt, milk and oil and
beat again. Add flour, water and
soda water and beat until well
mixed, then cover and stand for
1 hour. Beat briefly before using to
make thin pancakes, preferably in a
non-stick pan. Fold each in four,
and arrange close together in a
shallow baking dish – a 9-in pie
dish is a good size. The batter will
make 12 large or 18 medium
crêpes.
    To make the sauce, melt butter
and allow it to brown lightly.
Remove from heat and add orange
juice and zest, honey, liqueur and a
little sugar if necessary. Pour over
crêpes, sprinkle with cinnamon and
sugar and cover.
    Bake, covered, at 325°F for
about 30 minutes or until very hot.
Remove, uncover and flame with
warmed brandy. Serve with vanilla
ice cream.
Serves 6.

Ginger Brandy Torte

## *Ginger Brandy Torte*

**This is a strange looking dessert, as desserts go, but absolutely scrumptious. The base can be made a day or two in advance and stored in an airtight container.**

**4 egg whites**
**½ tsp cream of tartar**
**½ tsp salt**
**¾ cup granulated sugar**
**few drops of vanilla extract**
**1 tsp ground ginger**
**16 gingersnap cookies, finely crushed**
**scant ½ cup walnuts or pecans, chopped**

TOPPING
**1 tsp powdered gelatin**
**¼ cup water**
**good ¾ cup whipping cream**
**¼ cup confectioners' sugar**
**1 tbsp brandy**
**candied ginger to decorate**

Beat egg whites with cream of tartar and salt until soft peaks form. Slowly add granulated sugar, beating constantly, and continue beating until stiff. Beat in vanilla. Fold in ginger, cookies and walnuts. Spoon evenly into a lightly oiled and floured, loose-bottomed 9-in cake pan, and bake at 325°F for 25 minutes. Cool for 5 minutes, then invert and cool on rack.

For the topping, soften gelatin in the water and dissolve over low heat. Whip cream with confectioners' sugar, and gradually beat in dissolved gelatin. Add brandy and whip until thick. Spread over cold cake base. Decorate with slivers of candied ginger and refrigerate for a few hours before serving.
Serves about 8.

## *Tipsy Tart*

**A traditional old favorite, this time with a hint of orange.**

**1 cup pitted dates, chopped**
**½ tsp baking soda**
**½ cup boiling water**
**3 tbsp butter**
**¼ cup sugar**
**1 egg**
**1 cup flour**
**1 tsp baking powder**
**pinch of salt**
**1 tsp finely grated orange zest**
**½ tsp vanilla extract**
**½ cup chopped walnuts**

SYRUP
**½ cup water**
**knob of butter**
**¼ cup sugar**
**scant ⅓ cup brandy**
**scant ⅓ cup orange-flavored liqueur**

Put dates into bowl, sprinkle with baking soda and pour boiling water over. Cool, stirring and mashing a bit. Cream butter and sugar, add egg and beat well. Sift flour, baking powder and salt. Add dates to egg mixture, then stir in flour mixture. Add orange zest, vanilla and nuts. Pour evenly into greased 8-in pie dish and bake at 350°F on middle shelf for 25 minutes.

Meanwhile, make the syrup by boiling water, butter and sugar for 3 minutes. Stir at first to dissolve the sugar, and then boil rapidly. Remove from heat, add brandy and liqueur. Prick the hot tart when it is taken from the oven and pour syrup over slowly until it is all absorbed. Leave for a day to mature, if possible, then serve at room temperature, with a bowl of thick cream.
Serves 6–8.

# Cinnamon-Coffee Hot Water Sponge Cake

**A light and spicy cake in pale café au lait.**

3 eggs, separated
1 cup granulated sugar
1½ cups all-purpose flour
generous pinch of salt
1 tsp ground cinnamon
½ tsp ground nutmeg
2 tbsp butter
½ cup very hot, strong black
   coffee
1 tbsp baking powder

FROSTING
**1 lb sifted confectioners' sugar**
**3 tbsp butter, softened**
**½ tsp ground cinnamon**
**1 tsp instant coffee powder**
**¼ cup milk or single cream**
**walnuts to decorate**

Using an electric beater, beat egg
yolks and sugar until thick and
pale. Sift together flour, salt and
spices. Add to first mixture and
beat again — the mixture will be
crumbly. Melt butter in coffee and
add to cake mixture, beating just
until smooth. Fold in the stiffly
beaten egg whites and lastly the
baking powder.

   Pour batter into two 8-in oiled
and floured cake pans. Bake at
350°F for 25–30 minutes. Cool for
5 minutes, then invert onto cake
rack.

   To make the frosting, beat
confectioners' sugar, butter,
cinnamon and coffee powder
dissolved in 1 tsp hot water, and
then add enough milk or cream to
moisten. Fill and ice cake, and
decorate with walnuts.

## *Variation*
NUTMEG-BRANDY FROSTING
**1 lb sifted confectioners' sugar**
**3 tbsp butter, softened**
**freshly grated nutmeg to taste**
**3 tbsp brandy**
**3 tbsp milk**

Beat confectioners' sugar with
butter and nutmeg, then add
brandy and milk. Mix to a creamy
consistency.

Beat and Bake Coffee-Pecan Cake (left) and Instant Spice Cake (right)

# Instant Spice Cake

A large, moist, stick-to-the-ribs sort of cake, with a delicious flavor. One of my favorites, especially when in a hurry, as it is mixed in minutes.

2 tsp baking powder
1½ cups brown sugar
2 eggs
3⅔ cups sifted flour
1⅓ cups buttermilk
½ cup oil
2 tsp ground nutmeg
1 tsp ground cinnamon
generous pinch of ground
  cloves
2 tsp baking soda
1 cup seedless raisins
1 cup chopped nuts

FROSTING
scant 1 cup butter
2½ cups sifted confectioners'
  sugar

2 tsp mixed spice
about 1 tbsp orange-flavored
  liqueur
light cream to moisten

Put baking powder, sugar, eggs, flour, buttermilk, oil, spices and baking soda into a large mixing bowl. Mix with electric beater on medium speed for about 1 minute or until well blended. Fold in raisins and nuts and pour into a deep, oiled 9-in ring pan. Bake at 350°F for 1 hour. Stand for 5 minutes before inverting onto cake rack.

To make the frosting, cream together butter and confectioners' sugar. Add mixed spice, liqueur, and cream. Frost top and sides of cake, swirling with prongs of fork dipped in hot water. Cover and stand for a day if possible.

# Beat and Bake Coffee-Pecan Cake

This is a marvelously quick and versatile recipe. Oil is used instead of butter, so there's no creaming, and the flavors may be changed by omitting cinnamon, coffee and pecans and substituting vanilla extract, or grated lemon or orange zest. Altogether a real boon for the busy cook.

3 eggs, separated
¾ cup granulated sugar
scant 1 cup oil
½ tsp salt
⅔ cup milk
1½ cups all-purpose flour
2 tsp baking powder
1 tsp ground cinnamon
2 tsp instant coffee powder
1 tsp water
½ cup chopped pecan nuts

FROSTING
2 tsp instant coffee powder
3 tbsp water
4 tbsp butter, softened
3 ⅔ cups sifted confectioners'
  sugar
few drops of vanilla extract

Put egg yolks into bowl and add all the ingredients, except the egg whites, coffee, water and nuts, in the order listed. Dissolve coffee in water and add. Mix on medium speed for 90 seconds. Fold in stiffly beaten egg whites and nuts. Pour into two greased and lined 7-in cake pans and bake at 350°F in the center of the oven for 30 minutes. Stand for 5 minutes, then invert onto cake rack, remove paper, and cool.

Make frosting by dissolving coffee in water, adding remaining ingredients and creaming, adding a little more water if necessary. Decorate with pecan halves.

## Carrot Cake with Cream Cheese Frosting

Some carrot cakes are too dry, some too sticky. After endless creating and baking and sifting and sorting, this one has emerged as my favorite, which may be served frosted or plain.

3 eggs
1½ cups sugar
1 cup oil
1 cup all-purpose flour
1 cup wholewheat flour
1 tsp baking soda
2 tsp baking powder
1½ tsp ground cinnamon
1 tsp ground nutmeg
pinch of ground cloves
4 medium carrots, coarsely grated
1 cup seedless raisins
½ cup chopped walnuts

FROSTING
3 cups sifted confectioners' sugar
3 tbsp butter, softened
6 tbsp cream cheese or low-fat soft cheese
few drops of vanilla extract

Beat eggs and sugar until pale, then beat in oil. Sift dry ingredients and add. Mix well, then add carrots, raisins and walnuts. Line base of 7-in square pan with waxed paper and oil lightly. Pour in cake mixture, which will be thickish and tacky. Spread evenly, and make a small depression in the center. Bake at 325°F for 1¼ hours or until firm and brown. Stand for 5 minutes before turning out onto cake rack. Remove paper, then ice when cold.

Using a wooden spoon, mix confectioners' sugar and butter. Slowly beat in just enough cream or cheese to give a spreading consistency. Add vanilla. To frost, turn cake right side up onto serving plate. Cover top and sides with frosting, decorate with nuts, if desired, and cut into squares to serve.

# Chocolate Chiffon Cake

This light cake is baked in a ring pan and covered with a creamy chocolate frosting spiked with rum.

½ cup oil
¾ cup granulated sugar
4 eggs, separated
½ cup water
1 cup all-purpose flour
1 tsp instant coffee powder
1 tbsp baking powder
¼ cup cocoa powder
generous pinch of salt
few drops of vanilla extract

FROSTING
3 cups sifted confectioners' sugar
3 tbsp butter, softened
3 squares bittersweet chocolate
3 tbsp dark rum

few drops of vanilla extract
about 3 tbsp milk

Stir oil and sugar together until creamy. Add yolks one at a time, beating well. Slowly beat in the water. Sift together the flour, coffee powder, baking powder and cocoa three times, and fold in. Stiffly beat egg whites with the salt and fold in. Finally add the vanilla. Pour into a deep, ungreased 8-in ring pan and bake at 350°F in the center of the oven for 1 hour.

Turn upside down on cake rack. Air must circulate freely around cake. Leave until absolutely cold, then ease out of pan and frost, using a knife dipped in hot water.

For the frosting, cream confectioners' sugar with butter. Melt chocolate in the rum over hot water and add. Stir in vanilla and just enough milk to give a spreading consistency. Frost top and sides, roughing up with prongs of a fork, and garnish with shaved chocolate or walnut halves.

# Feather Sponge Cake

This is quite the lightest of cakes. Usually, sponge cakes are made with just three ingredients – flour, eggs and sugar – but Americans often include a rising agent, as in this recipe. It rises dramatically in the oven, but will settle, once cooled, into the traditional, flat-topped sponge cake. This type of cake should be eaten very fresh, as rising agents tend to make it dry.

4 eggs, separated
½ cup granulated sugar
6 tbsp cornstarch
4 tbsp all-purpose flour
½ tsp baking soda
1 tsp cream of tartar
pinch of salt
few drops of vanilla extract
strawberry jam
sweetened whipped cream
confectioners' sugar

Using an electric beater, beat egg whites until stiff but not dry. Slowly add sugar and beat until very stiff. Add yolks one at a time, beating well. Sift dry ingredients twice, fold in very lightly and quickly, and then fold in vanilla. Turn into two 8-in cake pans lined with rounds of waxed paper and lightly oiled and floured. Bake at 350°F in the center of the oven for 20 minutes. Stand for 2 minutes, then turn out onto a cake rack to cool.

Spread with warmed strawberry jam, and sandwich together with whipped cream. Position a paper doily on the top layer, dust with confectioners' sugar, and then carefully remove doily to create an attractive design.

## Coffee Liqueur Cream Cake

This is a rich and boozy sponge, doused with coffee and liqueur and covered with whipped cream. It may be served as a dessert or take pride of place at a lavish tea, where calorie-counting doesn't matter.

7 tbsp butter, softened
⅓ cup granulated sugar
1 cup self-rising flour
½ tsp ground cinnamon
generous pinch of salt
2 eggs
3 tbsp coarsely crushed pecans (optional)
2 tsp instant coffee powder
⅔ cup cold water
5 tbsp Tia Maria
cream
confectioners' sugar

Cream butter and sugar until very light. Sift flour, cinnamon and salt. Add eggs to creamed mixture, one at a time, together with 1 tsp of the flour mixture. Fold in remaining flour and pecans, if using. Spread batter, which will be stiffish, into a 7-in cake pan, base lined with waxed paper and oiled. Bake at 350°F for 25–30 minutes. Stand for 5 minutes before turning out onto cake rack. Remove base paper and cool, then tip back into tin.

Mix coffee powder, water and liqueur and slowly spoon over cake, as evenly as possible. It will be a tight fit, as the cake swells, but this is correct for in this way all the liquid will be absorbed. Turn out onto serving dish. Whip cream stiffly with a little confectioners' sugar and, if desired, flavor with coffee. Cover cake with cream and decorate with a few pecan halves.

## Dark Chocolate Cake

This cake is of the old, family favorite variety. It's not as light as a hot milk sponge cake, but then it's beautifully moist and keeps well.

½ cup butter, softened
1 cup granulated sugar
3 eggs, separated
3 tbsp cocoa powder
½ cup boiling water
2¼ cups all-purpose flour
1 tsp cream of tartar
1 tsp baking soda
1 tsp instant coffee powder
½ tsp salt
½ cup yogurt

FROSTING
2½ cups sifted confectioners' sugar
1 tbsp cocoa powder
3 tbsp butter, softened
1 tsp rum or few drops of vanilla extract

little milk or cream

Cream butter and beat in sugar. Add yolks one at a time, beating well between each addition, adding at the same time 1 tsp of the flour with each egg. Dissolve cocoa in boiling water and beat in slowly. Sift dry ingredients and add alternately with yogurt, beginning and ending with flour. Beat egg whites stiffly and fold in. Spoon mixture, which will be thickish, into two 7-in oiled and floured cake pans, and bake at 350°F for 25–30 minutes. Stand for 5 minutes, then invert onto cake rack to cool.

Mix frosting ingredients to desired consistency. Sandwich layers and ice the top, roughening with a fork, then decorate, if desired, with chocolate curls.

Orange, Date and Rum Cake (left) and Brandy Syrup Cake (right)

## Orange, Date and Rum Cake

2¾ cups all-purpose flour
1 tsp baking powder
½ tsp salt
1 tsp ground cinnamon
1 tsp ground ginger
½ tsp ground nutmeg
1½ cups pitted dates, chopped
½ cup walnuts or pecan nuts, chopped
1 cup + 2 tbsp butter, softened
¾ cup granulated sugar
2 eggs
1 cup buttermilk
1 tsp baking soda
1 tsp finely grated orange zest
few drops of vanilla extract
¾ cup sugar
¾ cup fresh orange juice
¼ cup dark rum

Sift together the flour, baking powder, salt and spices. Mix dates and nuts, toss with a little of the flour mixture and set aside. Cream butter and granulated sugar. Add eggs one at a time, beating well between additions. Mix buttermilk with baking soda and add to creamed mixture alternately with flour mixture, beginning and ending with flour. Finally stir in orange zest, vanilla, dates and nuts.

Spoon into a deep, oiled and floured 9-in ring pan, spreading batter evenly. Bake at 325°F on middle shelf for 1 hour. Five minutes before cake is ready, mix ¾ cup sugar and orange juice in a saucepan and bring to a boil slowly, stirring to dissolve the sugar. Remove from heat and stir in the rum. Cool cake for 5 minutes before turning out onto large plate. Prick top with a skewer and slowly trickle the hot syrup over until it is all absorbed.

## Brandy Syrup Cake

2¾ cups all-purpose flour
1 tsp baking powder
½ tsp ground cinnamon
½ tsp ground nutmeg
½ tsp salt
½ cup pitted dates, chopped
⅓ cup seedless raisins
⅓ cup chopped walnuts or pecan nuts
12 maraschino cherries, chopped
¼ cup butter
1 cup granulated sugar
2 eggs
1 tsp baking soda
1 cup skimmed milk soured with 1 tsp vinegar
few drops of vanilla extract

SYRUP
1 cup water
½ cup sugar
⅓–½ cup brandy

Sift flour with baking powder, spices and salt. Add dates, raisins, nuts and cherries. Cream butter with granulated sugar until light. Add eggs one at a time, beating well, adding 1 tsp of the flour mixture with each egg. Stir baking soda into soured milk and add to creamed mixture alternately with flour. Finally add vanilla.

Spoon into an oiled and floured 9-in ring pan. Smooth top and bake at 325°F for 50–60 minutes or until done.

Just before cake is done, make the syrup by boiling the water and sugar together rapidly, uncovered, for 5 minutes. Remove from stove and add brandy. Pour hot syrup slowly over cake in pan, waiting as each spoonful is absorbed. Cool cake in pan for about an hour, then invert and release spring. Stand for about 8 hours for flavor to mellow, then serve with whipped cream.

## Last Minute Cake

Dark and moist, this cake can be made the week before Christmas.

¼ lb butter
3 cups mixed dried fruit
¾ cup dates, pitted and chopped
¾ cup brown sugar
1 tsp baking soda
good ¾ cup water
½ tsp ground mixed spice
1 tsp ground cinnamon
⅓ cup maraschino cherries, chopped
½ cup nuts, chopped
¼ cup brandy
2¼ cups all-purpose flour
pinch of salt
2 eggs, beaten
1 tsp baking powder

Melt butter. Add washed dried fruit, dates, sugar, baking soda stirred into the water, and spices.

Bring to a boil, then cover and simmer for 15 minutes. Leave in a mixing bowl overnight. Next day add cherries, nuts and brandy. Sift flour with salt and fold in. Add eggs and finally add baking powder.

Line a deep 8-in cake pan with one layer of foil, shiny-side down, and two layers of waxed paper, and brush base and sides with oil. Spread batter evenly and make a small dent in the middle. Place a small cake pan filled with water on the bottom shelf of the oven, to prevent the cake from drying out. Bake at 300°F on middle shelf for a total of about 2½ hours – test with a skewer – and cover top loosely with foil after 1 hour. Cool in pan before turning out, then dose with a little sherry or brandy before wrapping in waxed paper and storing.

## Light Fruitcake

The word light in the title refers only to the color – for this cake is very fruity, large and moist, with a lovely flavor.

2¾ cups all-purpose flour
½ tsp salt
2 tsp baking powder
1 cup + 2 tbsp butter
1 cup sugar
finely grated zest of 1 orange
few drops of vanilla extract
3 eggs
3 lb mixed dried fruit, washed and dried
⅓ cup maraschino cherries, chopped
2 large rings candied pineapple, finely chopped
½–1 cup nuts, chopped
1 cup milk
¼ cup brandy

Sift flour, salt and baking powder. Cream butter, sugar, orange zest and vanilla until light. Add eggs one at a time, beating well between additions and adding 1 tsp of the flour mixture with each egg. Stir in the sifted dry ingredients, all the fruit and nuts. The mixture will be very stiff. Slowly stir in milk until completely absorbed, and finally add brandy.

Line a deep 9-in cake pan with one layer of foil, shiny-side down, and two of waxed paper. Brush well with oil, and spoon in cake mixture. Place a cake pan of water on the shelf below the cake, to prevent it drying out while baking. Bake at 300°F on middle shelf for 2–2¼ hours, covering loosely with foil after 1½ hours. Test with a skewer before removing from oven. Cool in pan before turning out.

### Variation
Sift 2 tsp ground mixed spice with the flour and add a knob of slivered, preserved ginger with the fruit.

Favorite Fruitcake

## Favorite Fruitcake

Like all good fruitcakes, this one
needs to be unwrapped and dosed
with a dash of brandy or sherry.
Serve plain or covered with
marzipan and fondant icing.

3 cups mixed dried fruit, washed
bare ½ cup maraschino cherries,
   chopped
2 knobs preserved ginger,
   chopped
scant ½ cup sherry
½ cup butter
⅔ cup light brown sugar
few drops of vanilla extract
3 tbsp orange marmalade
2 eggs
1¾ cups all-purpose flour
1 tsp baking powder
pinch of salt
1 tsp ground cinnamon
½ tsp ground nutmeg
generous pinch of ground cloves
1 cup nuts, chopped

Put dried fruit, cherries and ginger
into bowl. Pour sherry over and
leave overnight.

Cream butter, sugar, vanilla and
marmalade. Drop in eggs, one at a
time, beating well after each
addition and adding 1 tsp of the
flour with each egg. Sift flour,
baking powder, salt and spices and
fold into creamed mixture
alternately with fruit. Finally add
nuts.

Line a deep, round 8-in cake pan
with one layer of foil, shiny-side
down, topped with two layers of
waxed paper. Brush base and sides
with oil. Spoon in the cake mixture,
and level top with the back of a
spoon dipped in hot water. Place a
cake pan of water in the oven on
the shelf below the fruitcake and
bake at 300°F on the middle shelf
for about 2½ hours or until done.
Cool in pan. Turn out, sprinkle
with brandy or sherry and store,
well wrapped in waxed paper.

## Quick Coffee Cake

**This type of cake does not contain
coffee. The name is derived from
the fact that it is meant to be
served, freshly baked and cut into
squares, with morning coffee.
The texture is light and moist and
it does not require frosting.**

1 cup all-purpose flour
½ tsp salt
1 tsp ground mixed spice
1 tsp baking soda
1 tsp baking powder
1 cup wholewheat flour
½ cup seedless raisins
1 cup sugar
chopped nuts (optional)
1 cup buttermilk
2 eggs
1 cup oil
cinnamon/sugar

Sift all-purpose flour with salt,
spice, baking soda and baking
powder. Add wholewheat flour.
Stir in raisins, sugar and nuts if
using. Beat together the buttermilk,
eggs and oil. Stir into dry
ingredients and mix very lightly
and quickly as though making
English muffins.

Line base of an 8-in square pan
with waxed paper and brush with
oil. Pour in cake mixture, spreading
evenly, dust top with a little
cinnamon/sugar and bake at 350°F
on middle shelf of oven for about
35 minutes — test with a skewer.
Stand for a few minutes before
inverting onto cake rack. Cut into
squares to serve.
Makes 16 squares.

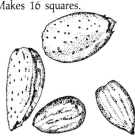

## Orange Loaf Cake

2¼ cups all-purpose flour
¾ cup granulated sugar
2 tsp baking powder
generous pinch of salt
½ cup oil
½ cup fresh orange juice
1 tsp finely grated orange zest
2 eggs
few drops of vanilla extract

ORANGE GLAZE
3 tbsp orange juice
1 tbsp butter
1 cup sifted confectioners' sugar

Sift dry ingredients into bowl. Add oil, juice and zest. Using an electric beater, mix for 1 minute on medium speed. Add eggs and vanilla. Beat for 45 seconds until well mixed. Pour into oiled, floured and lined bread pan — 9 x 3 ½ x 3-in — and bake at 325°F on middle shelf for 1 hour. Stand for 5 minutes, turn out and cool on cake rack.

Heat butter and juice in small saucepan, add confectioners' sugar and stir over very low heat until smooth. Pour over top of cold cake, allowing glaze to trickle down the sides.

## Nutty Dark Gingerbread

¾ cup brown sugar
½ lb butter
3 tbsp syrup or honey
3 tbsp molasses
¼ cup milk
¼ cup water
1 cup brown flour
1 cup plain flour
½ tsp salt
½ tsp ground nutmeg
1 tbsp ground ginger
1½ tsp baking powder
½ tsp baking soda
½ cup filberts, chopped
1 egg, beaten

Heat the sugar, butter, syrup, molasses, milk and water gently. Mix remaining ingredients, except egg. Pour the hot, melted ingredients into dry ingredients and mix well. Stir in egg. Pour into oiled and floured bread pan — 8 x 3½ x 3-in — and bake at 350°F for 45 minutes.

## Lemon Coconut Loaf

**A butter-rich, lemony loaf.
Serve plain.**

½ cup butter
1 cup + 2 tbsp granulated sugar
2 cups all-purpose flour
2 tsp baking powder
generous pinch of salt
2 eggs
finely grated zest of 1 lemon
¼ cup shredded coconut
½ cup water
½ cup milk
few drops of vanilla extract

Cream butter and sugar until light.
Sift flour, baking powder and salt.
Add eggs to creamed mixture, one
at a time, together with 1 tsp of the
sifted mixture. Mix in sifted
mixture and then add remaining
ingredients, beating until just
mixed. Pour into oiled, floured and
base-lined bread pan – 9 x 3 x 3-in.

Smooth the top with the back of a
spoon dipped in hot water.
Sprinkle with extra coconut and
bake at 350°F for 1 hour. Stand for
5 minutes, then turn out and cool
on cake rack.

### Variation

This mixture may also be used to
make small, flat-topped cup cakes.
Make as above and use to fill 24
muffin pans, two-thirds full. Omit
coconut topping. Bake for 20–25
minutes and allow to cool for a few
minutes before removing.
Decorate, if desired, with butter
frosting flavored with grated
lemon zest.

## Banana Loaf

**Banana loaves are all much the
same, but this is the one I like
best, especially with the
addition of a handful of chopped
walnuts. The flour used may be
either white or plain brown.**

2¼ cups all-purpose flour
2 tsp baking powder
generous pinch of baking soda
½ tsp salt
1 tsp ground cinnamon
¼ lb butter
1 cup sugar
2 eggs
4 large, ripe bananas, mashed
½–1 cup nuts, chopped
  (optional)
few drops of vanilla extract

Sift flour with baking powder,
baking soda, salt and cinnamon.
Cream butter and sugar until light.
Add eggs, one at a time, beating

well between additions and adding
1 tsp of the flour mixture with each
egg. Add flour mixture to creamed
mixture alternately with bananas,
beating well until smooth. Stir in
nuts and vanilla.

Pour into a lined and lightly
oiled 10 x 3½ x 3-in bread pan.
Smooth top and bake at 350°F in
center of oven for 50 minutes to
1 hour. Turn out, remove paper
and cool. Serve sliced and buttered.

## Spiced Carrot and Raisin Loaf

A large, moist loaf. Serve in slices, lightly buttered.

2¾ cups water
1½ cups light brown sugar
1½ cups seedless raisins
5 medium carrots, coarsely grated
2 tbsp butter
1 tsp ground cinnamon
½ tsp ground nutmeg
pinch of ground cloves
1 lb all-purpose flour †
2 tsp baking soda
2 tsp baking powder
generous pinch of salt
1 cup walnuts or pecan nuts, chopped

Combine water, sugar, raisins, carrots, butter, cinnamon, nutmeg and cloves in a large saucepan.

Bring to a boil, cover and simmer for 10 minutes. Pour into large mixing bowl and leave until completely cooled. Sift dry ingredients. Stir into carrot mixture and add the nuts.

Pour into a base-lined and lightly oiled bread pan – 10 x 3½ x 3-in. Bake at 325°F for 1 hour or until firm. Turn out on cake rack and cool.

† Brown or wholewheat flour may be substituted for some or all of the flour.

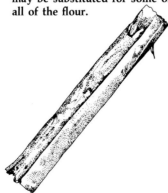

## Brown Fruit Loaf

A simple, reliable loaf to serve sliced and buttered for tea or for packed lunches.

1½ cups mixed dried fruit
¾ cup brown sugar
1 cup water
¼ cup oil
½ tsp ground nutmeg
1 tsp ground cinnamon
½ tsp ground ginger
½ tsp salt
½ cup walnuts, pecan nuts or brazil nuts, chopped
½ cup yogurt
1 egg
1 tsp baking soda
2¼ cups brown bread flour
1 tsp baking powder
few drops of vanilla extract

Put dried fruit, sugar, water, oil, spices and salt into a saucepan, bring to a boil and simmer for

5 minutes. Cool thoroughly. Add nuts. Beat yogurt, egg and baking soda and add to fruit mixture alternately with flour. Finally add baking powder and vanilla.

Spoon into oiled and floured 8 x 3½ x 3-in bread pan and smooth top with back of spoon dipped in hot water. Bake at 325°F for about 45 minutes or until skewer comes out clean. Invert and cool on cake rack.

### Note
The flavor of freshly grated nutmeg is far superior to that of pre-ground nutmeg. Buy the nutmegs whole and grate as needed – small nutmeg graters are manufactured specially for this purpose.

## Zucchini Bread

Serve this large, spicy loaf sliced and buttered.

3 eggs
1 cup oil
1 cup sugar
few drops of vanilla extract
¾ lb zucchini
2½ cups flour (half brown flour may be used)
1 tsp baking soda
1 tsp baking powder
½ tsp salt
1 tsp ground cinnamon
1 tsp ground mixed spice
½–1 cup pecans or walnuts, chopped

Beat eggs, oil, sugar and vanilla together until light. Trim, peel and coarsely grate raw zucchini and stir in. Sift dry ingredients together and add. Finally stir in nuts. Combine thoroughly and turn into a base-lined, oiled and floured bread pan – 10 x 3½ x 3-in. Bake at 350°F on middle shelf of oven for 1 hour to 1 hour 10 minutes. Cool for 5 minutes, then turn out onto cake rack, remove paper and cool.

## Date and Pecan Loaf

1½ cups pitted dates, finely chopped
2 tbsp butter
¾ cup light brown sugar
½ tsp baking soda
1 cup boiling water
2¼ cups flour (half brown flour may be used)
generous pinch of salt
1 tsp baking powder
few drops of vanilla extract
½ cup pecans, chopped

Put dates into bowl with butter and sugar. Sprinkle with baking soda and pour boiling water over. Leave to cool, stirring occasionally. Sift flour, salt and baking powder. Add cooled date mixture. Add vanilla and pecans and mix well. Pour into oiled and base-lined 8 x 3½ x 3-in bread pan. Level top with back of spoon dipped in hot water and bake at 325°F in the center of the oven for 1 hour. Turn out onto cake rack, remove paper and cool.

Wholewheat Scones

## Wholewheat Scones

Raisins, dates, orange zest, or nuts may be added.

2¾ cups wholewheat flour
4 tsp baking powder
½ tsp salt
1 egg
scant ⅓ cup milk
scant ⅓ cup water
3 tbsp honey
¼ cup oil

Mix flour, baking powder and salt in a bowl. Beat remaining ingredients together. Add to flour mixture and mix to a soft dough with a fork. Turn onto a floured board and pat into a round, adding more flour if necessary, to make a manageable dough. Brush surface with milk or eggwash and cut into 8 wedges with a knife. Place on oiled cookie sheet and bake at 425°F for 12 minutes.
Makes 8.

## Cheese Scones

1 cup all-purpose flour
1 tbsp baking powder
½ tsp salt
2 tsp sugar
1 tsp dry mustard
1 cup wholewheat flour
3 tbsp butter
1¼ cup grated Cheddar cheese
1 egg
¼ cup milk
¼ cup water
Paprika

Sift plain flour, baking powder, salt, sugar and mustard. Add wholewheat flour. Rub in butter, add cheese. Beat egg, milk and water and add. Mix with a fork and then lightly form into a ball, adding, if necessary, an extra 1–2 tsp water. Pat out lightly and cut into squares. Place on oiled cookie sheet. Brush tops with eggwash. Sprinkle with paprika and bake at 425°F for 12 minutes.
Makes 9.

## Quick Breakfast Scones

The only time-consuming aspect of this recipe is heating the oven. After that, these feather-light "drop" scones are made and baked in a jiffy.

2¼ cups all-purpose flour
1 tbsp baking powder
1 tsp sugar
½ tsp salt
1 tsp dry mustard
½ cup grated mature Cheddar cheese
1 egg
scant ½ cup milk
scant ½ cup water
¼ cup oil
paprika

Sift flour, baking powder, sugar, salt and mustard. Add cheese. Beat egg, milk, water and oil. Make a well in center of dry ingredients and pour in the liquid. Mix quickly to a soft dough, using a fork. Drop spoonfuls onto oiled cookie sheet, dust tops with paprika and bake at 425°F for 10–12 minutes. Serve hot with butter.
Makes 12.

## Wholewheat Nutty Pulled Breads

**Crisp and wholesome, these can be dunked in hot drinks.**

**2¼ lb wholewheat flour**
**2 cups all-purpose flour**
**1 cup sugar**
**1 tsp salt**
**2 tsp baking powder**
**1 tsp baking soda**
**1 tsp cream of tartar**
**1 cup + 2 tbsp butter, melted**
**⅔ cup seedless raisins**
**½ cup pecan nuts, chopped**
**2 cups buttermilk**
**2 eggs**
**good ¾ cup oil**

In a large bowl mix flours, sugar, salt, baking powder, baking soda and cream of tartar. Stir in butter. Add raisins and nuts. Beat buttermilk, eggs and oil. Stir into

dry mixture, knead into a dough and roll into balls a little bigger than a golf ball. Pack closely into two base-lined and oiled 9 x 3½ x 3½-in bread pans.

Bake at 350°F for 1 hour. Turn out, break apart, nick in half and then carefully break again. Use a knife to help, but don't actually slice them – for some reason they are always better if broken. Arrange on flat cookie sheets and dry out in a very low oven of 250–275°F. They taste even better if allowed to toast slightly.
Makes about 72.

## Old-Fashioned Buttermilk Pulled Breads

**3 lb self-rising flour**
**2 tsp salt**
**1 cup sugar**
**1⅝ cup butter**
**2 cups buttermilk**
**3 eggs**

Mix flour, salt and sugar in a large mixing bowl. Rub in the butter – or if you're in a hurry you can melt the butter first. Mix well. Beat buttermilk with eggs and add. Knead well – the more you knead, the higher they'll rise. If the dough seems a little dry, rinse the buttermilk carton out with a little water and add to the mixture to make a medium-soft but not a slippery dough. Continue kneading until the dough forms a ball and

leaves the sides of the bowl clean, then roll into balls about twice the size of golf balls and pack closely into two base-lined, oiled and floured bread pans – 10 x 3½ x 3-in.

Bake at 400°F for 30 minutes, then reduce heat to 350°F and bake for a further 30 minutes. Turn out and break apart and then, with the help of a knife, break into pieces. Arrange on cookie sheets and dry out at 250°F or in a warming drawer.
Makes 84–96.

## Date, Nut and Oat Biscuits

½ cup butter
½ cup sugar
1 egg, beaten
½ cup pitted dates, chopped
½ cup walnuts, chopped
1 cup brown flour
½ tsp baking powder
½ tsp baking soda
pinch of salt
1 cup porridge oats
¼ cup shredded coconut
few drops of vanilla extract

Melt butter, add sugar and mix well. Pour into mixing bowl and add egg. Stir in dates together with walnuts.

Sift flour, baking powder, baking soda and salt and add to above mixture, tipping in any bran left in strainer. Add porridge oats, coconut and vanilla. Mix thoroughly – the mixture will be soft but firms up on cooling. Form into about 30 balls and place on lightly oiled cookie sheets, not too close together. Flatten lightly with a fork and bake at 350°F for 12 minutes or until golden brown. Cool on cake rack.
Makes about 30.

## Cinnamon Jam Bars

2¼ cups butter, softened
⅞ cup sugar
1 egg
few drops of vanilla extract
2¾ cups all-purpose flour
1 tsp baking powder
pinch of salt
1 tsp ground cinnamon
¾ cup smooth apricot jam
½ cup shredded coconut

Cream butter and sugar. Beat egg with vanilla and add. Sift dry ingredients and add. Work into a soft dough and pinch off two-thirds. With floured hands, press into lightly greased 13 x 8-in jelly roll pan.

Spread evenly with jam. Add coconut to remaining dough and mix in thoroughly. Grate coarsely over top of jam. Dust with a little cinnamon and bake at 350°F for 20–25 minutes until golden brown. Cut into small bars and allow to cool in pan, then remove to cake rack and leave until cold.
Makes 32.

Cinnamon Squares

# Chocolate Crunchies

A different method and a different flavor from the usual brown crunchie. The recipe is easily doubled for a larger batch.

½ cup sugar
1 cup white or brown flour
⅓ cup shredded coconut
3 tbsp cocoa powder
½ tsp baking soda
1 cup porridge oats
½ cup butter, softened
few drops of vanilla extract
½ cup nuts, chopped (optional)
few squares of bitter-sweet
   chocolate

In a large mixing bowl, combine sugar, flour, coconut, cocoa, baking soda and porridge oats. Using an electric beater, mix in butter and vanilla. When well mixed, add nuts, if using. Press into a greased 13 x 8-in jelly roll pan and top with coarsely grated chocolate. Bake at 350°F for 20 minutes, cut into squares and leave to cool in pan. Makes 24–30.

### Note
If preferred, chocolate topping may be omitted and replaced by mixing 2⅓ cups confectioners' sugar with 4 tsp cocoa and just enough boiling water to make spreadable. Spread evenly over slightly cooled crunchies and cut into squares when set.

# Cinnamon Squares

½ cup butter, softened
1 cup light brown sugar
1 egg, beaten
1 cup brown flour
1 cup porridge oats
1 cup muesli
2 tbsp shredded coconut
⅓ cup seedless raisins
1 tsp baking powder
1½ tsp ground cinnamon
½ cup Brazil nuts, chopped

Using an electric beater, cream butter and sugar. Add egg, and beat well. Add remaining ingredients and mix to a fairly soft dough. Press out flat into a lightly oiled cookie sheet or large jelly roll pan, and bake at 350°F for 20 minutes. Cut into large squares and remove from pan when cooled, then leave on cake rack until cold. Makes 20.

# Crunchies

2 cups porridge oats
½ cup + 2 tbsp sugar
1 cup white or brown bread
   flour
1 cup shredded coconut
½ cup + 2 tbsp butter
3 tbsp corn syrup
1 tsp baking soda

Mix porridge oats, sugar, flour and coconut. Melt butter, stir in syrup, then add baking soda. When mixture foams, stir into dry ingredients, mix well and press into a medium-sized, greased cookie sheet. Bake at 350°F for 15 minutes or until lightly browned. Cut into squares and remove from pan when cold.
Makes 30.

### Variation
Add a handful of seedless raisins and/or sunflower seeds to dry mixture.

Coconut Slices

Spiced Pecan Crisps

## Coconut Slices

½ cup + 2 tbsp butter, softened
1 cup sugar
1 egg
few drops of vanilla extract
2⅓ cups all-purpose flour
generous pinch of salt
½ tsp baking soda
⅓ cup shredded coconut

Cream butter and sugar until light. Add egg and vanilla and beat well. Sift flour with salt and baking soda and mix into creamed mixture, then add coconut. Roll dough into two 1¼-in wide sausages. Wrap in waxed paper and chill for 1 hour. Using a sharp knife, cut into ¼-in slices and place fairly far apart on an ungreased cookie sheet. Bake at 325°F in the center of the oven for about 12 minutes.
Makes about 60.

## Spicy Brown Cookies

Economical, Continental-type cookies.

½ cup butter, softened
¾ cup sugar
1 egg, beaten
¼ cup corn syrup
3¼ cup flour
1 tsp baking soda
½ tsp salt
1 tsp ground cinnamon
2 tsp mixed ground spice
whole cloves

Cream butter, sugar, egg and syrup. Sift dry ingredients together and add. Mix into a ball, pinch off pieces and place on oiled cookie sheet. Press a clove into the middle of each and bake in the center of the oven at 350°F for 12 minutes, or until lightly browned. Store in airtight container for a few days for best flavor.
Makes 40.

## Spiced Pecan Crisps

½ cup butter
¾ cup light brown sugar
1 egg
few drops of vanilla extract
2½ cups all-purpose flour
½ tsp baking powder
generous pinch of baking soda
1 tsp ground cinnamon
½ tsp ground nutmeg
½ cup pecan nuts, chopped

Cream butter with sugar until fluffy. Beat in egg and vanilla. Sift dry ingredients and add to creamed mixture, combining thoroughly. Lastly stir in pecans. Form into sausages, wrap in waxed paper and freeze for about 45 minutes, until firm.

To bake, slice into fairly thin rounds and place on lightly oiled cookie sheet. Bake at 350°F for 12–15 minutes, until a pale golden brown.
Makes about 54.

## Chocolate Kisses

When the tiny meringues are cold, carefully pierce the bottoms to form hollows. Fill with whipped cream, then sandwich two together.

½ cup granulated sugar
2 tsp cocoa powder
2 egg whites

Mix sugar and cocoa. Beat egg whites with a pinch of salt until stiff but not dry. Gradually beat in half the sugar-cocoa mixture. When very stiff, fold in the remainder, using a metal spoon and being careful not to over-mix. Lightly oil a large cookie sheet, sprinkle with cornstarch, dust off excess. Pipe or drop teaspoonfuls of meringue onto prepared sheet and bake in center of oven at 250°F for 2 hours. Turn off heat and leave in oven until cold.
Makes 24.

## Walnut Fridge Crisps

**Delicious, crisp cookies.**

**2¼ cups all-purpose flour**
**1 tsp baking powder**
**generous pinch of salt**
**½ tsp baking soda**
**1 tsp ground mixed spice**
**½ cup butter**
**⅓ cup light brown sugar**
**2 tbsp granulated sugar**
**1 egg**
**few drops of vanilla extract**
**⅓ cup finely chopped walnuts**

Sift flour, baking powder, salt, baking soda and mixed spice. Cream butter and slowly add brown and white sugar, beating well. Beat egg with vanilla and add to butter mixture, then mix in the flour mixture – an electric beater is perfect for the job. Lastly add walnuts.

Form into 2 long sausages, wrap in waxed paper and chill until firm enough to slice. Cut into thin rounds and bake on an ungreased cookie sheet at 350°F for about 15 minutes. Cool on cake rack. Makes about 54.

### Hint

**Lightly toasting nuts before using brings out the flavor. Using the grinding blade, chop coarsely in a food processor, taking care not to reduce to a fine powder – which can happen very quickly. Spread them out on cookie sheets and place in a moderate oven until lightly browned. Pecan and Brazil nuts respond particularly well to toasting, although, when nibbled purely for nourishment, nuts should be eaten fresh.**

## Orange Wafers

**Thin, feather-light cookies to serve with delicate desserts or ice cream**

**½ cup butter, softened**
**½ cup granulated sugar**
**3 tbsp orange-flavored liqueur**
**1 cup all-purpose flour**
**¼ cup cornstarch**
**pinch of salt**
**1 tsp finely grated orange zest**

Cream butter, sugar and liqueur until fluffy. Sift flour, cornstarch and salt and blend into butter mixture. Mix in orange zest and shape into a ball, then roll into a long, smooth sausage. Wrap in waxed paper and chill for about 1 hour. Slice thinly, using a sharp knife, and arrange on an ungreased cookie sheet, leaving plenty of room for spreading. Bake at 350°F for 10–12 minutes, or until pale gold. Dust with granulated sugar and leave on cookie sheet to cool slightly, then lift carefully onto cake rack and leave until cold. Makes 42–48.

### Note

**When grating orange zest, be sure not to include any of the white pith. Half an orange should provide 1 tsp finely grated zest.**

## *Oat Cookies*

**Large, crunchy cookies.**

1 cup + 2 tbsp butter, softened
¾ cup light brown sugar
1 cup all-purpose brown flour
  (not wholewheat)
2 cups porridge oats
⅓ cup shredded coconut
½ tsp salt
few drops of vanilla extract
½ tsp baking soda
¼ cup hot water

Cream butter and sugar very well. Add flour, porridge oats, coconut, salt and vanilla. Dissolve baking soda in the hot water and add. Mix well. Roll into balls or push from teaspoon into rough heaps on oiled cookie sheet and flatten slightly with a fork. Leave plenty of room for spreading. Bake at 350°F for 15 minutes or until a pale brown color. Remove carefully with a spatula and leave to crisp on cake rack. Makes 36.

## *Wholewheat Raisin Drops*

½ cup butter, softened
1 tbsp honey
⅓ cup light brown sugar
1 egg
½ cup all-purpose flour
pinch of salt
1 tsp baking soda
1 tsp ground mixed spice
½ cup wholewheat flour
1½ cups porridge oats
2 tbsp shredded coconut
½ cup seedless raisins
chopped nuts (optional)

Cream butter with honey and brown sugar. Add egg and beat well. Sift flour, salt, baking soda and mixed spice, add to creamed mixture and beat. Add wholewheat flour, porridge oats, coconut, raisins and nuts, if using. Mix well and then push off the end of a teaspoon onto a lightly oiled cookie sheet, leaving room for spreading. Bake at 350°F for 15 minutes, until browned. Cool on cake rack, then store in airtight container with a little sugar sprinkled between layers. Makes 30.

Oat Cookies (top) and Wholewheat Raisin Drop Cookies (bottom)

# Namib Knobs

**Crisp little cakes, stuffed with dates, and very like mincemeat pies in appearance.**

PASTRY
**2 cups all-purpose flour**
**¼ cup cornstarch**
**¼ cup confectioners' sugar**
**¾ cup butter**
**1 egg**
**few drops of vanilla extract**

FILLING
**1½ cups pitted dates, chopped**
**1 tsp lemon juice**
**¼ cup water**
**½ cup walnuts, chopped**

First make the filling. Put dates, lemon juice and water into a small saucepan and heat gently until dates are soft enough to be mashed with a wooden spoon. Add nuts and set aside to cool.

Sift flour, cornstarch and confectioners' sugar. Rub in butter. Beat egg and vanilla and add. Mix well and then knead into a ball with your hands – do not add any liquid. Roll out thinly on a floured board and cut into 2–3-in circles. Re-roll off-cuts until all the dough has been used. Place a heaped spoon of filling in the middle of each pastry round, cover with a second round and press edges together with the prongs of a fork. Prick each top twice. Arrange on oiled cookie sheet and bake at 350°F for 18–20 minutes or until pale gold. Remove to cake rack and dust thickly with sifted confectioners' sugar. Makes about 14.

## Hint
**A light dusting of sugar between the layers of cookies in a container will help to keep them crisp.**

# Butter Cookies

**½ cup butter, softened**
**¾ cup granulated sugar**
**1 egg**
**few drops of vanilla extract**
**2 cups flour (half brown flour may be used)**
**1 tsp cream of tartar**
**½ tsp baking soda**
**halved almonds or maraschino cherries**

Cream butter with sugar until light. Add egg and vanilla and beat well. Sift dry ingredients, add to creamed mixture and knead until smooth. Form into walnut-sized balls and place on oiled cookie sheet, leaving room for spreading. Flatten lightly with a fork and top each with an almond or cherry. Bake at 350°F for 12–15 minutes until golden brown. Cool on cake rack.
Makes 30.

# Chocolate Cookies

**good 1 cup porridge oats**
**1¼ cups all-purpose flour**
**⅓ cup shredded coconut**
**1 cup sugar**
**generous pinch of salt**
**½ cup butter, softened**
**1 egg**
**1 tbsp honey**
**½ tsp baking soda**
**5 tsp boiling water**
**5 tsp cocoa powder**

Mix oats, flour, coconut, sugar and salt. Rub in butter. Mix in egg beaten with honey. Dissolve soda in boiling water. Add to cocoa, mix to a thick paste, then combine with flour mixture. Roll into small balls, place on oiled cookie sheet and flatten with a fork. Bake at 350°F for 12–15 minutes. Cool on rack. Makes 40.

Shortbread Cookies

## Shortbread Cookies

**Crisp, buttery cookies served in wedges like shortbread.**

**2¼ cups all-purpose flour**
**3 tbsp cornstarch**
**pinch of salt**
**1 cup confectioners' sugar**
**¾ cup butter**
**few drops of vanilla extract**

Sift together the flour, cornstarch, salt and confectioners' sugar. Rub in butter until crumbly. Add vanilla. Knead well, then roll out to about ½-in thickness onto the ungreased base of a loose-bottomed 9-in cake pan. Crimp the edges, prick well and mark into 12 wedges. Bake at 300°F for 45 minutes and allow to crisp on pan for 5 minutes before cutting through slices and removing.
Makes 12.

## Coconut Shortbread Fingers

**2¼ cups all-purpose flour**
**¾ cup granulated sugar**
**⅓ cup shredded coconut**
**½ cup butter, softened**

Mix dry ingredients. Rub in butter thoroughly until mixture has a fine, crumbly consistency, then knead for 5–10 minutes until dough clings together and forms a smooth ball. Press evenly into an ungreased 8-in square pan. Mark into fingers and prick well. Bake on the middle shelf of oven at 300°F for 50–60 minutes. Cut into fingers, sprinkle with extra sugar and leave in pan to cool. Remove to cake rack and leave until cold and crisp before storing in airtight container.
Makes 21 fingers.

## Coconut Tartlets

**Sweet and delicious: crisp pastry shells hold a dollop of jam and a coconut-meringue topping.**

PASTRY
**½ cup butter**
**good ½ cup granulated sugar**
**2 egg yolks**
**few drops of vanilla extract**
**1½ cups flour**
**1 tsp baking powder**

FILLING
**smooth apricot jam**
**2 egg whites**
**⅓ cup shredded coconut**
**good ½ cup granulated sugar**
**few drops of vanilla extract**

Cream butter and sugar, add yolks one at a time, beating well. Add vanilla. Sift flour and baking powder, add and mix to a dough. Knead, adding a little more flour if

necessary. Roll out thinly on a floured board, cut out circles, and line oiled tart pans. Put 1 tsp jam in the center of each.

Beat egg whites with a pinch of salt until stiff. Gradually beat in coconut, sugar and vanilla. Cover jam with meringue mixture and bake at 400°F for 16–18 minutes until lightly browned. Leave for a few minutes before removing to cake rack.
Makes 18 medium tartlets.

Yankee Overnight Muffins

## Yankee Overnight Muffins

1 cup wholewheat flour
1 cup all-purpose flour
½ cup sugar
¼ cup oil
few drops of vanilla extract
1½ tsp baking soda
1 egg, beaten
generous pinch of salt
1 cup milk
1 tsp ground cinnamon
½ tsp ground nutmeg
⅔ cup seedless raisins
½ cup walnuts, chopped

Mix together all the ingredients, except the raisins and nuts. Stir in raisins and nuts. Mix, cover and leave in refrigerator overnight. Fill greased muffin pans three-quarters full, and bake at 400°F for 15–20 minutes, until well risen and browned.
Makes about 18.

## Old-Fashioned Jam Muffins

2¼ cups all-purpose flour
¼ cup sugar
1 tbsp baking powder
generous pinch of salt
1 tsp finely grated orange zest
½ cup milk
½ cup water
⅓ cup oil
1 egg
jam or marmalade
cinnamon/sugar

Stir dry ingredients. Add zest. Beat together milk, water, oil and egg and pour into a well in the center of sifted mixture. Mix quickly and lightly. Drop a little batter into oiled muffin pans, add 1 tsp jam, cover with more batter and top with a little cinnamon/sugar. Bake at 400°F for 25 minutes.
Makes 12–16.

## Spiced Raisin Bars

**Soft bars with a cake-like texture, which may be served either plain, dusted with sifted confectioners' sugar, or topped with vanilla or orange butter frosting.**

¼ cup butter
3 tbsp light brown sugar
4 tbsp corn syrup
2 eggs
few drops of vanilla extract
1 cup flour (half brown flour may be used)
1 tsp baking powder
½ tsp ground cinnamon
½ tsp ground nutmeg
pinch of ground cloves
⅔ cup seedless raisins
chopped nuts (optional)

Cream butter and sugar until light. Add syrup, eggs and vanilla and mix well. Sift dry ingredients, toss in the raisins, and stir into creamed mixture. Add nuts, if using. Line base of a 8-in square pan with waxed paper and brush with oil. Pour in mixture and spread evenly. Bake at 350°F for 25 minutes. Turn out carefully onto cake rack, remove paper and cool. Turn right side up, spread with frosting, if using, and, using a sharp knife, cut into bars.
Makes 24.

## Flour-Topped Rolls

These are soft, floury rolls similar to the "baps" which the Scots serve warm for breakfast.

good ¾ cup milk
scant ½ cup water
1 tsp sugar
1½ tsp dried yeast
1 lb all-purpose flour
1 tsp salt
3 tbsp butter, softened

Scald milk with water and leave until lukewarm. Sprinkle in the sugar and yeast, stir, then cover and leave until frothy. Sift flour and salt into a large bowl. Rub in butter. Pour yeast mixture into the center, mix and then knead very well until smooth and pliable, adding a little extra warm water if necessary. Return to bowl, brush top with oil, then cover with a cloth and leave to rise in a warm place for 1½ to 2 hours, until doubled.

Knock down, knead briefly, and divide into 12 pieces. Flatten between the palms of the hands into rounds, then using a rolling pin roll lightly into ovals and place on a cookie sheet dusted with flour. With your thumb make a deep dent in the center of each, then leave to rise for about 25 minutes in a warm place. Just before baking, brush with milk and, using a strainer, sift a little flour evenly over the tops. Bake in center of oven at 425°F for 10 minutes.
Makes 12.

### Hint
Dried yeast stays fresh for much longer than cubes of fresh yeast. Never leave the container standing open, and store in the refrigerator, where it will keep for a few months if kept dry and tightly covered.

Brown Soda Bread

## Brown Soda Bread

1½ cups white bread flour
1½ cups wholewheat flour
½ tsp salt
1 tsp brown sugar
1 tsp baking soda
scant 1½ cups buttermilk
milk or egg yolk

Mix both flours, salt and sugar. Stir baking soda into buttermilk until dissolved, then add to flour mixture and mix to a soft dough. Shape into a large round with floured hands, and place on an oiled and floured cookie sheet.

Brush with milk or beaten egg yolk and score into quarters or eighths with the back of a knife. Bake at 400°F for about 40 minutes or until crusty and brown. Serve as soon as possible, broken into sections.
Serves about 8.
Makes 1 round loaf.

## Wholewheat Pitta

1 tsp instant dried yeast
1 tsp sugar
1½ cups wholewheat flour
1½ cups all-purpose flour
1 tbsp oil
1 cup warm water
½ tsp salt

Mix ingredients. Knead well for 5–10 minutes, adding extra flour if necessary, to make a soft, pliable dough. Place in bowl and brush top with oil. Cover and leave to rise in a warm place for about 1 hour until doubled. Knock down, divide into 8 and shape into balls. Roll into flat ovals and place on cookie sheets dusted with flour. Cover and leave until slightly risen and puffy. Bake at 475°F for 10 minutes. Wrap in cloth to keep soft.

## Old-Fashioned Wholewheat Bread

**This takes a bit of mixing and kneading, but the result is a large, crunchy loaf with a traditional humped top.**

2½ tsp instant dried yeast
2¼ lb wholewheat flour
1½ tsp salt
2½ cups warm water
1 tbsp honey
5 tsp oil
2¼ cups all-purpose flour
⅔ cup crushed wheat
2 tsp water
1 tsp sugar

In a large bowl mix yeast, 13 oz wholewheat flour and the salt. Mix together the 2½ cups warm water, honey and oil. Stir thoroughly into the flour mixture to make a sloppy, porridge-like dough. Cover and leave in a warm place for 15 minutes. Add the all-purpose flour, crushed wheat and the remaining wholewheat flour, and knead very well until mixture makes a firm, smooth ball. You may have to add a little more water or a little more flour, as flours differ in their absorption capacity.

Shape dough into a loaf to fit one large or two medium oiled and floured bread pans. Cover and leave in a warm place for 40 minutes to 1 hour, until well risen. Mix the 2 tsp water with the sugar and brush the top to give it a good color when baked. Bake at 400°F for 30 minutes, then at 350°F for another 30 minutes. Turn out – the loaf should sound hollow when rapped on the bottom. Cool on cake rack.
Makes 1 large or 2 medium loaves.

## Wholewheat Nut and Raisin Bread

A very wholesome and spicy loaf.

4½ cups wholewheat flour
1 tsp salt
1½ tsp ground cinnamon
½ tsp ground nutmeg
generous pinch of ground cloves
3 tbsp oil
3 tbsp honey
¼ cup brown sugar
½ cup seedless raisins
½ cup walnuts, pecan nuts or
   Brazil nuts, chopped
2 cups yogurt or buttermilk
2 tsp baking soda

Put flour, salt, 1 tsp cinnamon, nutmeg, cloves, oil, honey, ¼ cup brown sugar, raisins and nuts into a large bowl and mix with a wooden spoon. Beat yogurt or buttermilk with baking soda. Pour into flour mixture and mix well. Spoon into an oiled and floured 9 x 3½ x 3-in bread pan. Sprinkle the top with remaining brown sugar and cinnamon and bake at 350°F for 1 hour. Turn out and cool on cake rack, then serve sliced and buttered.
Makes 1 loaf.

## Nutty Wholewheat Bread

This is a quick yeast bread, which requires no kneading.

1¾ cups warm water
1 tsp honey
2 tsp dried yeast
3¼ cups wholewheat flour
½ cup all-purpose flour
1 cup crushed wheat
1½ tsp salt
2 tsp brown sugar
1 tsp mixed dried herbs
   (optional)
1 tbsp oil
⅓ cup sunflower seeds

Mix 1 cup warm water with the honey. Sprinkle in dried yeast, stir, cover and leave to froth. Mix both flours, crushed wheat, salt, sugar, herbs (if using) and oil. Stir in dissolved yeast and sunflower seeds. Add just enough of the remaining warm water to make a soft dough. Spoon into an oiled and floured 9 x 3½ x 3-in bread pan, patting in firmly.

Sprinkle top with more sunflower seeds and leave to rise in a warm place for about 1 hour. Bake at 400°F for 45 minutes. Makes 1 medium loaf.

### Hint

When using sunflower seeds in one of these quick-bread recipes, use buttermilk, not yogurt, for the liquid – the latter tends to turn the sunflower seeds green.